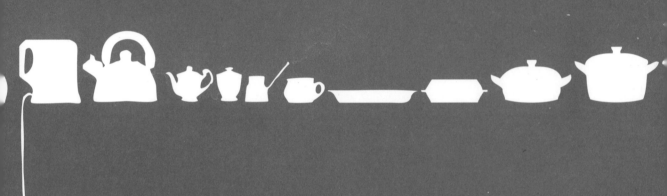

GIRL IN THE KITCHEN

GIRL IN THE KITCHEN

HOW A TOP CHEF COOKS, THINKS, SHOPS, EATS, AND DRINKS

BY **STEPHANIE IZARD**

WITH **HEATHER SHOUSE**   PHOTOGRAPHS BY **DAN GOLDBERG**

CHRONICLE BOOKS

SAN FRANCISCO

Library of Congress Cataloging-in-Publication
Data available.

ISBN 978-0-8118-7447-2

Manufactured in China

Design: ANNE DONNARD
Typesetting: RISE-AND-SHINE STUDIO
Food stylist: ERIN QUON
Food stylist assistant: CHRISTINA ZERKIS
Prop stylist: ANDREA KUHN
Photo assistant: DAMIEN THOMPSON
Photo assistant: BOB DOWLING
Digital tech: PATRICK KENNY
Producer: LINDSAY REGAN

The photographer would like to give special thanks to
JOSEPHINE ORBA, KELLY MCKAIG, KAREN BRODY, BRIAN EAVES, and
CONSTANCE PIKULAS.

10 9 8 7 6 5 4 3 2 1

CHRONICLE BOOKS
680 Second Street
San Francisco, California 94107
www.chroniclebooks.com

I WOULD LIKE TO THANK Dave Gollan for help with recipe testing, everyone at the Goat (I love you guys!), Heather for putting up with me and my procrastination, and my parents for putting up with me for the past 34 years.

—Stephanie Izard

THANK YOU to James Rahm for his help with the wine pairings, to Greg Hall for help with the beer pairings, to my agent Jane Dystel for going to bat for us whenever we asked, to my parents for unconditional love and support, and, of course, to Steph for believing that we could create an awesome book together and for sticking it out while we did.

—Heather Shouse

TABLE OF CONTENTS

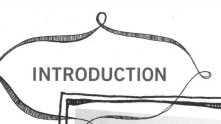

AS I AM WRITING THIS,

I'M SITTING IN THE BACKSEAT OF A CAR THAT'S PACKED WITH TWO GIRL & THE GOAT MANAGERS AND OUR HEAD MIXOLOGIST. WE ESCAPED FOR THE FIRST TIME SINCE OPENING IN JULY 2010, FOR A 24-HOUR ROAD TRIP TO FRANKFORT, KENTUCKY, TO BUY A BARREL OF BUFFALO TRACE WHISKEY FOR MY RESTAURANT. AND POSSIBLY ONE FOR MY HOUSE. BEN, THE MIXOLOGIST, IS RAMBLING ON WITH INTERESTING FACTS ABOUT THE HISTORY OF SAZERACS WHILE MY MANAGER DAN AND I ARE DISCUSSING THE DESIGN OF THE POWER-GENERATING WINDMILLS DOTTING THE INDIANA LANDSCAPE. IN THE MIDST OF THIS, I DECIDED TO PULL OUT MY LAPTOP AND FINALLY WRITE THIS INTRO, WHICH, OF COURSE, IS LONG OVERDUE. AFTER THIS I'LL PULL OUT LAST NIGHT'S MENU FROM THE RESTAURANT, COVERED IN VARIOUS SCRIBBLES AND IDEAS, AND TRY TO FINISH WRITING THE NEXT MENU THAT'S SET TO GO ON IN A FEW DAYS. THAT'S HOW I WORK: VERY LAST MINUTE, VERY SPUR OF THE MOMENT, ALWAYS A LITTLE NUTS, AND PRETTY MUCH ALWAYS HAVING A GOOD TIME.

This way of life is what got me into cooking in the first place. It's crazy hectic, but it's just plain fun. My first day of culinary school at Le Cordon Bleu in Scottsdale, Arizona, my teaching chef said, "Beware, 80 percent of chefs become alcoholics." I figured I was in the right place. It's no secret that I've always loved to party, but when it came to cooking, somehow I've always managed to put my head down, work hard, and have an awesome time doing it.

THE ETHIC OF THIS BOOK IS LIKE MINE: IT'S A SOLID COLLECTION OF RECIPES BUILT ON A FEW CLASSIC TECHNIQUES, SO THAT YOU WALK AWAY HAVING ACTUALLY LEARNED HOW TO BE A BETTER COOK, BUT WITH ENOUGH TIPS AND TRICKS TO HELP TAKE THE STRESS OUT OF COOKING AND TO ALLOW YOU TO JUST HAVE FUN.

And for those of you with cookbook addictions like me, whose shelves are buckling under the weight of books you never actually cook from, I wanted to make this more than just a bunch of recipes. Through personal stories, spotlights of my favorite ingredients, and simplified breakdowns of cool techniques, there's plenty to read from the comfort of your couch, and plenty of insight into my style of cooking to hopefully inspire you to find your own. (And even if you're *not* cooking, try out the beer and wine suggestions throughout the book—that always makes reading a bit more fun.)

Back to those books cluttering up my house. Before Heather and I started writing this, I looked through every book in my home collection, pulling out old ones stashed away in boxes, flipping through the stacks in my living room and the piles that leave little room for eating on my kitchen table (although what chef actually has time for eating at home?). One of the first books I remember reading still stands out as the book I enjoyed the most. It was *A Cricket in Times Square*, and it was the summer before third grade. It took me three library visits to finish it, since, of course, I kept finding other things to do that

summer, but I can still remember discovering the pure joy of reading because of that book, turning the pages while sitting in my bed, on my banana-yellow sheets with my purple-flowered walls all around. A bit later in life I switched over to cookbooks. My mom, sister, and I would sit at the kitchen table in my childhood home in Connecticut every Sunday, flipping through cookbooks and writing the week's menu to hang on the refrigerator. Pages were marked and recipes were followed to a T, and the posted menus helped my friends decide what night to come over for dinner (my friend Sue always made sure she was around for roast beef and Yorkshire pudding night).

A few of my friends thought I was weird for loving Julia Child, the Frugal Gourmet and Yan Can Cook, which weren't exactly on par with Michael Jackson and Michael J. Fox for most twelve-year-olds. Aside from swimming (which I did competitively for most of my life), food was my main interest through childhood. I was always helping out in the kitchen, but for some reason it didn't immediately occur to me to be a chef. I followed the norm and went to college, getting a sociology degree from the University of Michigan, but felt lost even before graduation, unsure of what I was going to do next.

It was my dad who suggested culinary school, saying "Why waste your time trying to be white collar when we all know you're more white coat?" I enrolled in Le Cordon Bleu and found the place I was supposed to be all along.

In culinary school, cookbooks became references for techniques and insight into the world of restaurants and chefs that I was about to enter. After school, when I was thrown into sixty-hour workweeks with little money or time for traveling, cookbooks became a way for me to understand food from all over the world, to visit foreign places through pages of culinary history. And now I use books for inspiration, flipping through and registering recipe titles while glancing at the pictures, being reminded that, "Hey, I haven't used grapefruit in a while" or "If beets with pistachios works and beets with oranges works why not pistachios with oranges?"

How I think about food and how I come up with dishes is the core of my career as a chef, and the core of this book. Since *Top Chef* wrapped and since the launch of Girl & the Goat, I've often been quoted saying that I just want to make your whole mouth happy. What I mean by this is that with each dish you want to find the right balance of savory, sweet, salty, and even a little spice. When all of your tastebuds are utilized, the experience is heightened, more intense, more memorable. By looking at a recipe and understanding why each ingredient is there, it makes it easier to substitute if something is not available.

Take the tuna salad on page 115 for example. We have beautiful fresh fish with nice rich texture. We add raw snap peas to bring a bit of crunch and freshness. We add blueberries to bring a bit of sweet and tart, and the sorrel helps bring out the tart notes even further. The fatty pine nuts round it all out. So let's say you have no blueberries. How about some diced tart plums, or some sliced strawberries? Both have the same sweet and tart notes. Or let's say you aren't able to get tuna, but you have some beautiful lump crab. Sub it in. Experiment. Go nuts. Above all,

KNOW THAT IT IS OKAY TO ADJUST RECIPES, TO PLAY AROUND WITH THEM TO FIND YOUR OWN FAVORITE TWIST.

I intend for this book to be a guide rather than a rule book. Mix and match sauces and sides, putting together flavors that you enjoy based on the "make your whole mouth happy" goal. You'll have more fun this way, and you'll become a better cook doing it. And as your confidence grows, you'll depend on the recipes less and less, using them as quick references while cooking more by feel. One of the ways I hope to help get you there—aside from explaining flavor profiles of ingredients and their effect on the overall dishes—is by encouraging you to cook using visual cues as opposed to watching the clock. Depending on your pan and the strength of your stove's flame, an onion might sweat in twice the time it takes to sweat

in my apartment, but if you know what it's supposed to look like before moving on to the next step, you know how to cook, not just how to follow a recipe.

Speaking of my apartment, I think the fact that we did all of the recipe testing out of my tiny Chicago home really helped shape this book as well. Sure, I've opened two restaurants and cooked in plenty of amazing kitchens, but these recipes are all geared toward the home cook, and they were created and tested using an average home kitchen. At the restaurant, we have purveyors that we work with to score hard-to-find ingredients, we have oversized equipment, and we are there to cook. All day, every day. So having dishes that take days to make is the norm. But having spent the two years between winning the Top Chef title and opening Girl & the Goat cooking at home, I was inevitably brought back to home cooking. Because of this,

I PROMISE YOU THAT EVEN THOUGH A COUPLE OF RECIPES MIGHT BE AIMED MORE AT A SPECIAL DINNER PARTY THAN TUESDAY NIGHT SUPPER, ALL ARE SIMPLE ENOUGH TO DO AT HOME AND ARE MADE WITH INGREDIENTS READILY AVAILABLE FROM YOUR LOCAL GROCERY STORE.

Granted, I bought a second refrigerator and had aisles of dry storage set up in my otherwise empty apartment while working on this, but as I think I mentioned before, I'm a bit obsessive . . . and not very practical, as I now just have two empty refrigerators serving little purpose (well, one has ranch dressing and beer in it).

Aside from giving you some interesting recipes and some insight into how to combine flavors and textures in your food, I want to stress a few key points that you'll see repeated throughout this book. The *most important* thing you can do is to season your food! There is nothing worse than an undersalted dish. I'm not suggesting to make it salty, just well seasoned, as salt brings out the natural flavors in food. At my restaurants, I have been known to ask cooks to season soup with me to learn to season well

by adding salt gradually, and tasting as you go, and noticing as the flavor becomes more and more vivid. That way you'll also know when to stop. Always use less pepper than salt, and if the dish has other spices that the pepper might compete with, omit it.

While we're on the topic of tasting as you go, remember to taste everything! Even if you've made a dish many times before, there are so many variables that can make it different, from the sweetness of your produce to the strength of your spices. That variance in produce is related to another key point: cooking in season. I'm not saying you can't serve apple pie in the spring if you're craving it, and apples are of course available at the grocery store all year long. But I would think twice before serving hot butternut squash soup on a warm summer night. It's just so much more enjoyable in the fall and winter.

When items are in season, you're getting food at its peak. And if you can seek out local ingredients and learn a bit about where your food comes from, even better. I've spent a lot of time at farms and with

fishermen, which translates into a deepened respect for the products I work with. If hanging out with cheesemakers and fishermen isn't a possibility for you, at least try to hit up a local farmers' market. You'll not only be supporting your local economy and environment, but also you might just come across a new favorite ingredient and inspiration for your next meal.

Above all, just keep in mind two words as you read and cook with this book: enjoy yourself. Pour a glass of wine or crack open a beer, invite some friends over, turn on some music, and have fun. With a little help from these pages and a hungry appetite for great flavors, you'll create your own good times. Just like I have.

CHEERS!

Steph T.

STARTERS

CALL IT MAIN-COURSE-LETDOWN SYNDROME, BUT A LOT OF RESTAURANTS CAN KNOCK THE STARTERS OUT OF THE PARK WHILE THE ENTRÉES JUST PALE IN COMPARISON.

Because of that, more often than not I'll go to a restaurant, order a bunch of starters to share with friends or a date, and just skip the main dishes altogether. Restaurants are catching on, though, so for the last few years small-plate menus have been popping up all over the country, letting chefs have more fun with ingredients and worry less about making a balanced entrée of a starch, protein, and vegetable. Plus when you're serving smaller portions, you can also get away with something totally rich and creamy like the Shallot Custard (page 33), where a few bites is all you need. And last, but definitely not least, starters are perfect drinking companions—munch on some Asian-Spiced English Peas (page 18), take a swig of beer, and repeat.

WARM MARINATED OLIVES

One night in Seattle, I had my olive epiphany. I was in town for the Washington Wine Commission's annual showcase and all of the panelists were invited to dine at the Corson Building, an amazing space created by Matt Dillon, a *Food & Wine* magazine "Best New Chef." Matt's vision of taking a rundown space in a random part of town and turning it into an amazing restaurant, complete with its own garden to feed the menu seasonally, left me so inspired. Not only was his food fantastic, but he figured out how to create the experience of being in a European farmhouse where guests could enjoy a casual family-style setting and local fare. I distinctly remember the first plates to be passed around were simple marinated olives, the slight heat bringing out the savory briny flavor to its fullest. This recipe is my take on those deliciously simple warm olives, with rich liquid you can sop up with freshly toasted bread. The roasted garlic adds a slight sweetness, but the meaty olives are truly the stars.

2 heads garlic, cloves separated and peeled	2 tablespoons sugar	1 Anaheim chile pepper, halved, seeded, and thinly sliced	1 tablespoon yellow mustard seeds
1 tablespoon extra-virgin olive oil	1 tablespoon sherry vinegar	1 tablespoon fennel seeds	1½ teaspoons pink peppercorns
¼ teaspoon salt	1 cup thinly sliced shallots	1 tablespoon coriander seeds	2 pounds whole olives, mixed (see Ingredient Spotlight, facing page)
2 oranges, zested and juiced			

1. Preheat the oven to 400°F. Put the garlic cloves on a sheet of aluminum foil, drizzle with the olive oil, and season with the salt. Fold the foil over to create a sealed pouch and roast the garlic until the cloves are lightly brown and very tender, 30 to 45 minutes.

2. Meanwhile, in a small nonreactive saucepan, bring the orange juice, sugar, and sherry vinegar to a boil. Stir in the shallots and sliced chile, return them to a boil, then remove from the heat and allow to cool to room temperature.

3. Heat a small sauté pan over medium heat. Add the fennel, coriander, mustard seeds, and peppercorns and toast for a few minutes, until lightly browned and very fragrant. Transfer the spices to a mortar and break up into smaller pieces with a pestle.

4. In a medium bowl, combine the garlic and olives with the orange juice mixture and spices. Refrigerate, letting the mixture marinate at least overnight.

5. Preheat the oven to 300°F. Put the olives and marinade in an ovenproof serving dish or other baking dish and heat for about 10 minutes, until warmed through. Serve.

DRINK TIP

There's a reason olives are the most common snack at wine bars—their salty goodness goes perfectly with many wines. If you're in the mood for red, a Sangiovese (or Chianti) has just the right amount of pucker to counter the salt in the olives. When it comes to whites, the acidity of Sauvignon Blancs will do the same, but with an additional crispness as well.

INGREDIENT SPOTLIGHT

OLIVES There are plenty of reasons I've always been drawn to Mediterranean food, but the liberal use of olives has to be top on the list. Throughout Spain, Greece, Italy, and France, you'll find so many varieties it'll make your head spin. To find your favorites, try going to an olive bar (they're pretty common in better grocery stores these days) and just load up a container with a couple of each. My favorites are *cerignolas* (huge, bright green Italian olives with plenty of flesh), *manzanillas* (a rich, thick-skinned, purplish green Spanish variety that tastes a bit like artichoke hearts), and *arbequina* (tiny pea-size brown olives that would be a pain to cook with but are excellent for eating). I like to chop up the olive flesh and add it to any dish where I need a hit of briny saltiness, but just remember to be careful to adjust your seasoning by using less salt that you normally would, as the olives will release plenty of it into the dish.

ASIAN-SPICED ENGLISH PEAS

SERVES 4

This recipe came to me one spring day when I was standing with some of my cooks, cleaning a very large case of English peas. While I love them, like other spring vegetables, they're pretty time-consuming to prepare. I started thinking about edamame and how addictive it is to eat, when you're sitting around drinking beer and mindlessly sucking the tasty sweet beans from inside the pod and getting all of the saltiness off the tough skin. So I thought, "Why not treat English peas the same way?" And this way, your friends won't even realize that they're doing half of the work for you.

1 lemon, juiced

3 garlic cloves, minced

2 tablespoons fish sauce

2 tablespoons olive oil

1 tablespoon Dijon mustard

1 tablespoon soy sauce

½ teaspoon sriracha (see Ingredient Spotlight, facing page)

1 pound English pea pods

1. In a large bowl, whisk together the lemon juice, garlic, fish sauce, olive oil, mustard, soy sauce, and sriracha. Add the pea pods, then toss to coat. Cover and refrigerate overnight or for at least 4 hours.

2. Bring the peas to room temperature and strain them, reserving the liquid. Heat a large sauté pan (with a lid) over medium-high heat. Add half of the peas and a small spoonful of the marinade to the pan. Sauté for 2 minutes, then reduce the heat to medium-low. Add ¼ cup water, then cover and let steam until just cooked through, 6 to 8 minutes. Repeat the process with the remaining peas.

3. Put the cooked pea pods in a serving bowl and drizzle them with the remaining marinade.

DRINK TIP

Wit beers (the Belgian take on wheat beers) have just enough spice to complement the spicing of these peas, but a good amount of crispness to keep your palate clean and wanting to go back for another bite.

INGREDIENT SPOTLIGHT

SRIRACHA Often called "rooster sauce" because of the strutting bird on the label of the most popular brand (Huy Fong Foods), sriracha is an Asian-style hot sauce. In countries like Thailand and Vietnam, it's commonly used to spice up soups or as a condiment for satay. Here in America, expats and adventurous eaters reach for it like the new ketchup, squirting the stuff over everything from fries to pizza. I cook with sriracha almost as often as I do with sambal (see page 47), but because sriracha is a bit spicier, I turn to it when I want a bolder flavor with more kick. In most cities, you should be able to find it in the Asian section of your local supermarket, but you can also order it online if you can't track it down where you live.

FRIED CHEESE WITH SPRING VEGGIES AND STRAWBERRY REDUCTION

SERVES ABOUT 10

During my first visit to the *Food & Wine* Classic in Aspen, the other *Top Chef* winners and I were asked to participate in a cocktail party where we would make hors d'oeuvres from various parts of the world. Out of the list, I chose Egypt. It was random to say the least, and a cuisine I knew nothing about. So I did what I do when I'm asked to cook food from a certain country—I do a little online research or flip through cookbooks and then just run with my own twist on a dish or set of flavors. For Egypt, I came across a recipe for fried cheese and I immediately got excited about it. I decided to start with the classic recipe but fit it into the spring season to lighten it up a bit and balance the salt with some seasonal veggies and strawberries. The end result was so tasty that I remember one guest came back for six helpings—another cheese lover indeed!

In this recipe (and in plenty of others to follow), you'll be making a reduction or gastrique, which might sound fancy but is basically just the result of cooking down fruit and sugar with vinegar. I probably use gastriques more often than any other type of reduced sauce, mainly because I love the bright sweet-and-sour balance they offer. You're adding flavor but not weighing the dish down as you would with some of the heavier classic sauces.

STRAWBERRY REDUCTION

1 cup white balsamic vinegar

1 cup sliced fresh strawberries

¼ cup packed fresh basil leaves

¼ cup sugar

¼ cup fresh lemon juice

TOPPING

½ cup shelled fresh fava beans (about 8 ounces)

½ cup shelled English peas (about 5 ounces pea pods)

½ cup thinly sliced raw asparagus spears

6 fresh basil leaves, cut in chiffonade (see Technique 101, page 73)

1 lemon, zested and juiced

2 tablespoons olive oil

Coarse salt

Freshly ground black pepper

FRIED CHEESE

1½ cups shredded haloumi cheese (about 4 ounces; see Ingredient Spotlight, page 23)

1 large egg, beaten

2 tablespoons all-purpose flour

freshly ground black pepper

2 tablespoons vegetable or peanut oil, plus more as needed

Coarse salt

Lavash or flatbread, broken into 1-inch pieces for hors d'oeuvres or 3-inch for starters

Continued . . .

1. To make the strawberry reduction: Combine the vinegar, strawberries, basil, sugar, and lemon juice in a medium saucepan. Bring them to a boil and then reduce the heat. Simmer to reduce the liquid by half, 25 to 30 minutes. Strain, discarding the solids, and let the liquid cool.

2. To make the topping: Remove the fava beans and the peas from their pods, discarding the pods.

3. Bring a medium stockpot of salted water to a boil. Prepare a bowl of ice water. Blanch the beans and peas by boiling them for about 4 minutes. Drain, then place the beans and peas in the ice bath to shock. Once chilled, you'll need to peel off the outer protective layer of the fava beans (see Technique 101, below). Roughly chop both the beans and peas.

4. Combine the favas, peas, asparagus, basil, and lemon zest in a large bowl. Whisk together 2 tablespoons of the lemon juice and the olive oil and drizzle over the veggies, tossing to combine. Season with salt and pepper.

5. To make the fried cheese: Prepare this just before serving. Combine the cheese, egg, flour, and ¼ teaspoon pepper in a medium bowl.

6. Heat the 2 tablespoons vegetable oil in a large sauté pan over medium-high heat. Form small, round, flat discs from teaspoon-sized scoops of the cheese mixture. (The less you handle the rounds, the better they stay together.) Add the discs to the hot sauté pan about 1 inch apart. Fry the cheese in batches until golden brown, about 1 minute per side. Transfer them to a paper towel–lined plate and sprinkle with salt and pepper.

7. To assemble as hors d'oeuvres, place a single cheese disc on a piece of lavash, top with about 1 teaspoon of vegetables, and drizzle with the gastrique. For starter portions, place three cheese discs on each 3-inch piece of lavash and top.

TECHNIQUE 101

Shelling Fava Beans: Favas are one of those delicious foods that unfortunately require a bit of work, as the frozen beans just won't have the same fresh pop to them and canned simply doesn't exist (even if it did, I wouldn't recommend it over fresh). But once you get the hang of shelling favas, it's actually quite simple. You've already removed the pods before boiling and shocking them in the ice bath as explained above, but now you'll need to free the bean from its protective coating. The easiest way to do this is to make a small incision with your thumbnail at the end of the bean with a little lip and then squeeze the opposite end with your thumb and forefinger. Voila! The bean should pop right out.

DRINK TIP

Rosé wines are as much a sign of spring in the wine world as asparagus is in the food world. Not only is this a great pairing of fresh, spring flavors, but the strawberries bring out the natural strawberry flavor in rosés.

INGREDIENT SPOTLIGHT

HALOUMI CHEESE Most of the time when you think of grilled cheese, you picture stuff that melts and turns good and gooey. But haloumi is a genius invention from the Mediterranean island country of Cyprus (it's also popular throughout the Middle East and Greece, as well as in Greek-American restaurants that torch the stuff with a loud "Opa!" and call it flaming saganaki). Made from both goat's and sheep's milk, this cheese has a super-high melting point, making it perfect for frying or grilling. For this recipe, I fry it, but I also like to slice it into slabs and toss it on the grill, cooking it just until it develops nice brown grill marks and is heated through. Top it with a fresh herb salad of mint and parsley, plus a squeeze of lemon juice and a splash of olive oil, and serve it with some crusty bread. Just remember that haloumi is pretty salty, so don't partner it up with anything aggressive (like olives) or it can be overwhelming.

SWEET-AND-SOUR EGGPLANT WITH TOMATILLOS

MAKES 1 QUART

This is a very simple recipe that celebrates the natural sweetness of eggplant by pairing it with tart tomatillos. I haven't worked with Mexican ingredients that much, but during the Chicago Gourmet event the summer before we opened Girl & the Goat restaurant, my sous chef suggested we use tomatillos in a chicken dish. I was a little hesitant, but the unique tartness and pulpy green-tomato texture was so great, I've been using them ever since. This preparation is easy and versatile; it's great tossed with hot pasta, as a pizza topper, or over grilled fish or meats, but I put it in the starters chapter because I usually just eat it spooned over crusty bread. If you wind up with leftovers, store them in the fridge where the flavors will continue to develop over a day or two, making it even better.

1 Japanese eggplant (about 2 pounds)

2 tablespoons olive oil

1 cup finely diced onion

2 garlic cloves, minced

Salt

Freshly ground black pepper

½ fresh poblano pepper, thinly sliced

2 cups diced fresh tomatillos (see Ingredient Spotlight, page 26)

1 cup grape tomatoes, halved

2 tablespoons sugar

2 tablespoons white wine

1 tablespoon champagne vinegar or white wine vinegar

1. Cut the eggplant lengthwise and then crosswise in ½-inch half-moons.

2. Heat a large sauté pan over medium-low heat. Add the olive oil, then the onion and garlic, and sweat until the onion is translucent, about 3 minutes. Season lightly with salt and pepper.

3. Increase the heat to medium-high, add the poblano pepper, and cook until softened, 2 minutes more.

4. Add the eggplant, tomatillos, and tomatoes and stir to thoroughly coat the vegetables with the oil. Cook until the vegetables start to soften, about 3 minutes more. Season lightly with salt and pepper, then add the sugar, wine, and vinegar. Cook for 3 minutes, then reduce the heat to medium-low. Continue cooking until the liquid has been soaked up by the vegetables and they have broken down to be nice and soft, 8 to 10 minutes. Adjust the salt and pepper, let the mixture cool to room temperature, and serve.

DRINK TIP

Rosé wines are as much a sign of spring in the wine world as asparagus is in the food world. Not only is this a great pairing of fresh, spring flavors, but the strawberries bring out the natural strawberry flavor in rosés.

INGREDIENT SPOTLIGHT

TOMATILLOS These little fruits look something like a small green tomato wearing a papery jacket, and they're essential to Mexican cooking, used in everything from green salsa to *mole verde.* You should be able to find them in most grocery stores these days, but definitely in Latin American produce markets. Choose tomatillos that are firm, with a snug husk. Pull the husks off before using the fruits, then try a slice of tomatillo raw to get an idea of the flavor so you can get creative with uses. What you'll taste is close to a green tomato but with a lemony tartness, so think about using it raw to brighten up salads and fresh pico de gallo–type salsas. For a quick sauce to pour over roasted meats, simply halve the tomatillos. Sweat some chopped garlic and onion, add the tomatillos, enough water to cover, and season with salt and pepper, then cook until they soften down into a delicious sauce.

TEMPURA ASPARAGUS WITH OLIVE AIOLI

SERVES 4 TO 6

Growing up, tempura was one of my favorite dinners. Yep, we made meals out of tempura. My mom would let us pick any vegetables we wanted, then we all gathered around the electric wok-turned-fryer and fried up our dinner. I think potatoes were one of my favorites to throw in, since french fries have always been on the top of my last-meal list, but really I loved it all. Although it's fried, tempura is not a heavy batter. The keys to keeping it light are using very cold sparkling water and equal parts cornstarch to flour, and being careful not to overmix the batter, which makes it doughy. And to get it super-crisp, make sure your oil is nice and hot—anything less that 375°F will result in soggy crust. Follow these tips and you'll get a perfectly light coating that won't overpower whatever vegetable or protein you decide to fry.

You can pretty much tempura anything, but for this book I decided to use the ultimate spring vegetable: asparagus. Although you can find it year-round, asparagus is best in the springtime in the Midwest, when it invites us into the new season as one of the first greens we see. Crisping up asparagus spears and dipping them in a rich and salty olive aioli makes for a perfect afternoon or pre-dinner snack—so good that one friend said to me after eating them, "The devil has a new pitchfork."

OLIVE AIOLI

1 head garlic

1 tablespoon olive oil

1 egg yolk

1 tablespoon Dijon mustard

1 tablespoon fresh lemon juice

½ cup blended vegetable oil (half olive oil, half vegetable oil)

½ cup chopped pitted niçoise or kalamata olives

TEMPURA

¾ cup all-purpose flour

¾ cup cornstarch

1½ teaspoons coarse salt

½ teaspoon freshly ground black pepper

1 cup cold soda water

About 1 cup canola or peanut oil

1 pound fresh asparagus (thin stalks about the size of a pencil)

Continued . . .

1. To make the aioli: Preheat the oven to 400°F. Cut the head of garlic in half horizontally and place the two halves on a piece of aluminum foil. Drizzle the olive oil over the garlic and then fold up all four sides of the foil, pinching them together to make a pouch around the garlic. Roast the garlic until the cloves are tender and slightly browned, about 40 minutes.

2. Let the garlic cool and then pop the cloves out of the skins. Smash the cloves into a paste and transfer them to a blender. Add the egg yolk, mustard, and lemon juice and pulse several times to combine the ingredients. With the blender running, add the blended oil in a slow, steady stream through the lid of the blender. Process until the aioli is thick and smooth. Transfer it to a small bowl and fold in the olives. Set aside or refrigerate until ready to use.

3. To make the tempura: Whisk together the flour, cornstarch, salt, and pepper in a large bowl. Add the soda water, whisking briskly until the batter is just slightly thinner than pancake batter.

4. Heat the canola oil to 375°F in a wide Dutch oven or large sauté pan with high sides. Using tongs or your fingers, dip the asparagus spears in the tempura batter to coat and fry them in batches, 6 to 8 spears at a time, depending on the size of the pot. (Slowly drop the asparagus in one at a time, being careful to not overcrowd the oil with spears, which will drop the oil temperature, resulting in a soggy coating.) When they are golden brown, remove the fried spears with tongs, transfer them to a paper towel to drain, and sprinkle with salt and pepper. Repeat the process in batches.

5. Serve immediately with the olive aioli.

DRINK TIP

Asparagus can be tough to pair, but the one wine that goes great with it is Sauvignon Blanc. Go for one from New Zealand since they're known to be really crisp and grassy, which will help cut through the fried tempura batter as well.

CRISPY CHICKPEA FRITTERS WITH SALSA VERDE

SERVES 4 TO 6

I absolutely love chickpeas. Growing up I would just eat them straight out of the can as a snack. (Although I remember once grabbing hominy off the shelf at the grocery store by accident, getting home, popping open the can to dig in, and spitting hominy all over the kitchen counter. Needless to say, I am not a hominy fan.) But back to the highlight of this dish—the chickpea. I love the nutty taste and texture of this little legume. For the full effect, start with dry chickpeas to give you a little more control over the seasoning and texture, but they do have to soak overnight before cooking, so if you forget, just grab a can.

This recipe is my version of a classic Sicilian dish, *panelle*, which uses chickpea flour to create a beautifully textured fritter. When you first make the batter, it may seem a bit on the gummy side and very dense, but just wait. Once the fritters are chilled and fried crisp on the outside, the inner texture becomes very creamy and light. Traditionally, the *panelle* is served with fresh parsley, but I like to use salsa verde—not the Mexican green salsa, but a classic Italian herb sauce that gets acidity from vinegar and a briny saltiness from anchovies. The acidity of the sauce cuts right through the rich fritter and the bit of feta adds a nice, bright, sour note. The crisp chickpeas are just an added bonus. You can even fry up a bowl's worth and top them with a little crumbled feta as a nice snack, but I promise, you can't eat just one.

FRITTERS

1 cup chicken broth

1½ teaspoons salt

1 cup chickpea flour

1 cup cooked or canned chickpeas, drained and roughly chopped

⅓ cup grated Parmesan cheese

Olive oil or other nonstick cooking spray

CRISPY CHICKPEAS

Blended oil (half vegetable, half olive oil) for frying

5 or 6 black peppercorns

1 teaspoon salt

1 teaspoon coriander seeds

¼ teaspoon red pepper flakes

¼ teaspoon paprika

1 cup cooked or canned chickpeas, drained

¼ cup buttermilk

¼ cup chickpea flour

¼ cup cornstarch

Blended oil (half vegetable, half olive oil) for frying

4 ounces feta cheese

6 tablespoons Salsa Verde (page 240)

Continued . . .

1. To make the fritters: Combine 1 cup water, the broth, and salt in a large saucepan over medium heat. Whisk in the chickpea flour and cook until the mixture thickens, 7 to 8 minutes, stirring often. Stir in the chopped chickpeas and Parmesan cheese.

2. Coat an 8-by-8-inch baking dish with cooking spray. Use a rubber spatula to spread the chickpea mixture into the dish evenly. Refrigerate until set and completely chilled.

3. Meanwhile, make the crispy chickpeas: Heat the blended oil to 375°F in a deep fryer or heavy-bottomed pan with high sides.

4. Combine the peppercorns, salt, coriander, red pepper flakes, and paprika in a spice grinder and finely grind them. Set aside.

5. Place the chickpeas in the buttermilk to soak for a few minutes. Meanwhile, mix together the chickpea flour and cornstarch in a medium bowl. Strain the chickpeas, shake off some of the excess buttermilk, and then place them in the flour mixture. In two batches, remove the chickpeas from the flour, shake off the excess, and fry them until crisp and light brown, 3 to 4 minutes. Transfer them to a kitchen towel to drain. Season well with the spice mixture.

6. Once the fritter batter is completely chilled, carefully invert the dish onto a cutting board. Cut the dough into a 4-by-4 grid of squares, then into thirty-two triangles. When ready to serve, heat the blended oil to 380°F in a deep fryer or heavy-bottomed pan with high sides. Fry the fritters a few at a time until crisp and just beginning to brown, 3 to 4 minutes. Remove, let them drain on a kitchen towel or paper towels, and then transfer them to plates or a serving platter. Top with the feta, fried chickpeas, and a heavy drizzle of the salsa verde.

DRINK TIP

Pinot Gris is another name for Pinot Grigio, and it's typically called Pinot Grigio when the grape is grown in Alsace and Oregon. There, they take on an awesome balance of brightness and fruit, perfect for pairing with the fresh herbs in the salsa verde.

SHALLOT CUSTARD WITH
APPLE-ENDIVE SALAD

This is a fun and simple first course I served at my former restaurant Scylla when autumn came along. It's a nice rich custard topped with a tart salad of apples and endive to start the meal. Although I'm not a pastry chef, I still find myself using pastry techniques in my savory dishes, like here where the creamy texture of custard is topped with the perfect crunch of torched sugar. It's a slightly savory take on the classic crème brûlée, with sherry to bring out the natural sweetness of the shallot, and nutmeg to add toasted-nut spice.

It also brings me back to the days when my dad made Sunday breakfast for the family. My sister and I would argue weekly over whether Dad should make waffles or pancakes, waffles being my choice since they have more nooks and crannies to hold plenty of butter and syrup. Regardless of who won, breakfast was always delicious, as Dad added in a hint of vanilla, cinnamon, and nutmeg to the batter. Even now, when I smell nutmeg, I'm brought back to those mornings.

1 tablespoon butter	Salt	1 Granny Smith apple, julienned	1 tablespoon extra-virgin olive oil
½ cup thinly sliced shallots	1½ cups heavy cream	1 head endive, julienned	4 tablespoons sugar, preferably turbinado (raw sugar; see Ingredient Spotlight, page 35)
1 tablespoon sugar	2 large eggs	8 to 10 chives, cut into 1-inch lengths	
1 tablespoon dry sherry	Freshly ground black pepper	¼ cup fresh lemon juice	
¼ teaspoon ground nutmeg	Vegetable oil spray		

Continued . . .

1. Preheat the oven to 275°F.

2. Heat the butter in a small pot over medium heat until melted. Add the shallots and sugar and stir until the sugar begins to dissolve and caramelize, which should take about 5 minutes. Add in the sherry and nutmeg and continue to reduce *au sec* (which means to cook until it's reduced to a quarter of its original amount). Season with a pinch of salt. Set aside.

3. In a small bowl, whisk together the cream and eggs, seasoning with salt and pepper. Set aside.

4. Divide the caramelized shallots evenly among four shallow 4- to 6-ounce ramekins that have been coated with oil spray, then divide the egg mixture among the ramekins as well. Fill a baking dish large enough to fit the ramekins with ½ inch of warm water. Place the ramekins into the dish, then cover the whole thing with aluminum foil. Carefully transfer the dish to the oven and bake until the custard just sets up, 20 to 25 minutes. To check for doneness, lift the foil and slightly jiggle a ramekin (use a potholder!). The set custard won't show much motion.

5. Once the custards have set, remove the baking dish from the oven and let the ramekins cool in the water for 10 minutes to finish setting. Cover each ramekin with plastic wrap and refrigerate until you're ready to serve. (They'll hold for 2 days.)

6. When you're ready to serve, remove the custards from the fridge and let them sit at room temperature for about 10 minutes. Meanwhile, toss the apple and endive with the chives, lemon juice, and olive oil and season with salt and pepper.

7. Sprinkle 1 tablespoon sugar on top of each custard and brown it with a torch (see Technique 101, below). Sprinkle each with a pinch of salt, top with apple salad, and serve.

TECHNIQUE 101

Caramelizing Sugar: For caramelizing sugar on custard, it's easiest to put the whole amount of sugar on the first custard, shake it around to coat, and then turn it over and tap it lightly over the next custard. Repeat through all of the custards and then discard any excess. To evenly caramelize the sugar, start in one place and slowly move the torch around in a circular motion so that you're constantly moving the flame. This will help avoid burning in spots and should give you a nice even brown coating. Also, I use a blowtorch that I purchased at my local hardware store. It's less expensive than those little pastry torches at fancy kitchen-supply stores, and it's durable enough to withstand the test of time (and the abuse of being in my messy kitchen cabinets).

DRINK TIP

Chardonnays come from many places, but in France they're known as White Burgundy. They tend to be rich enough to match this custard and the sweet shallots but they're not overly oaky, so they wouldn't compete with those flavors.

INGREDIENT SPOTLIGHT

TURBINADO SUGAR In the last few years, you've probably seen little brown packages marked "Sugar in the Raw" pop up in sugar caddies at restaurants. That's turbinado sugar, and while it is light brown in color, it's not the same as brown sugar, which is white sugar combined with molasses. Turbinado, usually from Hawaii, gets color from being unbleached and minimally processed. It actually comes from the first stage of sugar processing, just after the sugar is extracted from the canes. I prefer it mainly because of the coarse, crunchy crystals and the caramelly flavor, plus it melts faster so it's harder to burn. It's fairly widely available, but if you can't find it in stores, go to SugarInTheRaw.com.

MUSSELS ESCABECHE ON CROSTINI

Escabeche might be spelled or pronounced differently depending on where you find it, but whether it's referring to Puerto Rican, Jamaican, Spanish, or Provençal cuisine, it's generally the same thing: an acidic marinade on seafood. I ran into the Spanish version thanks to one of the perks of competing on *Top Chef*—winning a trip to Barcelona. Finally, I had the chance to taste foods I had only read about. My second night there we went out for tapas, and one of the first things to catch my eye was the mussels escabeche. Like many Spanish dishes, they arrived in a little tin, and while the sweet, sour, and spicy notes were there, I was a little disappointed. The texture was a bit off, and I kept thinking it really needed the contrast of some slightly crunchy vegetables. Sometimes even classics could use an update.

STEAMED MUSSELS

1 tablespoon olive oil

½ cup chopped onion

2 garlic cloves, sliced

2 pounds fresh mussels, cleaned and prepared (see Technique 101, facing page)

1 teaspoon salt

1 teaspoon freshly ground black pepper

¾ cup white wine (see Quick Tip, facing page)

2 sprigs fresh thyme

FENNEL ESCABECHE

1 tablespoon olive oil

1 cup thinly sliced fennel bulb

½ red bell pepper, julienned

¼ cup thinly sliced red onion

1 serrano chile, seeded and thinly sliced

1 garlic clove, minced

3 tablespoons white balsamic vinegar

1 tablespoon white wine

1 teaspoon sugar

Salt

Freshly ground black pepper

CROSTINI

Twelve ½-inch baguette slices, cut on a bias

1 tablespoon olive oil

Salt

3 large fresh basil leaves, cut in chiffonade (see Technique 101, page 73, for garnishing)

1. To make the mussels: Heat the olive oil over medium-low heat in a large pot, add the onion and garlic, and sweat until the onion is translucent, about 3 minutes. Increase the heat to high, add the mussels, stir to coat, add the salt and pepper, and stir again. Add the wine and thyme, cover, and steam until the shells just open, 3 to 5 minutes, depending on the size of the mussels. Discard any mussels that don't open.

2. Drain the mussels (you can reserve the cooking broth for a later use, such as for soup base) and pull the meat from the shells, discarding the shells and setting the mussels aside.

3. To make the escabeche: Heat the olive oil over medium heat in a large sauté pan. Add the fennel, bell pepper, onion, serrano, and garlic and sauté, without browning, until the bell pepper is tender, about 3 minutes. Add the balsamic vinegar, wine,

and sugar and season with salt and pepper. Cook for another minute, or until almost all of the liquid has evaporated.

4. Pour the mixture over the mussels, then refrigerate them for at least 1 hour, but no longer than overnight.

5. To make the crostini: Shortly before you want to serve the escabeche, preheat the oven to 375°F. Pull the escabeche from the fridge to bring it up closer to room temperature.

6. Brush the baguette slices with the olive oil, sprinkle with salt, and bake until the slices are just toasted, 6 to 8 minutes.

7. Place three toasts on each plate, top with a small pile of the mussel escabeche, and garnish with basil chiffonade to serve.

QUICK TIP ···

Cooking with Wine: You'll see that many of the recipes in this book call for a general white or red wine, but I don't want you to think too hard when it comes to picking out what type. Just keep in mind that you should never cook with a wine you wouldn't drink (meaning, leave that crappy, cheap cooking wine alone), but on the other hand, there's no reason to cook with expensive stuff, as the nuances are going to be lost in the final dish. I've always just gone with very middle-of-the-road flavors: For white, think "nothing too oaky or too sweet"—Pinot Grigio is ideal—and for reds, steer clear of something really bold and peppery like Shiraz and more toward medium-bodied wines like Merlot. Final note for home cooks: There are some pretty good-quality boxed wines out there these days, and these are perfect for keeping on hand to cook with, as the packaging keeps the wine fresher than an opened bottle will.

TECHNIQUE 101 ···

Bearding Mussels: Before cooking mussels, they have to be soaked, "bearded" (meaning you have to remove what's technically called the byssal threads), and then cleaned. First, soak the mussels in clean water for about 15 minutes to loosen any sand stowaways. Next, grab hold of the beard (using a dry towel or even tweezers helps keep your grip on the slippery sucker) and give it a yank, pulling toward the hinged end of the mussel. (Pulling toward the opening end can kill the mussel.) Last, clean the shells and edge with an abrasive scrub pad under running water. Now you're ready to cook.

DRINK TIP

A highly acidic sauce like this vinegar-based escabeche needs something sweet to counter it but nothing so overpowering that you won't taste the brininess of the mussels. Belgian *dubbel* beers have an ideal sweet maltiness just perfect for the job.

CLAMS STEAMED WITH CORN, BACON, AND FINGERLINGS

SERVES 2 TO 4

Growing up on the East Coast, we ate a lot of clam chowder (New England style, of course; in my mind, the red Manhattan style just doesn't even count). I loved it when my mom made her super-rich and creamy version, topped with little oyster crackers to add crunch and soak up a little broth. But the thing I loved most was the perfect pairing of bacon and clams, almost like they were created to be together. Taking that and adding in the natural sweetness of corn, I put together this simple starter. I think it's a great dish to serve family-style on a sunny summer evening, washed down with an ice-cold beer. Even if you're not sitting on a dock overlooking the Atlantic, you can feel like you are.

12 ounces fingerling potatoes	3 slices bacon, cut into ½-inch pieces	3 ears corn, kernels cut off the cob	2 tablespoons crème fraîche
1 tablespoon olive oil	1 small onion, finely chopped	24 fresh littleneck clams, scrubbed (see Ingredient Spotlight, page 40)	1 tablespoon butter
Salt	3 garlic cloves, minced	¼ cup dry white wine	Several sprigs fresh mint leaves, chopped, for garnishing
Freshly ground black pepper			

1. Preheat the oven to 400°F.

2. Toss the potatoes with the olive oil on a rimmed baking sheet or casserole dish and season with salt and pepper. Roast the potatoes until they are slightly tender, 45 minutes to 1 hour. Let cool, then slice into ½-inch rounds.

3. Heat a large Dutch oven or stockpot over medium heat. Add the bacon and cook it until the fat is rendered and the bacon is just browned, about 7 minutes. Add the onion and garlic and sweat by cooking them until they are tender but not browned, 3 to 5 minutes. Add the sliced potatoes, corn, and clams and season with salt and pepper. Pour in the wine and cover the pot to steam the clams for about 10 minutes. When the clams are completely open, use a slotted spoon to transfer them with the vegetables and bacon to serving bowls or plates, leaving the liquid in the pot. (Discard any clams that don't open).

4. Stir the crème fraîche and butter into the pot and simmer over medium-low heat until just thickened, 3 to 5 minutes. Adjust the seasoning with salt and pepper and spoon the sauce over the clams and veggies. Garnish with the mint and serve.

DRINK TIP

It sounds odd to think of it this way, but Irish stouts have the same creaminess that plump steamed clams do, plus the toasted malts go hand in hand with smoky bacon.

INGREDIENT SPOTLIGHT

CLAMS Clams come in all shapes and sizes. Clams Steamed with Corn, Bacon, and Fingerlings (page 38) calls for littlenecks, which are the smallest and most tender of clams, though they also tend to be the most expensive. The next size up is cherrystones, which are medium sized, moderately priced, and often served raw on the half shell. The largest are chowder clams, which, as their name implies, are often used chopped in chowders since they're a bit tougher and larger and can handle some slow simmering. For this dish, cherrystones will work just fine, but I would save the chowder clams for soup recipes. And remember, as with all shellfish, clams should be served only when they are live right up until cooking. When steaming the clams, discard any that don't open, as they were most likely dead to start off. If you have one or two that only partially open, it's fine to pry them open a bit to give them a little help.

OYSTERS THREE WAYS:
RAW OYSTERS WITH SOYBEAN TAPENADE

MAKES 24 OYSTERS

A simple fresh oyster on the half shell can sing on its own. The briny taste of the ocean, along with the richness of the meaty oyster, are all you really need, but it's fun to have a little topper to add another dimension of flavor as well. A simple *mignonette* sauce of vinegar, shallots, and black pepper is a classic, or you can try something fun like this soybean "tapenade" I developed. When I worked at Vong restaurant in Chicago, we had a soybean coulis made of ground soybeans with a hint of fish sauce and cilantro, and since it was my favorite sauce to dip seared tuna into, I figured those somewhat intense flavors would work just as well with fresh oysters.

½ cup cooked shelled soybeans (edamame), finely chopped	1 tablespoon minced Preserved Lemon (page 241)	¼ teaspoon sambal paste (see Ingredient Spotlight, page 47)	24 fresh, shucked oysters (see Technique 101, page 43; I like something delicate and smaller like Kusshi or Kumamotos when eating them raw), with half shells reserved and rinsed
3 tablespoons extra-virgin olive oil	1 garlic clove, minced		
1 tablespoon chopped fresh cilantro	½ teaspoon fish sauce		

1. In a small bowl, combine the soybeans, olive oil, cilantro, preserved lemon, garlic, fish sauce, and sambal and stir to combine well.

2. Place the oysters in their half shells on a serving platter and top each with a very small spoonful of the soybean "tapenade."

3. Serve immediately.

CRISP OYSTERS WITH BACON AIOLI AND QUAIL EGGS

While I love a fresh oyster and can appreciate the purist approach to enjoying them raw, I have trouble saying no to a fried one. Bite through the perfect crunch into the slightly warmed center and you'll find that the salty and briny notes have toned down and the texture has become perfectly creamy. This version of fried oysters appeared at one of our "Wandering Goat" dinners a few months before the opening of Girl & the Goat. I wanted to give guests a glimpse of what was to come with some fun, casual dinner parties at random locations around the city. The events were a great way for me to play around with different recipes, while also mingling with some folks from around Chicago and sipping on some Three Floyds beer brought by my friends at the brewery. This recipe was concocted for a bacon-themed Wandering Goat, so as you can probably guess, every dish included bacon in some way. The crisp oysters were topped with a bit of bacon aioli that lightly melted on the way to the guests. You can simplify things by omitting the quail eggs and the oysters will still be great, but the quarter-sized yolks add color for cute passed hors d'oeuvres and make the rich snack even richer.

BACON AIOLI

5 slices thick-cut bacon, cut into ½-inch pieces

¼ cup sherry vinegar

1 egg yolk

1 tablespoon Dijon mustard

1 teaspoon honey

1 cup blended oil (half vegetable, half olive oil) or grapeseed oil

Coarse salt

Freshly ground black pepper

OYSTERS

1 cup canola or peanut oil

⅓ cup cornstarch

⅓ cup all-purpose flour

½ cup wheat beer

24 fresh, shucked oysters (see Technique 101, facing page; medium sizes like Dabob Bay because they're uniformly sized, so they fry well), with half shells reserved and rinsed

Salt

Freshly ground black pepper

24 quail eggs

Salt

Freshly ground black pepper

Fresh chervil for garnishing

1. To make the aioli: Heat a large sauté pan over medium heat. Add the bacon and cook until crisp, 7 to 10 minutes. Lift the bacon out of the fat with a slotted spoon to a plate lined with paper towels. (Pour off some of the fat, leaving enough to coat the pan to fry the quail eggs.) Chop the bacon coarsely.

2. Put the vinegar, egg yolk, mustard, and honey into a blender and pulse several times to combine thoroughly. With the blender running, drizzle the blended oil through the lid until all of it has been incorporated and a thick emulsion forms. Add the bacon bits and blend again until smooth. Season with salt and pepper. Cover and refrigerate until needed.

3. To make the oysters: Heat the canola oil to about 365°F in a deep pot or Dutch oven.

4. In a large bowl, whisk together the cornstarch and flour. Fold in the beer to make a loose batter (add a little extra beer if the batter seems too thick).

5. Dunk the oyster meats in the batter, coating them thoroughly. Carefully drop the battered oysters into the hot oil in small batches, frying until they are crisp and golden. Lift them out with a slotted spoon, transfer to a plate lined with paper towels, and sprinkle with salt and pepper.

6. Reheat the sauté pan with the bacon fat over medium heat. Fry the quail eggs sunny-side up (until the whites are set and the yolk is bright and intact). Season with salt and pepper.

7. Put a spoonful of aioli on each of the oyster shells. Add a fried oyster, put a quail egg on top, and garnish with chervil to serve.

TECHNIQUE 101

Shucking Oysters: If you buy your oysters from a reputable fishmonger, or even a knowledgeable clerk at a grocery store like Whole Foods, they're likely to only sell you the "good" ones, meaning oysters that are clamped shut tightly. That's good because it means the liquid won't run out (especially if they're stored flat like they should be), but it also means that now you have to put some muscle into getting these suckers open. Now I'm not big on having a bunch of gadgets taking up drawer space in the kitchen, but if you're going to eat oysters at home, you really need an oyster knife with a nice solid handle. You don't have to go all out and get one of those high-tech oyster gloves; just be sure to protect the hand that's holding the oyster with a thick towel. With the hinge pointed away from you, wedge the tip of the knife into the hinge and wiggle it back and forth until the top shell starts to give. Slide the full length of the knife along the bottom edge of the top shell to separate it completely. Rinse the oyster under cold water to remove any gritty sand, then use the knife to detach the oyster from the bottom shell. There's a tough little knob there called the abductor muscle that attaches the oyster to its shell, so be sure and slide the knife under it to sever it completely. As with all shellfish, freshness is key, so don't shuck the oysters until just before you're going to use them.

GRILLED OYSTERS WITH HORSERADISH AIOLI AND PANCETTA

MAKES 24 OYSTERS

I had my first grilled oyster in Manhattan at Savoy restaurant, where my good friend Chef Ryan Tate was serving these slightly warmed delicacies with just a bit of herb aioli melted over the top. I fell in love with the texture that the oysters take on when they're allowed to steam over the heat of the grill in their own briny juices and how the aioli melts to join them for a light sauce. A bit of crispy pancetta adds a little peppery crunch.

4 ounces thick-cut pancetta, diced into ⅛-inch cubes

HORSERADISH AIOLI

¼ cup sherry vinegar

2 egg yolks

2 tablespoons prepared horseradish, plus more if needed

1 tablespoon Dijon mustard

½ teaspoon coarse salt

¼ teaspoon freshly ground black pepper

1 cup blended oil (half vegetable, half olive oil)

OYSTERS

24 fresh, shucked oysters (see Technique 101, page 43; Wiley Points and Wellfleets are good for this because their plumpness can stand up to grilling), with half shells reserved and rinsed

1 small bunch fresh chives (about 10), sliced into ½-inch pieces

1. Heat a large sauté pan over medium-high heat. When the pan is hot, add the pancetta, reduce the heat to medium, and cook until the pancetta is very crispy, about 7 minutes. Transfer the pancetta to a plate lined with paper towels to drain. Once cool, chop the cubes into a very fine dust. Set aside.

2. To make the aioli: Combine the vinegar, egg yolks, horseradish, mustard, salt, and pepper in a blender. With the blender running, pour the blended oil through the opening in the lid in a slow, steady stream until a thick sauce forms. Adjust the seasoning and add extra horseradish for a more intense flavor. Cover and refrigerate for up to 5 days.

3. To make the oysters: Preheat the grill (gas or charcoal) to medium-high. Arrange the oysters on half shells in one layer on the grill grates. Close the lid and grill until the oysters are just warmed through, 2 to 3 minutes.

4. To serve, arrange the grilled oysters on a platter. Top each oyster with a dollop of the aioli, a sprinkle of pancetta dust, and a few pieces of chive.

DRINK TIP

When in doubt, go with bubbly. And no matter the type of oyster you're eating—again, go with bubbly. Blanc de Blanc is an affordable alternative to pricier Champagnes, but it still has that beautiful effervescence and dry crispness you're looking for.

SAUTÉED SHRIMP WITH BUTTERNUT PURÉE AND CIDER GASTRIQUE

This recipe may sound a bit strange, but it's actually built off of two classic flavor combinations: squash with apple and ginger with chile paste. Squash and apples are pretty much required fall menu items for any serious American restaurant, and the combo of ginger and chiles is popular throughout all of Asia. After cooking at two Asian-inspired restaurants—Vong and Spring, both in Chicago—ginger and chiles slowly started creeping into my cooking as additions that could cut through rich flavors. Back when I owned Scylla, I tried to hide my love of cooking with Asian flavors, as the restaurant was branded "Mediterranean" from the beginning. These days, I try not to categorize my food to any specific region. I just like to cook things that I enjoy, and I use fun flavors that work well together, no matter what part of the world they come from.

BUTTERNUT PURÉE

½ small butternut squash (about 8 ounces)

1½ tablespoons butter

¼ cup chopped onion

1 garlic clove, minced

1½ teaspoons minced peeled fresh ginger (see Quick Tip, page 46)

⅓ cup vegetable broth or water

⅓ cup heavy cream

Salt

Freshly ground black pepper

CIDER GASTRIQUE

½ cup cider vinegar

3 tablespoons sugar

¼ teaspoon freshly ground black pepper

APPLE FRISÉE SALAD

½ Granny Smith apple, julienned

½ head frisée lettuce, dark green ends and base trimmed, remainder shredded

6 to 8 fresh chives, cut into 1-inch pieces

1 teaspoon olive oil

SHRIMP

3 tablespoons olive oil

2 garlic cloves, minced

½ teaspoon sambal paste (see Ingredient Spotlight, page 47)

12 fresh jumbo (11 to 15 count) tail-on shrimp, peeled and deveined

2 tablespoons butter

Salt

1. Preheat the oven to 375°F.

2. To make the purée: Scoop out the seeds and guts of the squash (reserve the other half for another day). Place ½ tablespoon of the butter in the cavity, then flip the squash over so it's flesh-side down on a rimmed baking sheet. Bake until the skin browns and the squash is slightly soft to the touch, about 45 minutes.

3. Melt the remaining 1 tablespoon butter in a small saucepan over medium heat. Add the onion, garlic, and ginger. Once the onion is translucent, scoop out the butternut squash flesh from the skin and add it to the pan. Add the broth and cream, then simmer the mixture over low heat until the cream has taken a nutty smell and the soup has thickened, about 25 minutes. Use an immersion blender or transfer everything to a tabletop blender to purée until smooth. Season with salt and pepper.

Continued . . .

4. To make the gastrique: Cook the vinegar and sugar in a small pot over medium heat until it reduces to a syrupy consistency thick enough to coat the back of a spoon, 5 to 7 minutes. Add the pepper, remove the gastrique from the heat, and let it cool to room temperature before serving. (For more on gastriques, see page 22.)

5. To make the salad: Toss all the ingredients together in a small bowl.

6. To make the shrimp: In a large bowl, stir together the olive oil, garlic, and sambal, then toss the shrimp in the marinade to coat. Cover and refrigerate for at least 1 hour and up to overnight.

7. Pull the shrimp from the fridge. Melt the butter in a large sauté pan over medium heat. Season the shrimp with a bit of salt and sauté until pink but still slightly translucent in the middle, about 1 minute on each side.

8. To serve, make a small circle on each plate with a heaping spoonful of the squash purée. Lay three shrimp over the purée on each plate, drizzle about 1 teaspoon of gastrique over the shrimp, and divide the frisée salad evenly among the plates.

PLAN OF ATTACK

- Up to 2 weeks ahead: Make the Cider Gastrique. Store it covered in the refrigerator.
- Up to 3 days in advance: Make the squash purée.
- The night before: Marinate the shrimp.
- Cook time: Prepare the frisée salad. Warm up the reduction and the purée on the stovetop while sautéing the shrimp.

 QUICK TIP ....

Fresh ginger is a knobby little root, making it a bit tough to peel. What I do is ditch the peeler and use the edge of a teaspoon; its rounded edges help you get into all the crevices of the ginger. Also, slicing or mincing ginger can give you a bunch of annoying threads, so grate it on a Microplane grater, and you'll have these awesome fine shavings that will almost melt into whatever you're cooking— much better than picking ginger threads from your teeth.

DRINK TIP

As rich as squash is, you want something nice and crisp to cut through this purée. Kölsch beers are a summery German style that's less bitter than pilsners, but they still have a good amount of bite to complement the ginger.

INGREDIENT SPOTLIGHT

SAMBAL To put it simply, this stuff kicks ass. It's essentially a Southeast Asian chile paste (common in Indonesia and Malaysia, to be specific), and I use it more than any other type of chile paste out there. There are a ton of different kinds, but the majority of what you'll see in stores is labeled *sambal oelek* (although you might also come across *sambal badjak*, which includes onions). It's pretty much just ground chiles with salt and a bit of vinegar. It's traditionally used as a condiment, but most often I use it as a marinade. My go-to brand is Huy Fong Foods, which some larger grocery stores now carry in the Asian foods aisle. Most Asian markets will either have it or something comparable.

GRILLED LAMB-STUFFED CALAMARI
WITH CRISPY SHALLOTS

SERVES 6

This is a dish I've been playing around with since my Scylla days. I remember sitting on the couch on one of my days off (Monday was pretty much always the couch surfing/refuel/ work-on-menu day), and I was trying to come up with something new to do with squid, as we always had some version of it on the menu. Often when I'm writing new menus, I make lists of all of the ingredients I want to include (mainly things that are in season), then I sort of play a matching game, crossing off ingredients as I go, as in "this will go with this, and that with that." I had lamb on the list because it was spring—a great time for lamb—and I decided to try the lamb and squid together. I'm a big fan of combining two proteins on one plate (often seafood and meat, a bit of a surf and turf—which I'm sure bugs the hell out of those who don't eat meat).

So I got to work making the lamb filling, and it needed a bit of a salty kick, but something earthy to complement the subtle gaminess. Miso was just the trick. Like using tamari in hummus, adding that little extra bit of miso paste makes a huge difference. If you can, try to make each component of the dish so you get how the flavors work together, but you can also simplify by serving it with either the almond butter sauce or the vinaigrette as opposed to both. The squid is also great topped with other sauces like the Pistachio Picada (page 227), the Romesco (page 133), or just with a simple salad.

FILLING

2 teaspoons olive oil

1 shallot, minced

2 garlic cloves, minced

8 ounces ground lamb

2 teaspoons Dijon mustard

2 teaspoons white miso paste

1 teaspoon sambal paste (see Ingredient Spotlight, page 47)

½ teaspoon soy sauce

CRISPY SHALLOTS

2 cups peanut or vegetable oil

¾ cup rice flour

¼ cup cornstarch

4 shallots, sliced into very thin rounds

Coarse salt

Freshly ground black pepper

12 medium squid tubes, plus tentacles (about 1 pound; see Ingredient Spotlight, page 51)

Peanut or vegetable oil

1 cup Miso–Marcona Almond Butter (page 238)

6 tablespoons Cilantro Vinaigrette (page 236)

Continued . . .

1. To make the filling: Heat the olive oil in a large sauté pan over medium-low heat. Sweat the shallot and garlic by cooking them until they are translucent, about 5 minutes. Increase heat to medium-high, add the lamb, mustard, miso, sambal, and soy sauce and cook to brown lightly, 7 to 10 minutes. Remove from the heat and cool slightly.

2. Meanwhile, to make the crispy shallots: Heat the peanut oil in a deep, heavy-bottomed medium saucepot until it registers 375°F on a deep-fry thermometer (see Quick Tip, below).

3. Mix together the rice flour and cornstarch in a medium bowl. Coat the shallots in the flour mixture and then shake them in a sieve to remove any excess flour. Carefully add the shallots to the hot oil in two batches and move them around with tongs as they fry to avoid clumping. When each batch is lightly browned and crispy, remove the shallots to drain on a paper towel and season with salt and pepper.

4. Preheat the grill (charcoal or gas) to medium. When the lamb mixture is cool enough to handle, stuff it into the squid tubes. Brush the outside of each tube with the peanut oil and toss the tentacles in oil as well. Grill the stuffed tubes and tentacles until just cooked through, turning once or twice, 2 to 3 minutes.

5. Serve the squid over a smear of the almond butter and top with a drizzle of the cilantro vinaigrette and the crispy fried shallots.

QUICK TIP

If you don't have a deep-fry thermometer, put the handle end of a wooden spoon in the hot oil to test the temperature instead. When a steady stream of bubbles forms around the handle, the oil is hot enough.

DRINK TIP

There's a lot going on in this dish, so when you're facing a ton of different flavors to pair with, the best solution is to go with something fairly innocuous that won't clash. Grüner Veltliners from Austria are perfect wines for this: not too dry, not too sweet, not too acidic . . . just nice and fresh to let the food come through.

INGREDIENT SPOTLIGHT

SQUID (A.K.A. CALAMARI) Most people only associate squid with the fried rings at red-sauce Italian joints, which is also why there's often confusion over whether squid and calamari are the same thing. They are; *calamari* is simply the Italian term for "squid." These slippery cephalopods (say that ten times fast) are cousins to both octopus and cuttlefish, and they're actually much more versatile than you'd think. The tubes are perfect for stuffing and grilling, but they will overcook quickly and become rubbery so you want to make sure your stuffing is precooked and that you're cooking the filled tubes just long enough to heat them through. Don't be nervous about selecting them, as most squid will be sold "refreshed" anyway (meaning they've been flash-frozen and then thawed before sale) and that's okay; most restaurants get it that way, too. If they're still frozen, just let them thaw under running water and make sure to rinse them inside and out—just like finding the occasional pit in pitted olives, there could be a few things hiding in the tubes.

BRAISED PIG TONGUES WITH QUICK-PICKLED SUNCHOKES AND BRUSSELS SPROUTS

SERVES 6

I firmly believe that every single part of the pig is tasty, from the snout to the tail, but I realize that not all of you are going to run right out and make pig tongue for dinner. Still, I want this book to be a true reflection of how I cook and eat, and I hope that at least some of you will give this recipe a try. I've been fortunate to have access to farms where they raise pigs very humanely to sell to chefs who respect the practices of small local farmers. A few of my chef friends and I have even visited the farms to participate in the slaughter and breakdown of the pig, which is a very interesting process to be a part of and a true testament to supporting the use of whole animals so as to avoid waste. Working with a whole animal means that you can cure legs and rumps into hams and prosciutto, turn shoulders into sausages, fat into lardo, belly into bacon, and so forth. Not to be forgotten is the part we are celebrating here, the tongue, which has an unbelievable rich meaty flavor and nice tender texture, so long as it's cooked right. Talk to your local butcher about special ordering tongue or approach a meat stand at a farmers' market—asking for a little tongue is a great way to start up a conversation.

2 or 3 pig tongues (1½ to 2 pounds)

2 tablespoons vegetable oil

1 medium onion, diced

2 garlic cloves, chopped

1 cup sliced fresh strawberries, plus 1 sliced for garnishing

1 cup diced fresh pineapple

1 cup dry sherry

1 cup white wine

4 cups veal stock or dark chicken stock (see Quick Tip, facing page)

½ cup white balsamic vinegar

1 tablespoon sugar

8 ounces sunchokes (see page 64), peeled and sliced very thin (or shaved on a mandoline)

4 ounces fresh Brussels sprouts, sliced very thin (or shaved on a mandoline)

¼ cup lightly packed fresh mint

2 tablespoons extra-virgin olive oil

Coarse salt

Freshly ground black pepper

2 tablespoons butter

1. Rinse the tongues under cold water and pat dry. Heat the vegetable oil in a large stockpot or Dutch oven over medium-low heat. Add the onion and garlic and sweat them until they start to soften but not brown, 3 to 5 minutes. Add the 1 cup strawberries and the pineapple and sauté for 1 minute. Pour in the sherry and wine, increase the heat to bring to a boil, then reduce to a simmer. Cook until the liquid is reduced by half, about 10 minutes.

2. Add the tongues and the stock, bring to a boil, then reduce the heat to low. Cover the pot and simmer the tongues until tender, 2 to 2½ hours.

3. When the tongues are soft and tender, remove them from the liquid and set aside. When they're cool enough to handle, carefully peel off the outer layer (the taste buds) and discard.

4. Bring the liquid to a boil and reduce to about one fourth of the original to create a rich sauce. Strain the sauce and discard the solids. Keep the sauce warm until ready to use.

5. Combine the vinegar and sugar in a small pot over medium-high heat. Bring the mixture to a boil, then simmer until the sugar is completely dissolved, about 2 minutes. Pour the mixture over the sunchokes in a medium bowl. Let the mixture sit for about 5 minutes to pickle the sunchokes. Strain the liquid off and set the sunchokes aside (you can reserve the pickling liquid for up to three additional uses; beyond that, it loses its potency).

6. Put the Brussels sprouts in a medium bowl. Tear the mint leaves and toss them with the shaved sprouts. Add the pickled sunchokes to the mixture, drizzle with the olive oil, and season with salt and pepper.

7. Cut the tongues into ¼-inch slices. Heat the butter in a large sauté pan over high heat. Add slices of tongue in a single layer and sauté to just lightly crisp the edges. Arrange the slices on plates or a serving platter, drizzle with the sauce, top with the sunchoke–Brussels sprouts salad, and garnish with sliced strawberry.

 QUICK TIP ·

Some recipes, like this one, really need the oomph of a dark stock like veal or beef or they just won't reduce down into the rich, concentrated sauce that you want. Veal stock is pricier and can be tougher to find (although most specialty stores and butchers carry it), but it's definitely worth it when it comes to full flavor. If you don't want to go that route, you can use chicken stock, but try to use a dark version like the one on page 232. It might seem like an extra step, but you can make a big batch and freeze it to have on hand. A good trick is to pour the stock into ice cube trays to freeze them so that it's already measured out for you when you need it. Each cube in a standard-size tray holds a little more than 1 ounce, and since there are 8 ounces in a cup, using a half dozen cubes will give you roughly 1 cup of stock.

 **DRINK TIP**

American pale ales work with this dish on two levels: They're crisp enough to cut through the richness of the braised tongue, and they also have a great grassy hoppiness that goes well with these tart veggies.

CHA
TWO

SOUPS

THINKING BACK TO MY CHILDHOOD, I HAD TWO FAVORITE SOUPS. ONE WAS FROM A WELL-WORN INDEX CARD LABELED SIMPLY "MEXICAN SOUP"—A RICH TOMATO BASE WITH GROUND BEEF, BEANS, AND A BIT OF SPICE—LIKE CHILI, BUT SOUPIER.

(I think the real reason I loved it was because my mom let me top it with a fistful of shredded Cheddar cheese and crumbled Doritos.) So that was my football-season soup, but during summers, my mom made big batches of vichyssoise and left a bowl of it in the fridge that we would dip into for meals and snacks. Even as a kid, these soups taught me that the seasons make you crave different flavors and temperatures. That's one of the main principles of my style of cooking today and why the recipes in this chapter range from a springy celebration of peas to a hearty beef stew brightened up with apples, pears, and pineapple. But before you dive in and start whipping up a batch, the one major rule I can tell you about soup is to taste everything! Even after you've made a soup a dozen times, there are so many variables that can make it different, from the sweetness of the vegetables to the saltiness of the stock. When I worked at Vong, we took a spoonful from each bowl of the chicken-lemongrass soup before we put it up in the window, and then the head chef would taste it again before sending it to the table. It was our last chance to adjust it—and I, for one, didn't mind tasting delicious soup all night long.

MANGO AND MARCONA ALMOND GAZPACHO

SERVES 4

Back during the days of my restaurant Scylla, I was asked to participate in a trade show event by my good friend Chandra Ram, who had just become the editor of *Plate* magazine. The event was all about the sponsors, and each chef was given some donated ingredients to work with. I was given mango, almonds, and shrimp. Now shrimp and mango are a pretty common combination—grilled shrimp with a little mango salsa or something like that—but I had the almonds to use as well. I still wanted to keep it simple, and I remember that I had just been watching some morning show where the guest made a white gazpacho with almonds and grapes. I thought, "Why not take the mango, get rid of the grapes, and make a variation on the classic Spanish cold soup?" To keep everything balanced when using ripe, sweet fruit in savory dishes, I always counter with a bit of spice. Here, the sambal shrimp do the trick.

¾ cup fresh orange juice

½ cup fresh or day-old bread cubes

2 very ripe mangos, diced (see Technique 101, facing page)

2 garlic cloves, minced

Coarse salt

1 English cucumber, peeled and diced (1½ to 2 cups)

1 cup unsalted Marcona almonds (see Ingredient Spotlight, page 239)

3 tablespoons extra-virgin olive oil

2 teaspoons sherry vinegar

Freshly ground black pepper

4 ounces large (21 to 30) shrimp, peeled and deveined

½ teaspoon sambal paste (see Ingredient Spotlight, page 47)

5 basil leaves, cut into chiffonade (see Technique 101, page 73)

1. Pour the orange juice over the bread cubes in a small bowl and set aside to soak.

2. Set aside 2 tablespoons of the mangos, dice them finely, and refrigerate for garnish. Mash 1 garlic clove to a paste with ¼ teaspoon salt. Put the garlic in a blender or food processor with the remaining mango, cucumber, almonds, 2 tablespoons of the olive oil, and 1 cup water. Add the bread and juice and process until very smooth. Stir in the vinegar, 2 teaspoons salt, and ¼ teaspoon pepper. Adjust the seasonings and refrigerate the soup for at least 30 minutes before serving.

3. Toss the shrimp with the sambal and remaining garlic clove and season with salt and pepper. Heat the remaining 1 tablespoon olive oil in a sauté pan over medium-high heat. Add the shrimp and sauté until cooked through, 1 to 2 minutes. Remove the shrimp from the pan to let cool slightly.

4. Divide the gazpacho between serving bowls. Slice the sautéed shrimp crosswise in coins and toss with the reserved mango and the basil. Garnish each serving with a spoonful of the shrimp and mango mixture.

TECHNIQUE 101 ·······························

Cutting Mango: Mangos are delicious, but they can be tough to slice because of their oval-shaped pit and slippery flesh. The easiest way to cut a mango is to cube it. Slice off one of the flat sides, then the other flat side, so that you're essentially making two halves but cutting around the wide, flat pit. (If you don't want the flesh around the pit to go to waste, peel the skin off the remaining sides with a knife and nibble around the pit as you would a peach.) Hold a mango half in one hand, flesh-side up, and with your hand protected by a thick towel, make score marks the length of the mango, being careful not to cut through the skin. Now score crosswise to create a crosshatch. Push up on the skin-side's center as if you're trying to turn it inside out until it's inverted, then slide the knife just above the skin's surface to free the cubes. Repeat with the other half. Use the cubed mango to top ice cream; throw some in a smoothie; or toss with diced avocado, salt, and pepper and toss with mixed greens for a quick salad.

DRINK TIP

Sometimes pairings are more about gut feelings than any kind of scientific match, and because this gazpacho is just made for sitting outside on a summery night, it goes well with light and refreshing Pinot Blancs.

SWEET GARLIC VICHYSOISSE

Vichysoisse (pronounced vih-shee-SWAHZ), a fancy name for chilled potato-leek soup, was often in the fridge when I was growing up. My mom would make a big batch for dinner, then we would sip on leftovers for a few days afterward. It's hard to take something as rich as potatoes and make them refreshing, but somehow vichysoisse always cut through the 95-degree heat (with 95 percent humidity, no less) on a hot Northeastern summer day. So we may have had vichysoisse, but one thing I did miss out on growing up was garlic. My mom always said, "I love garlic, but garlic doesn't love me." I never quite understood what she meant until I got older, but I knew not to order the garlic-lover's pizza. These days, I like to use garlic in just about everything. In this recipe in particular, the harshness of the garlic is subdued and the natural sweetness is allowed to shine through. This is achieved through blanching the garlic multiple times in heavily salted water, a method I learned from Shawn McClain when I worked at Spring in Chicago. The first time I did this, I was amazed at the outcome—all of the flavors we garlic freaks love with none of the bitterness.

2 heads garlic, peeled (12 to 15 cloves)

¼ cup olive oil

3 leeks, halved lengthwise and whites sliced into half moons

1 small fennel bulb, cored and thinly sliced

½ cup dry white wine

6 medium (about 2 pounds) Yukon gold potatoes, peeled and cut into 1-inch dice

2 cups chicken broth

2 cups half-and-half

¼ cup heavy cream

Salt

Freshly ground black pepper

1. Bring a medium pot of heavily salted water to a boil. Blanch the garlic three times by dropping into the water and cooking for 2 to 3 minutes, then draining the garlic, changing the water, and bringing it back to a boil before blanching the garlic again. Do not shock the garlic under cold water in between blanchings. (This process is time consuming, but it's worth it.)

2. Heat the olive oil in a large sauté pan over medium-low heat, add the leeks and fennel, and sweat them for a few minutes by cooking until the leeks are translucent. Add the wine and cook until nearly all of the wine has evaporated.

3. Add the potatoes and garlic to the pan. Cover with the broth, half-and-half, and 2 cups water. Simmer until the potatoes are very tender, 45 to 60 minutes.

4. Working in batches in a blender or food processor, purée the soup until smooth, adding half of the cream with each batch. Season with salt and pepper. Cool completely and as rapidly as possible (see Technique 101, facing page).

5. Refrigerate the soup and serve as desired.

TECHNIQUE 101

Cooling Soups: Soups are one of the best things to make ahead of time because they hold their flavor so well simply stored in the fridge, and you can quickly rewarm them to serve in about the same amount of time it takes you and a few friends to finish your first beer. In restaurants, we make soups in big batches (which you can do, too, by doubling any of the recipes in this chapter) but we don't put them in the walk-in to cool them—that would actually bring up the temperature of everything else in the fridge. Instead, we transfer the soup from the cooking vessel into a cold pot sitting in an ice bath (you can do this in a sink with a stopper; just add ice and water), then we stir the soup until it's nice and cool. Now it's ready for storage, but here's one other tip: Be sure to taste the soup again just before you're about to serve it because the seasonings may need readjusting as the fluctuating temperature can sometimes gobble up salt.

DRINK TIP

Sancerre wines are a very elegant style of Sauvignon Blanc from the Loire Valley of France, and they're ideal for bringing out the natural sweetness of garlic.

PEAR-PISTACHIO-PARSNIP SOUP

SERVES 4 TO 6

A few years ago, my sister asked if I would cook for some of her friends and coworkers for a Christmas party at her house. I think her words were, "No big deal; keep it simple, just make a couple of appetizers and dips," but of course I never keep things that simple. For some reason I decided to make nearly a dozen dishes, ranging from finger foods to pastas (although with all the wine there, I could have just set out some artichoke dip and everyone would still have had a great time). One of the simplest dishes I made was this soup, and it turned out to be the biggest hit. Even with such a small list of ingredients, this soup comes out great because the flavors all work well together: The sweetness and texture of the pears and parsnips are a good match, while the pistachios bring an unexpected salty note to the soup. And I know you'll hear me say this over and over, but anytime you have sweetness in a dish like you'll get from the fruit here, you really want to balance that out with a bit of heat—this time delivered by Thai chile.

1 tablespoon butter	8 ounces parsnips, peeled and sliced	¾ cup roasted, salted pistachios	1 cup milk
⅓ cup diced yellow onion	2 ripe Anjou pears, peeled and diced	½ cup white wine	1 dried red Thai chile (see Ingredient Spotlight, facing page)
2 garlic cloves, sliced		3½ cups chicken broth	

1. Melt the butter over medium heat in a medium soup pot. Add the onion and garlic and sweat by cooking until they are translucent but not browned, 3 to 5 minutes.

2. Stir in the parsnips, pears, and ½ cup of the pistachios. Add the wine and simmer to reduce the liquid by three fourths (meaning almost dry, a technique often referred to as reducing *au sec).*

3. Add the broth, milk, and chile, and bring everything to a boil. Reduce the heat and simmer the soup until the parsnips are very soft, about 1 hour.

4. Working in batches with a tabletop or immersion blender, purée the soup, then divide among four bowls. Garnish with the remaining ¼ cup pistachios and serve.

DRINK TIP

There's a pronounced sweetness to this soup, so while you might want a wine like Riesling with a similar sweetness to complement your food, try to find one from Alsace, which will tend to be drier than other Rieslings.

INGREDIENT SPOTLIGHT

THAI CHILES There are plenty of chile varieties out there, but I tend to gravitate toward Thai chiles, mainly for their versatility and the fact that they give good heat without the bitterness found in some dried chiles. You should be able to find these at better grocery stores and definitely in Asian markets (they might be labeled as "bird chiles"). I like to add them to sauces and soups for earthy heat, but remember that a little goes a long way.

EQUIPMENT SPOTLIGHT

IMMERSION BLENDERS The last thing I want is for any of you to avoid making a soup because of the hassle of transferring it to a blender to purée it in batches, then having to pass it through a sieve as we do in restaurants. There are definitely times when a velvety smooth soup is nice (especially if you're making it for a special party), but most of the time you can get away with a bit more texture. The easiest way to purée soups is using a handheld immersion blender. This tool is fairly inexpensive (you can get a good one for under $40) and a cinch to use. The best part is that you can purée the soup right in its cooking pot, so you don't need to wait until the liquid has cooled. Submerge the wand into the soup and move it around to make sure any hunks get caught up into the blade—just be careful not to pull the blender above the surface of the soup while it's still on, or you'll have one heck of a mess on your hands.

CHILLED WALLA WALLA ONION SOUP SERVES 4 TO 6

This is one of the easiest soups to make and even self-professed onion haters have loved it. Try to use Walla Walla onions if you can find them, and Vidalias if you can't; both have the sweet characteristics of other onion varieties but none of the harshness. Walla Walla onions are named for a great town in the wine country of Washington state, where I've become friends with some awesome winemakers (we even blended our first house wine for Girl & the Goat in that area at Seviah Vineyards). So whether you go with Walla Wallas or Vidalias, this soup is going to have a delicate, sweet flavor, and it's very light and velvety, making it an ideal chilled soup. (By comparison, a classic French onion soup is hearty and rich with a lot of caramel notes, so it's better served warm.) Plus, it's always nice to have something other than gazpacho to cool you off on a hot summer day.

2 tablespoons butter 1 tablespoon olive oil	4 Walla Walla or Vidalia onions, thinly sliced (see Technique 101, facing page)	2 garlic cloves, minced Salt Freshly ground black pepper	1 cup white dessert wine or sweeter white wine like Riesling

1. Melt the butter into the olive oil in a medium or large soup pot over medium-low heat. Add the onions and garlic, and sweat them slowly by cooking and stirring often until the onions are soft, about 20 minutes. Season lightly with salt and pepper.

2. Add the wine and simmer for 5 more minutes.

3. Add 6 cups water, bring the soup to a boil, and simmer until the flavors all come together, about 1 hour.

4. Working in batches with a tabletop or immersion blender, purée the soup.

5. Refrigerate the soup until it's well chilled, then taste it again and adjust the seasonings with salt and pepper. Divide the soup evenly among 4 to 6 bowls to serve.

TECHNIQUE 101 ··

Cutting Onions: Talk about a dork! When I was a kid, I used to volunteer to chop onions, then rummage through my mom's crazy collection of sunglasses and pick out the biggest pair to wear like goggles while I sat on a counter stool cutting onions. It did keep me from crying, but it's not really a look I could get away with later in professional kitchens. Most old wives' tales about how to keep from crying while cutting onions aren't going to work for people with sensitive eyes, but it does seem to help a bit to use a super-sharp knife and make sure the onion is good and cold. Always start by cutting the onion in half from tip to root, peel it, and then place it cut-side down on a cutting board and trim off just the tip of the end opposite the root. If you want slices, slice thinly against the grain, cutting as close to the root end as possible without cutting through the root. After slicing, cut the root off to free the slices. If you want to dice the onion, first turn the knife on its side and cut through the onion half horizontally, again leaving the root intact. Next, slice with the knife in the normal upright position and your dices will fall onto the cutting board naturally.

DRINK TIP

There's a theory of wine pairing that things that grow together go together. This might sound like a very specific pairing, but if you can find K Vintner's Kung Fu Girl Riesling, which is also grown in Walla Walla, you'll see how well this works. If you can't find that, sub your favorite Riesling.

SUNCHOKE SOUP WITH OLIVES AND GRAPEFRUIT

SERVES 4

I absolutely love this soup. Sunchokes (also called Jerusalem artichokes, although they're not an artichoke; they're actually related to the sunflower) are knobby roots that resemble ginger. They have an amazing nutty-sweet flavor and a texture similar to a potato, so they're ideal to cook and purée—in fact, cooking them brings out their nuttiness even more. This soup is great in small cappuccino cups served as hors d'oeuvres. I've served it hot or cold, and it's delicious both ways, but if you serve it cold, the soup will have to be thinned out a bit more with a touch of milk. And be sure to adjust the seasoning once the soup has chilled, as cold foods often need more salt than hot foods. Also, never cook with a wine you wouldn't drink. I always save any wine that I don't finish drinking for cooking with later (who am I kidding? I've never had trouble finishing a bottle of wine).

2 tablespoons butter	2 pounds sunchokes, peeled and cut into ½-inch rounds	3¾ cups chicken broth	8 Ruby Red grapefruit supremes (see Technique 101, page 76)
1 cup diced onion		¾ cup heavy cream	
2 garlic cloves, sliced	Salt	4 tablespoons cerignola olives, pitted and sliced (see Ingredient Spotlight, page 17)	
1 cup dry sparkling wine or dry white wine	Freshly ground black pepper		

1. Melt the butter over medium heat in a large stockpot. Add the onion and garlic and sweat them by cooking until the onion is translucent, 3 to 5 minutes.

2. Add the wine and simmer to reduce the liquid by two-thirds.

3. Add the sunchokes and season with salt and pepper.

4. Add 3 cups of the broth and 2 cups water and bring the mixture to a boil. Reduce the heat and simmer until the sunchokes are tender, about 1½ hours.

5. Add the remaining ¾ cup broth and the cream and purée the soup with a tabletop or immersion blender. Season with salt and pepper.

6. Divide the soup among bowls and top with the olives and grapefruit segments.

DRINK TIP

This is a fairly rich soup, one that works well with a lightly oaked California Chardonnay. Even one with a bit of butteriness will do fine here because you'll have the saltiness of the olives and the tart citrus to help balance everything out.

APPLE SOUP WITH TARRAGON YOGURT

SERVES 4

Once the end of summer comes around and fall starts to roll in, apples are in abundance in the Midwest. They've always been one of my favorite fruits to munch on—a little peanut butter on them, and I'm happy until dinner. The first time I turned apples into soup was for my friend James, who asked me to cook for a group of his friends, including his girlfriend, whom he planned to propose to later that night. Serving the soup as an appetizer, I made sure not to make it too sweet, balancing it with the vegetables, broth, and a good dose of salt and pepper. It must have been good, because James and Carly are now happily married.

1½ teaspoons olive oil	3 garlic cloves, minced	½ cup white wine	½ cup Greek-style yogurt
1½ teaspoons butter	2 Honeycrisp apples, peeled and thinly sliced	½ cup heavy cream	2 tablespoons minced fresh tarragon
1 cup chopped onion	Salt	1¾ cups chicken or vegetable broth	1 tablespoon milk
1 cup chopped fennel bulb	Freshly ground black pepper	1¼ cups apple cider	

1. Heat the olive oil and butter in a large soup pot over medium-low heat. Sweat the onion, fennel, and garlic by cooking them until the onion is translucent, 3 to 5 minutes.

2. Stir in the apples, season with salt and pepper, then add the wine. Simmer to reduce the liquid by half.

3. Meanwhile, cook the cream in a small saucepan over medium-low heat until it thickens, whisking periodically to loosen the little bits of browned cream that will impart a nutty flavor. Once it's reduced by half, set it aside for later.

4. Once the apple mixture has reduced, add the broth and cider and bring them to a boil. Reduce the heat and simmer until the apples and fennel are tender, about 1 hour.

5. While the soup is simmering, whisk together the yogurt, tarragon, and milk until evenly blended and smooth. Season with salt and pepper. Refrigerate until needed.

6. Once the soup is ready, purée it with a tabletop or immersion blender until smooth, then pass it through a fine-mesh sieve to remove any chunky bits. Of course, if you don't have a sieve and don't mind a slightly chunky soup, you can skip this step.

7. Transfer the soup back to the soup pot, whisk in the cooked cream, and season with salt and pepper. Divide the soup among bowls and top with a dollop of tarragon yogurt to serve.

DRINK TIP

Anytime you're dealing with apples, it's a pretty safe bet to go with German-style wheat beers, a.k.a. *weizens*. There's a fruity spiciness that is somewhat similar to apple cider—like the flavor of fall in a glass, but with a good dose of booze.

INGREDIENT SPOTLIGHT

BROTH VS. STOCK The terms *broth* and *stock* are used so interchangeably that it's become a bit muddy what the differences are between the two. Generally speaking, stocks are more concentrated and intense, typically because they're made with bones and animal parts with a lot of connective tissue plus chopped vegetables. Broth is usually just the liquid left after cooking whole pieces of meat or vegetables. I use the term *broth* in the recipes in this book because it's more readily available to home cooks, although more and more I've been seeing stocks (gelatin, frozen, and canned) popping up at grocery stores. For store-bought stuff, I like Swanson, but whatever you use, try to buy those marked "all natural" so that you're not getting a bunch of MSG and artificial flavorings. And remember, the flavor varies a lot from brand to brand, so be sure and taste it before cooking with it so you know how to adjust when seasoning with salt.

BROWN BUTTER–DELICATA SQUASH SOUP WITH SHERRY VINEGAR REDUCTION

SERVES 4 TO 6

Every fall, I look forward to squash soups. Winter squashes have the perfect texture to lead to a nice velvety soup, no cream needed. Almost any contemporary American restaurant will have some version of a squash soup during the cooler months, and it's usually a take on butternut. (In fact, you see butternut soup so often that I sought out Delicata squash just to give diners something a little different; Delicatas are a little less sweet and have a color and taste a bit closer to nutty corn kernels. My Aunt Marion makes a delicious butternut squash soup every year around the holidays, and a few years back she told me what a pain in the butt it can be to peel the squash for the soup. I gave her the tip that it's much easier to roast the squash ahead of time to loosen it from the skin, then simply scoop it out with a spoon. The next year when we all showed up for the holidays, she thanked me and said her annual routine had gotten a whole lot easier.

3 to 4 pounds Delicata squash

¾ cup unsalted butter plus 2 tablespoons

Salt

Freshly ground black pepper

½ cup pepitas (see Ingredient Spotlight, page 78)

1 teaspoon vegetable oil

¼ teaspoon minced fresh thyme

1 tablespoon olive oil

1 onion, finely diced

2 garlic cloves, sliced

1 Honeycrisp apple, peeled and finely diced

1 fennel bulb, finely diced

½ cup white wine

4 cups chicken broth or vegetable broth, plus more as needed

1 cup apple cider

1 to 2 tablespoons Sherry Vinegar Reduction (page 240)

1. Preheat the oven to 375°F and set two oven racks evenly apart. Cut each squash in half lengthwise and scoop out and discard the seeds and stringy pulp. Place 1½ teaspoons of butter inside each squash half and season with salt and pepper. Place the squash halves cut-side down in a baking dish large enough to hold all four (divide them among two baking dishes if they don't fit in one). Add enough water to go ½ inch up each squash half. Bake the squash until the skins start to brown and the flesh is tender, about 45 minutes. Remove from the oven (leaving the oven on), flip over so the flesh is exposed, and set aside to cool. When the squash halves are cool enough to handle, scoop out the flesh and discard the skins, reserving the flesh and baking liquid.

2. Toss the pepitas with the vegetable oil, ¼ teaspoon salt, and the thyme, then spread them out on a baking sheet. Bake until just lightly browned, 8 to 10 minutes. Remove and let cool.

3. Set a large soup pot over medium-low heat and add the olive oil. Add the onion and garlic and sweat by cooking them until the onions are translucent, about 5 minutes. Add the apple and fennel, season with salt and pepper, and sweat until the fennel is translucent, about 15 minutes more.

4. Add the wine and simmer to reduce almost all of the liquid. Add the broth, cider, reserved squash liquid, and the squash flesh. Bring them to a boil, then reduce the heat and simmer until the squash is very tender, about 1½ hours.

5. Meanwhile, slowly melt the remaining ¾ cup butter in a heavy-bottomed pot over medium heat. Continue heating until the milk solids begin to fall to the bottom of the pot and start to brown. Take care not to let the solids blacken, removing the butter from the heat when it is dark brown after 10 to 15 minutes. Strain the brown butter through a fine-mesh sieve and discard the solids.

6. Working with a tabletop or immersion blender, purée the soup until smooth. Add the brown butter slowly, stopping to loosen the ingredients with a wooden spoon, if necessary. Add additional broth to thin the soup if it's too thick. Adjust the seasoning with salt and pepper.

7. Ladle the soup into bowls, drizzle with sherry reduction, and sprinkle with the toasted pepitas.

DRINK TIP

When brown butter comes into play, especially with squash, look for a fall-ish beer that can offer a foil for all that richness. Flanders red ale is ideal; its tart Belgian style nearly mimics the acid you'll find in the sherry reduction, cleansing your palate between spoonfuls so you can keep going back for more.

TRUFFLED WHITE ASPARAGUS SOUP

SERVES 4 TO 6

This is a soup that I used to serve in my Scylla restaurant days. It's really simple, focusing primarily on the sweetness of the white asparagus, but it's very rich and meant to be a small first course rather than a main-course soup. It's a great way to start off a dinner party on a beautiful spring evening.

I've actually used this soup as a sauce quite a few times as well, like when I was in Puerto Rico filming the *Top Chef* finale. I chose the legendary Eric Ripert to be my sous chef, so he helped me create seared snapper with truffled white asparagus broth. I felt a little weird hovering over Chef Ripert while he was cleaning the snapper, seeing as he owns one of the best seafood restaurants in the country (Le Bernadin), but I just wanted to make sure it was right because every chef has a different vision. I have to say that Chef Ripert is one of the nicest and most charming chefs I have been lucky enough to meet over the past few years, and it was a great experience to play his "boss" for a few hours.

⅓ cup extra-virgin olive oil	3 garlic cloves, minced	3 pounds white asparagus, peeled and cut into 1-inch lengths	½ cup heavy cream
2 cups chopped sweet onions	Salt	½ cup dry white wine	2 teaspoons white truffle oil
1 cup chopped fennel bulb	Freshly ground black pepper	5 cups vegetable broth or water	

1. Heat a large soup pot over medium-low heat. Add the oil, then add the onions, fennel, and garlic. Season with salt and pepper and sweat the vegetables by cooking them until they are translucent, about 10 minutes.

2. Add the asparagus and wine and cook for 15 minutes more.

3. Add the broth, then increase the heat to bring the soup to a boil. Reduce the heat to low, cover the soup, and simmer until the asparagus is very tender, about 90 minutes.

4. Working with a tabletop or immersion blender, add the cream and truffle oil to the soup. Blend until very smooth, pass the soup through a fine-mesh sieve, and season with salt and pepper before serving.

DRINK TIP

This is a very delicate soup, immediately calling for a white wine, but you really want to taste the touch of truffle here so you should try to avoid both heavily oaked or strongly acidic wines. Go with Semillon, a beautiful grape that isn't too tart and isn't too buttery, but typically falls right in that sweet spot between.

CHILLED YELLOW TOMATO AND VANILLA BEAN SOUP WITH LUMP CRAB AND BASIL

SERVES 4 TO 6

In the early days of cooking at Spring, I was the "hot app" girl, which meant I was responsible for hot appetizers and worked a station that didn't really have a designated area; I had hotel pans filled with ice to keep my prep in, a tray jack to plate on, and, if I was lucky, Dale Talde (fellow *Top Chef* Season 4 contestant) would give me two of his sauté station burners to cook on. It was the first time I was cooking at a place where the orders were called by the expediter and no tickets were given to us. With more than 300 guests dining with us each night, I found that the only way I could remember the orders was to repeat them to myself over and over in a very *Rain Man* sort of way: "springroll, springroll, ravioli, springroll." Eventually my nickname became Definitely Stephanie, as in "Definitely going to miss Wapner," and I still have a knife given to me by executive chef Shawn McClain when I left, with the nickname engraved on it. Oh, the memories.

During that hectic *Rain Man* era, one of the dishes I was responsible for was a shrimp dumpling with a yellow tomato and vanilla bean sauce, and it was always a favorite of mine. Eventually when Scylla went into its first summer, I took that flavor combination, tweaked it just a bit, and created this beautiful chilled soup. It's a great alternative to a standard tomato gazpacho on a hot summer night, as the vanilla gives just a hint of sweetness to work against the tartness of the tomatoes without overpowering them. After all, when you wait all year long for them, you really want to taste those tomatoes.

6 medium yellow tomatoes	½ vanilla bean, cut open lengthwise	Freshly ground black pepper	4 large basil leaves, cut in chiffonade (see Technique 101, page 73)
2 tablespoons olive oil	½ cup white wine	4 ounces lump crabmeat	
1 cup diced onion	¼ cup Pernod	2 tablespoons extra-virgin olive oil	1 plum tomato, halved lengthwise, seeded, and diced, for garnishing
1 fennel bulb, thinly sliced	½ cup half-and-half or heavy cream	1 lemon, zested	
2 garlic cloves, chopped	Coarse salt	1 tablespoon fresh lemon juice	

Continued . . .

1. Preheat the grill to medium-high or turn on the broiler. Char the yellow tomatoes, placing them on the hot grill grates or under the broiler until they are browned and blackened all over. Set them aside to cool slightly.

2. Heat the olive oil in a Dutch oven or large pot over medium-low heat. Add the onion, fennel, and garlic and sweat by cooking them until the onion is translucent and the fennel softens slightly, about 10 minutes.

3. Scrape the vanilla paste from the bean and add it and the pod to the pot. Add the charred tomatoes, wine, and Pernod. Simmer to reduce the liquid by half, about 10 minutes. Add enough water to just cover the ingredients in the pot. Simmer until all of the flavors come together and the fennel is very soft, about 45 minutes more.

4. Remove the vanilla pod and discard it. Working with a tabletop or immersion blender, add the half-and-half to the soup and purée until smooth. Season with salt and pepper. Refrigerate until the soup is cold.

5. While the soup chills, toss the crab with the extra-virgin olive oil, lemon zest, lemon juice, and basil. Season with salt and pepper.

6. Ladle the chilled soup into bowls and top with a few tablespoons of the crab. Garnish with the diced plum tomato and serve.

TECHNIQUE 101 ·

Chiffonade: To chiffonade something, you're essentially just cutting it into thin strips. This technique is mostly used when cutting broad-leaf herbs like basil or sorrel. It's really simple, and it's actually pretty cool. All you have to do is stack about six or so of the basil or sorrel leaves on top of each other so that they're pretty well aligned. Now tightly roll the leaves the long way into a cigar-shaped cylinder. Holding the cylinder in place with one hand, cut across it at very close intervals. You should have a nice little pile of herb strips, but don't cut them too far in advance, or they'll lose their pretty bright-green color.

DRINK TIP

Summery flavors like ripe tomatoes and fresh shell-fish are so good they can stand on their own, so stay out of the way with a light and crisp white wine like Pinot Gris. (Yes, it's the same grape as Pinot Grigio, but given a French spelling.) Seek out the stuff from Alsace, and you'll generally find a bit more structure and oomph than in Italian Pinot Grigios.

FENNEL-POTATO SOUP WITH BUTTER-POACHED LOBSTER AND BLOOD ORANGES

SERVES 4 TO 6

I've never liked black licorice, so I thought it was strange that I fell hard for fennel while working at Spring restaurant—the anise flavor is so much fresher than what you'd find in licorice. It adds a nice note to just about anything, but especially sauces, stocks, and soups. Now that I'm officially addicted to the stuff, I'm always trying to come up with new uses for it. I tend to think of it as an ideal partner for citrus, so I wind up using it more in winter when citrus fruits are at their peak. But because lemons can be purely sour and limes purely acidic, I've learned to turn to blood oranges for the right balance of sweet and tart. I also happen to think that blood oranges are awesome with buttery lobster, but when your wallet is light you could sub more affordable shrimp into the recipe. And if you're short on time, you could just have the soup all by itself.

FENNEL-POTATO SOUP

1 tablespoon olive oil

1 small onion, finely diced

2 garlic cloves, thinly sliced

2 fennel bulbs, thinly sliced (reserve some fronds for garnishing)

2 medium Yukon gold potatoes, peeled and cut into chunks

¼ cup dry white wine

2 tablespoons Pernod

Salt

Freshly ground black pepper

1 quart vegetable broth, plus more as needed

½ cup heavy cream

BLOOD ORANGE REDUCTION

2 blood oranges, juiced

½ lemon, juiced

2 tablespoons honey (see Quick Tip, page 76)

LOBSTER

Salt

1 lobster tail (6 to 7 ounces)

¼ cup unsalted butter

½ lemon, juiced

Freshly ground black pepper

1 blood orange, cut into supremes (optional; see Technique 101, page 76), for garnishing

1. To make the soup: Heat the olive oil in a large Dutch oven or soup pot over medium-low heat. Add the onion and garlic and sweat by cooking them until the onion is translucent, about 3 minutes. Add the fennel and sweat until it is tender, about 5 minutes. Add the potatoes, wine, and Pernod and simmer to reduce the liquid until it is nearly gone. Season with salt and pepper. Add the broth, bring it to a boil, and then reduce the heat and simmer, covered, until the potatoes are extremely soft, about 40 minutes.

2. Meanwhile, heat the cream in a small heavy-bottomed pot over medium heat. Simmer, stirring often, until it has thickened and has a rich nutty flavor, about 10 minutes. Remove from the heat and set aside.

3. While the soup is simmering, make the blood orange reduction: Whisk together the orange juice, lemon juice, and honey in small nonreactive pot. Simmer over medium heat to reduce the liquids to a syrup, about 15 minutes. Remove from the heat and set aside.

4. Working with a tabletop or immersion blender, process the soup until smooth. Pass each batch through a fine-mesh sieve, pushing it through with a rubber spatula. Discard the solids. Return the soup to the pot over medium-low heat. Whisk in the reduced cream and adjust the seasoning with salt and pepper. Adjust

Continued . . .

the consistency by adding a bit more broth to thin it, if needed. Keep the soup warm while preparing the lobster.

5. To make the lobster: Bring a medium pot of salted water to a boil. Add the lobster tail and boil for 2 minutes, just enough to be able to remove the meat from the shell, not to cook it through. Using tongs, remove the tail from the boiling water and submerge in an ice bath to stop cooking. Remove the meat from the shell, rinsing it if necessary. Slice the lobster into bite-size pieces.

6. Melt the butter in a small saucepan. Whisk in the lemon juice and season with salt and pepper. Add the lobster pieces and poach by cooking them over low heat until they are just cooked through, about 2 minutes.

7. Ladle the hot soup into bowls. Divide the poached lobster pieces between the bowls and drizzle the soup with a little of the blood orange reduction. Garnish with a blood orange segment and a couple of fennel fronds before serving.

QUICK TIP

I cook with honey a lot, and while for some recipes I'll use honey powder, sometimes there's no substitute for the sticky stuff. Unfortunately, honeybees are a dwindling lot, disappearing in pretty scary numbers. I really think that to support the honey industry, people need to know how to cook with it and be willing to use it more. One of the easiest ways to get in the habit of using it is to eliminate the mess. By simply dipping your measuring spoon in any cooking oil or rubbing a bit of the oil onto the spoon with a paper towel, your honey will slide right out in one quick swoop. Try it, and you'll be addicted to honey like I am in no time.

TECHNIQUE 101

"Supreming" Citrus: Any time you have citrus segments on a dish in a good restaurant, they've been "supremed," meaning their peel, pith, and membrane has been sliced off, leaving just the beautiful fruit. The easiest way to do this is to slice off the top and the bottom of the whole fruit, then set it on its end and trim off the rind, following the curve of the fruit. Finally, holding the fruit in one hand, carefully slice along the inside of each membrane (the white lines) to free each segment. Voilá! Citrus supremes.

DRINK TIP

A lighter wine will get obliterated by buttery lobster, but you don't want to coat your palate with an equally buttery wine. Pinot Blanc to the rescue! This lightly fruity white wine is full bodied enough to stand up to the lobster but also dry enough to not duplicate its richness.

PUMPKIN–SALT COD SOUP

When fall comes around, chefs go squash crazy. But one year, I decided I really wanted to take pumpkin in a different direction by bringing in a salty element to balance the pumpkin's sweetness (and who's not bored with plain old pumpkin soup by now?). Remember: When you're cooking with pumpkin, select pie pumpkins as opposed to decorative pumpkins; they're smaller and have tastier, meatier flesh. Concocting a soup with salt cod made me a little nervous at first, but I tried it anyway. With a touch of heat from sambal and some good crunch from pepitas, it all came together. You never know until you try!

6 ounces deboned salt cod	Salt	4 ounces Yukon gold potato, peeled and diced	4 teaspoons roasted, salted pepitas (see Ingredient Spotlight, page 78)
1 pie pumpkin (about 2 pounds)	Freshly ground black pepper	¼ cup heavy cream	
3 teaspoons butter	2 cups milk	1 teaspoon sambal paste (see Ingredient Spotlight, page 47)	
	¾ cup diced onion		

1. The night before you plan to make the soup, soak the salt cod in cold water, keeping it refrigerated overnight. This draws the hardened salt shell off from the fish.

2. Preheat the oven to 375°F. Cut the pumpkin in half and scoop out and discard the seeds and guts. Put 1½ teaspoons butter in each pumpkin half, season with salt and pepper, and then set the pumpkin flesh-side down in a shallow baking dish. Bake until the skin starts to brown and the pumpkin is soft to the touch, about 1 hour.

3. While the pumpkin is baking, drain the salt cod. Combine it with the milk, 1 cup water, the onion, potato, and cream in a medium soup pot. Bring to a boil and then reduce to a simmer. Cook until the potato is fully tender and the salt cod is falling apart, 30 to 45 minutes.

4. Once the pumpkin has cooled enough to handle, scrape the flesh into the soup and add the sambal. Working with a tabletop or immersion blender, purée the soup.

5. Divide the soup among four bowls and top each with the pepitas before serving.

DRINK TIP

One of the easiest beer pairings out there is pumpkin with *märzens*. Also known as *Oktoberfestbiers*, these toasty, coppery-colored German beers were historically brewed in March (a.k.a. *märzen*), stored all spring and summer, then consumed in fall. And we all know nothing says October more than pumpkin, so the two are a perfect pair.

PEPITAS (HULLED PUMPKIN SEEDS) *Pepitas* is the Spanish word for "small seeds," and these dark-green hulled pumpkin seeds are used a lot in Mexican cooking. You might be tempted to save a pumpkin's seeds and roast them for garnish (especially for a recipe like this), but I find that the hulls make them too chewy. You can salt those and roast them for snacking, but when it comes to garnishes, I recommend just buying pepitas, which give you texture and flavor without the outer layer of the seed. You should be able to find them in the Mexican food aisle of your local supermarket (most likely already roasted and salted, which is fine), and you'll definitely find them at any Mexican grocer.

SMOKED HAM HOCK AND LEEK SOUP

This soup makes me think of cold nights back in Connecticut. I was lucky enough to grow up with a mom who loved to cook, and soup was one of her favorites. During summer we would have vichyssoise at least every other week, and in winter mom would roll out nice hearty soups like classic French onion (I always thought the best part was the melted cheese over the floating crouton) or ham and split pea soup—which, to me, was just an excuse to eat big hunks of salty ham. So essentially, this soup takes the most memorable elements of my mom's soups and rolls them all into one. Once winter starts to creep in, there's nothing like it.

2 tablespoons butter	Salt	½ cup chopped canned tomatoes	2 cups medium-size crusty bread cubes (preferably ciabatta)
4 cups sliced leeks, white and light green parts (see Technique 101, page 81)	Freshly ground black pepper	½ cup thinly sliced caper berries, brined	Salt
1 large or 2 small carrots, peeled and cut into ⅛-inch rounds	⅓ cup white wine	**GARLIC CROUTONS**	
3 garlic cloves, minced	1 pound smoked ham hock	2 tablespoons butter	1 cup shredded Comté or Gruyère cheese
	2½ cups chicken or vegetable broth	1 garlic clove, minced	

1. Melt the butter over medium heat in a medium to large soup pot. Add the leeks, carrot, and garlic and sweat by cooking them until the leeks are translucent, about 5 minutes. Season lightly with salt and pepper.

2. Add the wine and reduce *au sec* (by three-fourths, or until liquid nearly evaporates).

3. Add the ham hock, broth, and tomatoes. Bring the mixture to a boil, cover, and simmer until the ham pulls easily away from the bone, about 1 hour.

4. Turn off the heat under the soup, remove the ham hock, and add the caper berries.

5. To make the garlic croutons: Preheat the oven to 350°F.

Continued . . .

6. Slowly melt the butter with the garlic in a small skillet or sauté pan over low heat. Pour the garlic butter over the bread cubes on a nonstick baking sheet, toss to evenly coat, and season with salt. Bake until golden brown and crisp, about 12 minutes, turning the croutons about halfway through for even browning. Remove the pan to a rack to cool slightly.

7. Preheat the broiler. Once the ham hock is cool enough to handle, pull the meat from the bone, discarding any super-fatty bits, and add the pulled meat pieces back to the soup.

8. Divide the soup among ovenproof bowls. Top each with a handful of croutons and a hefty pinch of cheese and broil until the cheese is melted.

9. Serve immediately.

TECHNIQUE 101

Cleaning Leeks: Leeks look like giant green onions, and they're actually a cousin of both onions and garlic, with a milder flavor. Try to buy leeks that are bright in color, with no spotting. Don't be tempted to go for the biggest of the bunch; smaller leeks actually have more flavor. To clean them, cut off the dark green tips, cut them in half lengthwise, then slice each half into ¼-inch half moons. Soak the leek pieces in a bowl of cold water, using your hands to swirl any dirt from them, then lift the clean pieces from the water, leaving the grit behind. Pat dry before using.

DRINK TIP

Schwarzbier, German for "black beer," is a misleading name. This style is actually lighter than stouts, opaque, and not as malty as dark beers like porters. Still, schwarzbiers have just the right touch of smokiness to mimic the ham in this soup but are refreshing enough to get you through the gooey cheese.

BRAISED PORK AND COCONUT SOUP

This soup came about one afternoon when I was invited to a potluck party on the South Side of Chicago. My friend Giles, the genius cheesemonger behind The Great American Cheese Collection store, gets together with a group of his friends every couple of weeks to cook up a storm, with a different theme for each dinner. My first introduction to the group was the wide-open "Asian Night." I had some pork shoulder around, and some other staples I usually stock in my pantry, so this soup is what I put together. It's actually inspired by a coconut soup we made at Vong restaurant back in the day, which was based on the classic Thai soup *tom kha gai*. The combination and depth of flavors in coconut, chiles, fish sauce, and lime drew me into Southeast Asian cuisine, and I continue to be inspired by that food through travels to that area and by experimenting with these ingredients at home and in the restaurant. The addition of peanut butter to this soup actually happened because I had just done a blind tasting of peanut butters and had about twenty-five jars hanging around, but it stuck because it added a rich roasted saltiness that just can't be matched.

2½ pounds bone-in pork shoulder

⅓ cup packed brown sugar

4 garlic cloves, minced

Coarse salt

3 tablespoons olive oil

2 medium onions, finely diced

2¼ cups dry red wine

One 28-ounce can diced tomatoes

⅓ cup creamy natural peanut butter

1 quart chicken broth

2 tablespoons balsamic vinegar

1 tablespoon Dijon mustard

2 teaspoons fish sauce

1 tablespoon fennel seeds

2 teaspoons aji chile paste (see Ingredient Spotlight, page 162)

¾ cup canned coconut milk (see Ingredient Spotlight, page 85)

Freshly ground black pepper

1 small lime, juiced

⅓ cup roasted, salted peanuts, chopped

½ cup loosely packed cilantro, chopped

Continued . . .

1. Rub the pork with the brown sugar, one third of the garlic, and 1 teaspoon salt. Place it in a glass bowl, cover, and refrigerate overnight.

2. Preheat the oven to 350°F.

3. Heat 1 tablespoon of the oil in a large pot or Dutch oven over medium-high heat. Add the pork and brown it on all sides. Remove the pork and set it aside.

4. Add 1 tablespoon more oil to the pot and lower the heat to medium. Add half of the onions and another third of the garlic and sweat by cooking until the onions are translucent, about 5 minutes. Pour in 2 cups of the wine, increase the heat to a simmer, and reduce the liquid by half.

5. Reserve 1 cup of the tomatoes and add the rest to the pot. Add the peanut butter, stirring until it melts into the liquid. Add the broth, vinegar, mustard, fish sauce, fennel seeds, and chili paste. Bring the liquid to a boil, add the pork back in, cover the pot, and transfer it to the oven. Braise the pork until the meat is very tender, 3 to 3½ hours.

6. Remove the pork from the liquid and set it aside to cool slightly. Strain the liquid and skim off the fat with a slotted spoon (alternatively, let the liquid cool completely in the refrigerator and skim off the fat cap that forms once it's cold). Pull the meat away from the fat, discarding the fat. Cut the meat into bite-size pieces.

7. Heat the remaining 1 tablespoon oil in a medium pot over medium-low heat. Add the remaining onions and garlic and sweat by cooking them until the onions are translucent, about 5 minutes. Add the remaining ¼ cup wine, increase the heat to medium-high, and reduce the liquid by half. Add the reserved 1 cup tomatoes and the strained soup liquid. Simmer to reduce by one third, about 15 minutes.

8. Stir in the meat and coconut milk. Simmer the soup for an additional 15 to 20 minutes so the flavors come together. Season with salt and pepper. Divide the soup among bowls, squeeze a bit of lime juice over each serving, and sprinkle with chopped peanuts and cilantro before serving.

DRINK TIP

This soup packs complex flavors, and few beers are as complex as Belgian *tripels*, which earned their name because traditionally brewers used three times the amount of malt as they would for a "simple." In both the soup and the beer, you'll find earthiness, a touch of spice, and a bit of fruity sweetness.

INGREDIENT SPOTLIGHT

COCONUT MILK Some people think that coconut milk is the liquid that's stored inside a coconut, but actually that's coconut *water*, a super-refreshing drink that's becoming more and more popular these days. Coconut milk is the pulp of the coconut simmered with equal parts water and then strained (you can make it at home this way, but it's pretty convenient just to pick up a can at the store). You might be tempted to buy light coconut milk to cut calories, but for soups like this, you really need the richness of full-fat coconut milk. Keep some on hand and sub it for cream to add a slight tropical flavor to soups, use it to add extra richness to braised meats like pork and chicken while they cook, or add a bit to jasmine rice along with the water to steam it for an awesome flavor combined with Asian-style stir-fries. Another fun trick is to pour the coconut milk into an ice cube tray, freeze it, and then use the cubes to add a tropical twist to your favorite rum cocktails.

CHICKEN AND RAMP STEW
WITH CRISPY NOODLES

The spring before I opened Girl & the Goat, I seemed to be sick . . . a lot. I'm guessing it was the stress and lack of sleep, but whatever was causing it, I was in constant need of a bit of chicken noodle soup to get me through. Luckily it was that fantastic time of year when chefs get excited to see spring vegetables pop up, with the annual appearance of ramps (wild leeks) to start the season. One of the producers I work with, Spence Farm, invites all of the local chefs down to celebrate the start of ramp season with a little fun and a lot of picking. It's pretty cool—you can smell the fresh garlicky aroma of the ramps as the roots are pulled from the ground.

A couple of years ago, I was at Quality Meats in New York, a restaurant from the Smith & Wollensky chain, and one of the side dishes was crisp noodles. I absolutely loved them. I'm still not sure exactly how they prepare theirs, but I re-created them by boiling the noodles as usual, then letting them dry a bit before deep-frying them to a crispy golden brown. When they sit in this soup for a couple of minutes, they soak up a bit of the rampy chicken broth, while holding on to a bit of crunchy texture. I guess you could say it's a bit of a play on Chinese sizzling rice soup, although the noodles don't make that fun crackling sound (just close your eyes and imagine it).

1 tablespoon olive oil plus 1 teaspoon

2 chicken legs and thighs (about 1½ pounds)

Salt

Freshly ground black pepper

1 pound ramps or leeks, cleaned and chopped

⅓ cup white wine

2 quarts chicken broth

2 dried Thai chiles (see Ingredient Spotlight, page 61)

1½ cups dry elbow macaroni

Blended oil (half vegetable, half olive oil) for frying

⅓ cup chiffonade of ramp greens (see Technique 101, page 73; see Ingredient Spotlight, page 89) for garnishing

Continued . . .

1. Heat a large soup pot over medium heat. Add the 1 tablespoon olive oil. Season the chicken with salt and pepper and brown on all sides. Remove the chicken and set aside. Add the ramps and sweat them by cooking until they are slightly softened, about 3 minutes. Add the wine and simmer to reduce by half. Add the chicken, broth, and chiles, increase the heat, and bring everything to a boil. Reduce to low, cover, and simmer until the chicken easily pulls from the bone and is no longer pink inside, about 1½ hours.

2. Meanwhile, bring a large pot of salted water to a boil. Cook the macaroni to al dente according to the package instructions. Drain and toss the noodles with the remaining 1 teaspoon oil. Line a baking sheet with a kitchen towel and spread the noodles onto the towel to dry.

3. Heat the blended oil to 375°F in a deep fryer or heavy-bottomed pan with high sides. Once the noodles are fairly dry, fry them in small batches until crisp and light brown, draining them on a paper towel–lined plate.

4. Remove the soup from the heat. Remove the chicken and set aside to cool slightly. Strain the broth through a fine-mesh sieve into a clean pot. Discard the solids.

5. When the chicken is cool enough to handle, pull all the meat away from the bones and skin, then put the meat back into the broth.

6. When ready to serve, divide the crisp noodles among bowls and ladle the soup over the noodles. Garnish with the ramp greens. Let the soup sit for about 2 minutes to let the noodles slightly soften before serving.

DRINK TIP

If you're eating this super-simple chicken stew, you might just be sick, so you really don't need the alcohol, but if you're indeed healthy and looking to drink, go with your favorite New-World Chardonnay. Chicken soup is a pretty forgiving dish when it comes to pairing, so don't think about this one too hard.

INGREDIENT SPOTLIGHT

RAMPS These wild leeks are available for a very short period of time in early spring, and the unique taste—a cross between garlic and onion with an earthy sweetness—is highly anticipated all winter long. You might find them at specialty grocers, but you'll definitely find them at farmers' markets around April. Ramps look like a hybrid of a scallion and a leek, except that they have a really pretty purplish red part on the stalk just between the leaves and the small white bulbs. The white part is pretty intense to serve raw, so I usually roast them slowly with olive oil, salt, and pepper, and then purée the mixture like a pesto. You can add the purée to pastas or mashed potatoes for a hit of bright garlic flavor. You can also pickle the stems in a mixture of equal parts vinegar, water, and sugar and 1 tablespoon of salt for every 2 cups of brine. For the greens, chiffonade them and use as garnish or add them to a salad for a touch of bitter heat.

THE NEVER-ENDING-CHICAGO-WINTER BEEF STEW

I often donate a night of cooking to different charity auctions, so the winner gets a private dinner for a group of friends in their own home and the charity gets a nice donation. For one of these dinners just at the tail-end of a Chicago winter, I took some Allen Brothers beef, turned it into a nice warming stew, and then served it in a small portion topped with a dollop of sour cream as one of the courses. It's really simple, yet really flavorful, and a great way to use up various cuts of beef like chuck and short rib, which are both too tough to eat grilled or broiled. Those cuts of meat are filled with flavor that's best when cooked low and slow. You can eat this as a stew, over pasta, or even as a chunky sauce underneath your favorite fish as a comforting take on surf and turf. It holds up well in the refrigerator for about a week (actually the flavor is even better after a couple of days) and it will keep in the freezer for about one month.

3 tablespoons vegetable or canola oil

3 pounds beef, cubed

Salt

Freshly ground black pepper

1 small onion, finely diced

3 garlic cloves, minced

1 pineapple, finely diced (see Quick Tip, page 92)

1 apple, peeled and diced

1 pear, peeled and diced

½ cup red wine

1 quart chicken broth

2 cups apple cider

One 16-ounce can diced tomatoes, such as San Marzanos (see Ingredient Spotlight, page 93)

¾ cup fish sauce

¾ cup Worcestershire sauce

2 tablespoons balsamic vinegar

2 tablespoons Dijon mustard

1 tablespoon sambal paste (see Ingredient Spotlight, page 47)

Continued . . .

1. Heat 1 tablespoon of the vegetable oil over high heat in a large soup pot. Season half of the beef with salt and pepper and add it to the pot. Brown the beef and remove. Repeat with the rest of the meat, removing and setting it aside.

2. Add another 1 tablespoon vegetable oil to the soup pot and lower the heat to medium. Add the onion and garlic and sweat them by cooking until the onion is translucent, about 3 minutes. Add the pineapple, apple, pear, and wine and simmer to reduce the liquid by half. Add back the beef along with the broth, cider, tomatoes, fish sauce, Worcestershire sauce, vinegar, mustard, and sambal and bring to a boil. Reduce the heat to a simmer. Taste and adjust the salt and pepper. Cover and simmer until the beef cubes fall apart easily when poked with a fork, a little over 4 hours. Adjust the seasoning before serving.

 QUICK TIP ·······························

Adding pineapple to braised dishes actually helps tenderize the meat. I learned this the hard way one day at Scylla when I was using gelatin and pineapple juice to make a gelée, but the juice never set. I added more and more gelatin with no luck. Finally, my pastry chef reminded me that pineapple, along with other fruits such as papayas and figs, contains certain enzymes that break down connective tissues in meat, and since gelatin is essentially made from those connective tissues, natural pineapple gelée just won't work. The thing I took away from this, though, is that those enzymes are perfect for tenderizing, especially when you're going to be braising the meat low and slow as you do for this stew recipe. This trick works just as well on chicken and pork as it does for beef.

 **DRINK TIP**

Porter beer, the father of stouts, is a no-brainer go-to for beefy stews and chili. There's enough rich maltiness to stand up to these wintery foods but also a good dose of citrusy hops, so you won't fall into a coma before halftime.

INGREDIENT SPOTLIGHT

SAN MARZANO TOMATOES I once did a blind taste test of about twenty different brands of canned tomatoes to see if all the hype over San Marzano tomatoes was true, and the brand ended up being my favorite. A lot of the canned tomatoes I tasted were just too watery and didn't have that full flavor you need when you can't get fresh tomatoes in season. Others tasted like hard-as-a-rock underripe tomatoes with a ton of sugar added. But San Marzano, named for the location in Italy where they are produced, are canned at the peak of the growing season, locking in the best flavor you can get. If you can't find them, or if they're out of your price range, look for Red Gold, which are good quality for about half the price.

CHA
THREE

SALADS

DURING MY FRESHMAN YEAR IN A COLLEGE DORM, I RAIDED THE CAFETERIA SALAD BAR FOR THE SAME THING DAY AFTER DAY: A LITTLE LETTUCE PILED WITH GARBANZO BEANS, SLICED BUTTON MUSHROOMS, SHREDDED CHEDDAR CHEESE, AND CROUTONS, ALL DRIZZLED WITH A CLASSIC RANCH DRESSING.

And more often than not, the lettuce got left behind in the end (it just made me feel healthier to put it on the plate). But since then, I've discovered that there's a whole world of salads out there—and they don't even have to include lettuce. I got out of my cafeteria-salad rut by working in professional kitchens, where most new cooks start out in the *garde manger* (pronounced gahrd mahn-ZHAY) station working with salads and other cold foods. At first I was so anxious to get on the hot line where I could play with fire that I didn't fully appreciate the art of the salad. But eventually, I got it: Coming up with a great salad is all about combining a range of textures, flavors, and colors— the same rules that apply to putting together a successful entrée. Hopefully after making a few of my favorite salads

in this chapter, you'll have your "Aha!" moment, too, so that you can start experimenting on your own.

A few tips: Think about leaving raw vegetables that you would normally cook—like Brussels sprouts, asparagus, and corn—so that you're adding crunchy texture to the mix. Also, visit a farmers' market if you can, just to sample various greens so that you can understand the difference between peppery arugula, sweet butter lettuce, and so on. And don't lose the point that a salad should be refreshing and balanced, so even if you're not using a classic vinaigrette, use some seasonal fruits like blueberries to get the sweet and tart elements (or a spritz of lemon with a drizzle of honey), then bring out the flavors with a sprinkle of salt and some freshly cracked black pepper.

ESCAROLE AND FRISÉE SALAD WITH APPLE VINAIGRETTE

SERVES 4 TO 6

I always used to think of escarole as a green that was better sautéed or grilled—that is until I had lunch at Mario Batali's restaurant Otto in New York City a number of years ago and had a great escarole salad. To me, the bitterness that shines through when escarole is cooked is a bit milder when it's served raw, almost like slightly bitter butter lettuce. It's delicious. So to highlight that bitter note, I like to add a bit of frisée into my escarole salads. My relationship with frisée is strange, though. When I order a case of mixed greens or mesclun mix from a purveyor, I always get it without frisée. Not because I don't appreciate the squiggly little green, but I just think there is a time and place for it. Example: When I'm looking to create a nice bitter-greens salad with a bit of a sweet dressing, I reach for frisée. When I want a more delicate mix of baby greens and there won't be anything sweet to counter the bitterness, I prefer to omit it. So with this particular salad, the sweet and tangy dressing is balanced by the bitter greens, we get a bit of crunchy spice from the radish, and the croutons offer a nice texture contrast and saltiness. And in case you're wondering why I start off with an apple purée rather than just an apple-flavored vinegar, it's because I want a creamier texture and that real apple taste.

ESCAROLE SALAD

2 heads escarole (12 to 14 ounces each)

1 head frisée (about 6 ounces)

4 radishes, thinly shaved on a mandoline

2 tablespoons roughly chopped fresh tarragon

APPLE VINAIGRETTE

1 crisp apple (such as Stayman Winesap or Gala), peeled and finely diced

1 cup apple cider

¼ cup cider vinegar

1 tablespoon maple syrup

1 egg yolk

½ cup blended vegetable oil (half vegetable, half olive oil)

Salt

Freshly ground black pepper

GARLIC CROUTONS

¼ cup unsalted butter

5 sprigs fresh thyme

3 garlic cloves, smashed with the side of a knife

3 cups medium-dice ciabatta bread

1 teaspoon red pepper flakes

½ teaspoon salt

½ teaspoon freshly ground black pepper

¾ cup shaved Parmesan cheese

1. To make the salad: Cut the escarole in half lengthwise and then into quarters. Slice the quarters into 1-inch strips. Wash under cold water, drain, and pat dry.

2. Trim off the dark green ends of the frisée, cut off the bottom root area, and slice the rest of the head in half crosswise. Separate the leaves, then combine the escarole, frisée, radishes, and tarragon in a bowl and set aside.

3. To make the vinaigrette: Put the apples, cider, vinegar, and maple syrup in a medium pot. Cook slowly over medium heat until the apples are tender and about three-fourths of the liquid has been absorbed, 6 to 8 minutes. Remove from the heat and let cool. Once the mixture is cool, transfer everything to a blender, add the egg yolk and blended oil while the motor is running, and blend until smooth. Season with salt and pepper. (The dressing can be refrigerated, covered, for 3 to 4 days.)

4. To make the croutons: Preheat the oven to 350°F. Heat the butter, thyme, and garlic in a small pot over low heat. Steep the ingredients for about 5 minutes to infuse the flavors. Strain out the garlic and thyme with a slotted spoon and toss the bread with the flavored butter, red pepper flakes, salt, and pepper. Spread the bread out on a baking sheet and toast in the oven until the bread begins to brown, about 15 minutes. Let the croutons cool slightly.

5. To serve, toss the salad with enough dressing to just lightly coat the leaves. Top with the garlic croutons and Parmesan.

TECHNIQUE 101

Infusing Butter: I love having infused butter on hand to add instant flavor when cooking vegetables or to finish sautéing fish or meats. It's really easy to do, lasts for quite awhile in the refrigerator, and is a good way to use up herbs that aren't pretty enough to go into a dish fresh. Simply melt butter in a saucepan over medium-low heat, then add your favorite herb or combination of herbs (I like parsley or rosemary). Let the flavor infuse over the heat for 5 minutes, then strain the butter, discarding the herbs. You can also make a spiced butter with dry spices like fennel seed, cumin, and coriander, which can be a great addition to a dish with Indian or Mexican flavors. Just be sure to refrigerate the infused butter in an airtight container so it doesn't pick up other flavors.

DRINK TIP

Bitter salad greens like escarole can clash with the standard "salad wines" people gravitate toward like Sauvignon Blanc. Instead, try this salad with a lightly oaked Chardonnay, which should have just enough round sweetness to balance out everything.

ASPARAGUS, GOAT CHEESE, AND RHUBARB SALAD

SERVES 6

Chicago's Green City Market has continued to grow over the years with the support of many local chefs, who not only shop there for their restaurants but also do cooking demonstrations throughout the season highlighting local ingredients. A few years ago, I did one of these cooking demos in the spring, when asparagus and rhubarb were both flooding the market, so I decided to combine them into this very simple, refreshing salad. Rhubarb can be a bit tricky, as it has such a strong bitter taste to it, so I do a sort of quick pickle to bring out the natural sweetness and tenderize it just a bit. The sweet-and-sour rhubarb, the tart and creamy goat cheese, the crunch of the almonds, and the beautiful asparagus all come together so well, you'll wish it was spring all year.

1 cup white balsamic vinegar	¼ cup olive oil plus 2 tablespoons	Freshly ground black pepper	¾ cup sliced almonds, toasted
½ cup sugar	2 pounds fresh asparagus	4 cups baby arugula	
1½ cups sliced rhubarb (about 1 pound)	Coarse salt	1 cup (about 2 ounces) crumbled goat cheese	

1. Combine the vinegar and sugar in a small saucepan over medium-high heat. Bring to a boil, stirring occasionally, until the sugar is dissolved. Pour the hot liquid over the rhubarb in a medium bowl and let it sit until the liquid has cooled and the rhubarb is slightly tender.

2. Strain the liquid from the rhubarb, reserving both. Make a vinaigrette by whisking 2 tablespoons of the pickling liquid with the ¼ cup olive oil in a small bowl. Refrigerate the remaining liquid for another use.

3. Preheat the grill to medium-high or the oven to 350°F. Trim off and discard the woody ends of the asparagus and toss the spears with the remaining 2 tablespoons olive oil. Season lightly with salt and pepper.

4. Set the asparagus spears horizontally across the hot, oiled grill grates and grill until tender, 5 to 7 minutes, turning once or twice. Let the asparagus cool slightly, then cut the spears into 2-inch pieces. (If grilling isn't an option, roast them in the oven for 20 minutes.)

5. In a large bowl, combine the asparagus with the arugula, goat cheese, almonds, and reserved rhubarb slices. Drizzle in the vinaigrette, toss to coat, and serve.

DRINK TIP

Rhubarb is pretty tart on its own; throw goat cheese into the mix, and you have some serious tang going on. So when you think of countering this with a sweeter wine, you're on the right track. Just don't go too far—try an Austrian Riesling, which tends to be a little less cloying than a German Riesling.

HEIRLOOM TOMATO, MOZZARELLA, AND STONE FRUIT SALAD

SERVES 4

I love summertime, when heirloom tomatoes are at their peak here in the Midwest and we have beautiful stone fruits of all kinds. Hit the farmers' market and pick up what looks good to you; this recipe is really more of a simple outline to follow than a hard-and-fast set of rules. My only suggestion is to mix it up with various colors and sizes of tomatoes. While I really like this dish with nectarines and plums, feel free to add in apricots, peaches, or any other fun hybrids you come across, such as pluots or plumcots, which are a delicious cross between plums and apricots. The most important thing is to use ripe fruits, good-quality fresh mozzarella, and, as always, be sure to season with salt and pepper before dressing.

8 ounces fresh mozzarella, cut in ¼-inch slices

Salt

Freshly ground black pepper

1¼ pounds heirloom tomatoes, cut in ¼-inch slices

1 ripe nectarine, cut into thin wedges

2 ripe plums, cut into thin wedges

4 tablespoons Pistachio-Lemon Vinaigrette (page 237)

6 to 8 leaves fresh basil, torn

1. Divide the mozzarella among four plates. Season with salt and pepper. Top with the tomato slices, nectarine, and plums and season everything again with salt and pepper.

2. Drizzle the salads with the vinaigrette and scatter them with the torn basil before serving.

DRINK TIP

A summery wine is ideal for a summery salad, so think bright, clean, and crisp. In other words, pair it with a Sauvignon Blanc.

ARUGULA SALAD WITH WATERMELON AND FETA

SERVES 4

Watermelon always makes me think back to being a kid, playing silly games every Fourth of July at my swim club. One of these was a watermelon relay race. The melons got covered in grease to slick them up and we raced back and forth in the pool, trying to outswim the others while pushing a watermelon. It was fun stuff, plus it was pretty cool that a watermelon could float considering I could hardly lift one at the time. When I moved on to college, watermelon showed up again, only this time we pumped an entire melon full of vodka and I ate way too much of it, forgetting the melon was now 60 proof. That was a whole different kind of fun.

But through all that fun, I never appreciated the sweet and refreshing flavor of the watermelon as much as I did the first time I tried it with a bit of sea salt. It was a miracle! The melon was no longer overly sweet; instead it had a bit of salty crunch that balanced out the natural flavors. I realize that many chefs have their own takes on savory watermelon salads these days, but in case you have yet to try one, I really think you'll love this combination. The balsamic-honey reduction adds acidity, fresh arugula brings a bit of savory spice, and some salty and rich feta cheese ties it all together. There's really nothing better on a warm summer day.

1 small watermelon (4 to 5 pounds)	⅓ cup white balsamic vinegar	5 ounces baby arugula, stemmed	Freshly ground black pepper
Sea salt	1 tablespoon honey	¼ cup extra-virgin olive oil	1 cup (about 4 ounces) crumbled feta cheese

1. Cut the watermelon in half lengthwise, turn the halves cut-side down, and cut each into 1-inch slices. Trim the rind from the watermelon and then cut each half-moon of trimmed watermelon in ½-inch cubes by cutting crosswise and lengthwise in ½-inch increments (think checkerboard). Arrange the squares on a serving platter. Sprinkle each square with a few sea salt crystals.

2. Whisk together the vinegar and honey in a small pot over medium-high heat. Bring the mixture to a simmer and reduce until it is syrupy, 5 to 7 minutes. Let it cool to room temperature, then drizzle the watermelon with the vinegar syrup.

3. In a medium bowl, toss the arugula with the olive oil, season with salt and pepper, and pile the greens on top of the watermelon. Drizzle with the remaining vinegar syrup and sprinkle with the feta before serving.

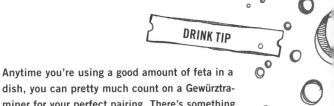

DRINK TIP

Anytime you're using a good amount of feta in a dish, you can pretty much count on a Gewürztraminer for your perfect pairing. There's something about the rich saltiness of the cheese that matches up with the honey notes in these straw-colored German wines that's tough to beat.

KOHLRABI, FENNEL, AND BING CHERRY SALAD

SERVES ABOUT 6

This salad is beyond simple, but that's what makes it so great. I love kohlrabi but feel like it often gets left behind because not many people recognize it. It's one of those vegetables that even some of my very knowledgeable friends working the Whole Foods check out line aren't sure about. (Although it is kind of fun to try and throw off the cashier a bit by coming through with odd stuff like this.) To me, kohlrabi tastes sort of like a cross between a broccoli stem and a turnip, with nice refreshing notes and just a bit of bite. Most people think you have to cook kohlrabi, but just like Brussels sprouts, it's great simply raw in a salad, so long as it's shaved thin and allowed to sit in the olive oil for just a minute to soften. So with kohlrabi as the slightly bitter note, I like the addition of very floral fennel, the sweet and tart notes of Bing cherries, and just a bit of acid from the preserved lemon. I'll admit that from time to time, I can overcomplicate dishes by bringing in a large number of ingredients, but this salad shows that when each item is hitting a different note, just a few elements are all you need for a great dish.

2 kohlrabi bulbs	16 Bing cherries, pitted (see Equipment Spotlight, page 106) and halved	1 tablespoon minced Preserved Lemon (page 241)	Freshly ground black pepper
1 fennel bulb	2 tablespoons extra-virgin olive oil	Salt	1 tablespoon torn fresh mint, for garnishing

1. Remove the stalks from the kohlrabi, as well as any hard stem ends still on the bulb. Cut the bulbs in half lengthwise and shave them very thinly on a mandoline, leaf-side down since the root side tends to be a bit woody.

2. Remove the stalks from the fennel, cut the bulb in half, and shave it very thinly on a mandoline, turning it to shave around the inner core.

3. Combine the kohlrabi and fennel in a large salad bowl. Add the cherries, olive oil, and preserved lemon and season with salt and pepper. Toss to combine and let the salad sit for about 5 minutes before serving to soften the kohlrabi. Garnish with the mint.

DRINK TIP

Dark mild ales are an English style known as "session beers," meaning you can have one hell of a drinking session with these brews without falling off your stool. They're low in alcohol, low in hops, and usually low in maltiness, so they won't get in the way of distinct flavors like fennel and cherries.

EQUIPMENT SPOTLIGHT

CHERRY PITTER A cherry pitter seems like such a random tool to keep in your drawer, but even if you only cook or bake with cherries a couple times a year, it's worth it (plus you can also use it for softer olives like manzanillas). Sure, you can try to use a small paring knife or the tear method with your fingers, but that's going to make a mess and it won't yield as much fruit as the pitter will give you. Keep in mind that cherries bleed a lot while you're pitting them, so do this over a bowl, letting the pits drop in and transferring the pitted cherries to a separate bowl. When you're done, you can always strain out the pits from the main bowl and use the juice to spike lemon-lime soda for Shirley Temples—my favorite drink as a kid.

SHAVED FENNEL AND BOK CHOY SALAD WITH GINGER VINAIGRETTE

SERVES 8

When I made this salad for the first time, I ate half the bowl myself. I just love it. The ginger vinaigrette is my take on the dressing you get drizzled over mixed greens at a sushi restaurant. Fresh ginger just has this amazing bite that clears your sinuses and makes you feel refreshed. And it's worlds apart from the powdered stuff I grew up with.

GINGER VINAIGRETTE

½ cup minced peeled fresh ginger (about 3 ounces; see Quick Tip, page 46)

½ cup minced shallot

2 tablespoons Dijon mustard

2 tablespoons white balsamic vinegar

1 egg yolk

1 tablespoon soy sauce

1 tablespoon maple syrup

1 cup grapeseed or blended oil (half vegetable, half olive oil)

Salt

Freshly ground black pepper

SALAD

1 fennel bulb

2 heads bok choy

2 tablespoons chiffonade of fresh basil

2 tablespoons roughly chopped fresh cilantro

Salt

Freshly ground black pepper

1. To make the vinaigrette: In a blender, combine the ginger, shallot, mustard, vinegar, egg yolk, soy sauce, and maple syrup. On low speed, slowly drizzle in the grapeseed oil until the dressing is smooth and thickened. Season with salt and pepper. Cover and refrigerate until needed.

2. To make the salad: Remove the stalks from the fennel, cut the bulb in half, and shave it thinly on a mandoline, shaving around the core.

3. Cut off the bottom couple of inches at the base of the bok choy and discard. Be sure to wash off any dirt and fully dry the leaves. Pile a few leaves on top of each other at a time and cut them crosswise very thinly.

4. Put the fennel and bok choy in a salad bowl with the basil and cilantro and toss with the dressing. Add as much as you like; I prefer this salad to be heavily dressed, like a slaw. Season with salt and pepper before serving.

DRINK TIP

Wit beer is pronounced just like wheat beer, and technically it is the same, but these Belgian-style wheats have less of the clove and banana notes you'd get out of German *hefeweizens* and more clean citrus notes that line up perfectly with fennel and ginger.

CELERY ROOT, SHIITAKE, AND PEARL ONION SALAD WITH CRISPY CAPERS

SERVES 4 TO 6

Celery root makes it into this book a few times (although in very different preparations) because it's one of my favorite root vegetables for its clean flavor and versatility. I know it gets skipped over a lot for its strange appearance, which can be a bit daunting if you're unsure what to do with it. This recipe is the simplest preparation of the root, cutting it into thin julienne strips and enjoying it raw. It needs just a minute or two in the dressing to soften up before it's ready to go, and it will still hold a great crunchy texture that's perfect for salad.

Roasted shiitakes are another love of mine. Often when I get Chinese food from Chen's (best crab rangoon in Chicago), there are dried shiitakes that have been rehydrated and added to the stir-fries. They soak up the sauce enough that they get a nice texture back and still have good mushroom flavor. Here I've done the opposite, taking fresh shiitakes; tossing them in a bit of oil, salt, and thyme; then dehydrating them a bit in the oven. They still hold on to their natural earthiness, but they lose some of their moisture so that you get a great crunchy texture—again, perfect for salads.

But with all that crunch, we need something sweet and smooth. Enter the pearl onion, one ingredient that I've often dreaded having on my station in a restaurant when I have to clean pounds and pounds a day. But I'll only make you clean just a few, enough to add a sweet onion flavor without having you slave away over these tiny guys.

1 pound fresh shiitake mushrooms, stemmed

4 tablespoons olive oil

¾ teaspoon salt

6 to 8 sprigs fresh thyme

8 ounces pearl onions

½ teaspoon mustard seeds

¼ teaspoon red pepper flakes

3 tablespoons sherry vinegar

2½ teaspoon brown sugar

1 head radicchio, quartered, cored, and cut into ½-inch strips

8 ounces celery root, peeled and julienned with a mandoline

½ cup Sherry-Thyme Vinaigrette (page 236)

3 ounces brined capers

½ cup canola oil

1. Preheat the oven to 325°F. In a large bowl, toss the mushrooms with 3 tablespoons of the olive oil and ½ teaspoon of the salt. Lay the mushrooms flat, tops up, on a baking sheet. Sprinkle with the thyme sprigs and bake until the mushrooms begin to crisp around the edges, 35 to 40 minutes.

2. Meanwhile, peel the pearl onions (see Quick Tip, below). In a dry 6-inch sauté pan over medium-high heat, toast the mustard seeds for 1 minute. Add the remaining 1 tablespoon olive oil and then add the onions and cook until they are lightly browned, about 2 minutes. Season with the red pepper flakes and remaining ¼ teaspoon salt. Add the vinegar and brown sugar and stir to coat. Reduce the heat and cook over low heat until the onions are tender and the liquid is thickened, 15 to 18 minutes. Let the onions cool to room temperature, then squeeze them into the bowl so that the inner layers come out, just to break the onions up.

3. Cut the shiitakes in half and add them to the bowl with the onions. Add the radicchio and celery root, then toss with the vinaigrette just to coat.

4. While the celery root and mushrooms are soaking up the dressing a bit, strain the capers and dry them on a paper towel, lightly pressing out some of the moisture. Heat the canola oil in a 6-inch sauté pan over high heat to 375°F on a deep-fry thermometer. You want the oil to be nice and hot, so test it by dropping in one caper to see if it begins to bubble. When the oil is ready, carefully add in the capers. Shake the pan slightly to continue to move the capers around and fry them until they're golden brown and crisp, about 5 minutes. Strain them out with a slotted spoon and drain them on paper towels. Let them cool for a couple of minutes, then toss them with the salad and serve.

QUICK TIP ·

Peeling pearl onions is always going to be a bit of a task. However, I have a trick I use to make this a little easier: Put the onions in a metal or heatproof bowl. Bring to a boil enough water to cover the onions, pour the water over them, and then let them sit for just a few minutes until the water has cooled enough for you to reach in and grab the onions. Cut off the root end of each onion, then the peel should just slide right off.

DRINK TIP

Earthy and salty flavors do best with beer, especially when we're talking caramelly onions and roasted mushrooms. German-style *dunkel* ("dark") beers are great for these flavors because while they can match up with the smooth, complex richness of the food, they aren't as sweet as brown ales and they aren't as bitter as stouts.

ARTICHOKE AND STRAWBERRY PANZANELLA

I grew up eating artichokes for dinner, with a side of lemony melted butter, racing my sister to the choke heart in the center. It wasn't until I brought my friend Maureen down to Florida to visit my Uncle Roger and Aunt Elizabeth that I realized not every family eats artichokes— Maureen had no idea what to do. (We quickly taught her how to use her teeth to get as much "meat" off of the leaves as possible, and she was hooked.) Whole artichokes are fun for a group, but for this recipe I decided to skip right to the best part: the hearts. It seemed obvious to me to combine the tart sweetness of the strawberries with the rich center of the artichokes, since they're both at their best in spring. And I wanted to incorporate those flavors into a twist on a classic panzanella, an Italian bread salad that's a perfect way to use up day-old bread. In many versions, the bread is soggy from the juice of the tomatoes that are tradition-ally included, but I've always liked to dress mine pretty minimally so you get good crunch, almost like giant croutons.

2 large artichokes

Juice of 2 lemons

½ cup olive oil plus ½ tablespoon

1 cup chicken broth

¾ cup white wine

4 garlic cloves, sliced

1 tablespoon salt plus ¼ teaspoon

3 cups cubed ciabatta or rustic Italian bread (½ to ¾-inch cubes)

8 fresh strawberries, thinly sliced

2 tablespoons chiffonade of fresh basil (see Technique 101, page 73)

1 tablespoon julienned Preserved Lemon (page 241) or zest of 1 lemon

8 ounces fresh mozzarella, cut into ¾-inch slices

Salt

Freshly ground black pepper

Continued . . .

1. Clean the artichokes (see Technique 101, below) and place the hearts in a deep bowl, adding enough cold water to cover them, plus the juice of 1 lemon. Letting them soak in the lemon water for an hour will improve their color and tenderness.

2. Cut each artichoke heart into eight wedges, then add them to a medium saucepan with the ½ cup of olive oil, broth, wine, remaining lemon juice, garlic, and 1 tablespoon salt. Bring the mixture to a boil, lower the heat, and allow it to simmer until the artichokes are just tender, 20 to 25 minutes.

3. While the artichokes are cooking, preheat the oven to 375°F.

4. Toss the bread cubes with the remaining 1½ tablespoons olive oil and the remaining ¼ teaspoon salt. Spread out the cubes on a baking sheet and bake until they are just crisped and browned, about 10 minutes.

5. Remove the artichokes from the pan with a slotted spoon and set them aside. Bring the liquid up to a boil and reduce until it looks like you have about ½ cup of liquid left. Strain, reserving the liquid, and let it cool to room temperature.

6. To serve, toss the artichokes, bread cubes, strawberries, basil, and lemon in a large bowl with the reserved cooking liquid. Divide the cheese slices among plates, season with salt and pepper, and top with a nice heap of salad.

TECHNIQUE 101

Cleaning Artichokes: Cooking an artichoke whole is easy—just slice off the stem so it'll stand upright and boil it, totally submerged, until a knife slides into the base easily, 20 to 25 minutes. Getting at the hearts (a.k.a. "cleaning" an artichoke) requires a bit more prep, but once you know what you're doing, it's easy. Hold the artichoke in one hand and trim off the outer leaves with a sharp knife by rotating the artichoke away from yourself. Keep trimming until you see the yellowish-white flesh, cleaning the base of all green patches as well. Cut off the top leaves so you're left with just the bottom and then scoop out the fuzzy central "choke" with a metal tablespoon, scraping off the dimpled layer beneath the choke as well until you see the smooth white flesh. Quickly submerge the cleaned artichoke in lemon water to keep it from turning brown.

DRINK TIP

They say artichokes are one of the hardest foods to pair with wine (along with asparagus), but keep in mind that "they" are usually attempting to pair with a white. To avoid acid overload, go red instead. Gamays are light-bodied, easy-drinking, fruity reds that are perfect with springy salads like this. And while this might sound strange, chilling the Gamay for just a few minutes before drinking will line up the flavors with the salad even better.

AVOCADO, ENDIVE, AND APPLE SALAD WITH GRAPEFRUIT VINAIGRETTE

SERVES 4

This salad actually came to me back when I was doing my first photo shoot for my Web site. I wanted to create dishes that represented my style with a great mix of texture and flavors but that were also just beautiful to look at. This salad is just that—a combination of various textures, vibrant colors, and also the many different, intense flavors of winter.

Often during the colder months, we get bogged down with overly heavy flavors, so I've always thought it's nice to start off the meal with a salad full of bright acidic notes, especially since citrus is at its peak this time of year. This grapefruit dressing achieves that bright acidity perfectly, and it also brings me back to my elementary school days. My sister and I grew up as competitive swimmers, and to raise money for the team we sold cases of ruby red grapefruit. I'm pretty sure we convinced our parents to buy multiple cases so that we could be the high sellers because I remember eating a grapefruit a day for months and months. It would have been nice if, at the time, my mom had a nice, simple dressing to make with some of my never-ending breakfast food—some days I just wanted to go back to my Rice Krispies.

GRAPEFRUIT VINAIGRETTE

2 tablespoons extra-virgin olive oil

1 teaspoon honey

1 ruby red grapefruit, cut in supremes (see Technique 101, page 76), juice reserved (cut over a bowl to catch the juice)

1 tablespoon chiffonade of basil (about 4 basil leaves)

Kosher salt

Freshly ground black pepper

SALAD

2 heads Belgian endive, cored and thinly sliced

1 Granny Smith apple, julienned

⅓ cup pomegranate seeds (about ¼ pomegranate)

2 radishes, thinly shaved

Salt

Freshly ground black pepper

1 ripe avocado

1. To make the vinaigrette: In a small bowl, whisk the olive oil and honey into the grapefruit juice, then stir in the grapefruit supremes and basil. Season with salt and pepper.

2. To make the salad: In a large bowl, gently toss together the endive, apple, pomegranate seeds, and radishes with the vinaigrette. Season with salt and pepper and set aside.

3. Cut the avocado in half and remove the seed. Cut each side in half again, creating four quarters. Scoop the flesh from the skin with a large spoon. Thinly slice each quarter of avocado lengthwise and fan the pieces onto four plates. Top the avocado slices with evenly divided portions of the salad and serve.

DRINK TIP

If you're ever in doubt, go with bubbly. Sparkling wines go with just about everything, and a nice cava (Spanish sparkling) has a fresh grapefruit-like flavor to mimic this tart dressing and just enough fizz to counter the rich and oily avocado.

SEARED TUNA WITH BLUEBERRIES AND SNAP PEAS

SERVES 4

This dish came about when I was visiting my parents during the Scottsdale Food and Wine Festival (it's always an experience partying with your parents). The annual event takes place in the spring, just when snap peas and blueberries are coming into season. Blueberries also have a touch of tartness, so they work well with a bright and lightly bitter green like sorrel, which to me has clean acidity that's almost like a cross between lemon and green apple peel. The combination of sorrel, crunchy pea pods, and juicy berries proved my theory that fruit is a totally underused ingredient in savory dishes—it can add just the right touch of natural sweetness that can simply be balanced out with a hint of spice (hence the sriracha in the salad's dressing). As long as you keep balance in mind, I'd encourage you to play around with berries in savory dishes, too. You might just come up with your own masterpiece.

DRESSING

3 tablespoons rice vinegar

2 tablespoons extra-virgin olive oil

1 tablespoon minced shallot

½ lemon, zested

1 teaspoon Dijon mustard

1 teaspoon honey

¼ teaspoon sriracha (see Ingredient Spotlight, page 19)

Salt

Freshly ground black pepper

SALAD

1 pound ahi tuna, blood line and skin removed, cut into 4 rectangles

1 tablespoon canola oil

Salt

Freshly ground black pepper

8 ounces sugar snap peas, cut on a bias into thin strips

1 cup shaved radish

1 cup fresh blueberries

⅔ cup chiffonade of sorrel (see Technique 101, page 73)

½ cup pine nuts, toasted

1. To make the dressing: In a small bowl, whisk together the vinegar, olive oil, shallot, lemon zest, mustard, honey, and sriracha until the dressing has emulsified. Season with salt and pepper.

2. To make the salad: Season the tuna with salt and pepper. Heat the canola oil in a large nonstick skillet over high heat. Sear the tuna, turning to brown each piece on all sides, being sure not to overcook it (you want the interior of the fish to be rare, bright pink). Transfer the tuna to a cutting board and cut it into ¼-inch slices.

3. In a medium bowl, carefully toss the peas, radish, blueberries, sorrel, and pine nuts with the dressing. Distribute the salad among plates and top with the seared tuna slices to serve.

DRINK TIP

Delicate flavors like sushi-grade tuna and springy peas should speak for themselves without your drink getting in the way. American wheat beers are incredibly good about taking a backseat to food, while offering a bit of mild creaminess countered by a touch of lemon zing to cleanse your palate for the next bite.

SMOKED TROUT, FINGERLING, AND BACON SALAD

SERVES 4

I was inspired to do a recipe for a smoked trout and bacon salad after a visit to Walla Walla, Washington, my favorite little town in the Pacific Northwest. I met some awesome people there years ago and have been getting back there as much as possible ever since. The restaurant I usually start my Walla Walla visits with is the Whitehouse-Crawford, which is where I fell in love with a simple smoked trout salad. I've since started smoking my own trout at my restaurant, which you can do at home fairly easily, but the salad is great with a high-quality store-bought smoked trout as well.

1 pound fingerling potatoes

2 tablespoons olive oil

8 ounces fresh green beans

6 ounces thick-cut bacon (about 7 slices), cut into ½-inch pieces

8 ounces smoked trout (see page 242)

6 ounces arugula

1 Preserved Lemon (page 241), sliced into thin strips, or the zest of 1 lemon

¾ cup Lemon-Maple Vinaigrette (page 234)

1. Preheat the oven to 400°F. Toss the potatoes with the olive oil and arrange them in a single layer on a baking sheet. Roast them until the potatoes are fork tender, about 30 minutes. Set aside to cool completely and then slice them into ½-inch rounds.

2. While the potatoes are roasting, bring a large pot of salted water to a rapid boil. Fill a bowl halfway with ice and cold water. Add the green beans to the boiling water and blanch them by cooking until they are just tender, 2 to 3 minutes. Drain the beans and put them in the ice bath to shock them. When they are completely cool, strain them again and refrigerate until ready to use.

3. Heat a large sauté pan over medium heat. Add the bacon and cook until the fat is rendered and the bacon is crispy, 7 to 10 minutes. Remove the crisp bacon with a slotted spoon to a plate lined with paper towels.

4. In a large bowl, toss together the potato rounds, beans, bacon, trout, arugula, and lemon. Drizzle the salad greens with the vinaigrette and toss again to coat the ingredients before serving.

DRINK TIP

Smoke on top of smoke. Looks like a job for a nut brown ale. To avoid smoky overload with your bacon and trout, you want a beer with enough creaminess to "put out the fire" so to speak, and nut browns tend to have a knack for balancing strong flavors.

SHRIMP, CORN, AND GREEN TOMATO SALAD

SERVES 4 TO 6

This is a simple recipe that reminds me of my days in Arizona, where everything has a hint of Mexico. Although it's not very complex, this salad is packed with bold and refreshing flavors, and it's ideal in summer when sweet corn is at its best. (Cooking the corn for just a minute or two allows the sweetness to come out while holding on to the natural crunchy texture.) The tart green tomato and lime juice lend the dish some nice acidity, while the poblano peppers add just the right amount of spice. And if you're not in the mood for shrimp, try the salad with some sliced grilled beef or a bit of roasted chicken—or just leave the meat off altogether and eat it right out of the bowl on the front porch on a hot summer day.

2 poblano peppers, roasted (see Technique 101, facing page)

1 pound extra-large (16 to 20) shrimp, peeled and deveined

¼ teaspoon coriander seeds, toasted

¼ teaspoon mustard seeds, toasted

3 or 4 black peppercorns

Pinch red pepper flakes

Salt

⅓ cup plus 2 tablespoons olive oil

2 ears corn, kernels removed

Freshly ground black pepper

⅓ cup fresh lime juice

2 tablespoons chopped fresh cilantro, plus 1 tablespoon leaves for garnishing

1 tablespoon honey

1 mango, diced (see Technique 101, page 57)

2 green tomatoes, seeded and diced

1. Finely dice one of the roasted peppers and put it in a salad bowl. Reserve the other pepper for the salad dressing.

2. Rinse the shrimp and dab them dry. In a spice grinder or blender, grind together the coriander, mustard seeds, peppercorns, and red pepper flakes. Toss the spices with the shrimp and season with salt.

3. Heat a large sauté pan over high heat. Add 1 tablespoon of the oil. Add the shrimp and sauté until they're just cooked through, about 3 minutes. Transfer them to a plate and refrigerate to chill.

4. Heat another 1 tablespoon oil in the same sauté pan over medium-high heat, add the corn, and sauté until it is just cooked, about 2 minutes. Season with salt and pepper. Transfer to a bowl and refrigerate.

5. Put the remaining roasted pepper, the lime juice, remaining ⅓ cup olive oil, the chopped cilantro, and honey in a blender and blend until smooth. Season with salt and pepper.

6. Once the shrimp and corn are cooled, transfer them to the salad bowl with the diced roasted pepper and add the mango and tomatoes. Toss with just enough of the dressing to coat (refrigerate any leftover for another use) and adjust the seasoning. Transfer the salad to plates or a serving dish and garnish with the cilantro leaves before serving.

TECHNIQUE 101

Roasting Peppers: It's definitely convenient to pop open a jar of roasted peppers, but it's not only more expensive than roasting them yourself, it's not going to give you the full roasted flavor you'll get by holding them over flames just minutes before you eat. Plus, you'll typically only find jarred roasted *red* peppers, so you're pretty limited on variety. I've found that the easiest and fastest way to roast peppers is to brush them with oil then, using tongs, hold each one over the flame of a stovetop burner and blacken it on all sides. Remove it from the flame and place it in a plastic bag, or a bowl covered with plastic wrap, until the pepper cools to room temperature. This method helps to somewhat steam the skin away from the flesh, making it much easier to peel off. Skin the pepper, remove the stem and seeds, and either use the pepper immediately or store it in an airtight container in the refrigerator for a few days.

DRINK TIP

Pilsners are one of the most popular lager beers in Germany, and for good reason: They're incredibly food friendly. Try one of these crisp, golden beers with this dish, and you'll see that the bright hops line right up with the green tomatoes and that the slightly spicy notes will complement the shrimp perfectly.

CHA
FOUR

PTER

PASTAS

I THINK I COULD EAT PASTA EVERY DAY FOR THE REST OF MY LIFE. I JUST LOVE IT. IT DOESN'T ALWAYS FIT INTO THE LOW-CARB LIFESTYLE WE'D ALL LIKE TO HAVE THE WILL-POWER TO FOLLOW, BUT SO WHAT? I JUST CAN'T SAY "NO" TO NOODLES.

We make our own pasta at Girl & the Goat, and there really is something rewarding about rolling out the perfect dough. If you want to give it a shot, try the Basic Pasta Dough recipe (page 230). But if you're short on time or just want to keep things simple, the fresh pasta you can find at specialty markets or even dry pasta like Barilla, DeCecco, and Trader Joe's will do just fine. And don't forget that Italians don't own the noodle—simple Asian stir-fries you might normally eat with rice are usually even better tossed with soba or ramen. When it comes to serving size for this chapter, keep in mind that in a lot of restaurants, including mine, pastas are served family-style as a midcourse, so that's how these recipes were written. Still, I realize some people like to eat pasta as the main event, so each recipe yield will list two serving sizes: the first for entrée portions and the second for appetizers or mid-courses. And if you wind up eating a whole batch straight out of the pan for breakfast, well, you're on your own.

OLIVE OIL–POACHED SHRIMP WITH SOBA NOODLES

SERVES 4 AS AN ENTRÉE, 6 AS AN APPETIZER

Just after *Top Chef* wrapped, I was doing a small tour of cooking demonstrations that took me to Michigan (any excuse to get back to Ann Arbor, where I went to college, is worth it. Go Blue!). It was during early spring, so what I wanted to create was a simple and refreshing cold noodle salad with Asian flavors that highlighted the season, when asparagus is at its peak. The soy sauce, shiitake mushrooms, and soba noodles are pure umami—that savory fifth taste often connected with Japanese food. Poaching the shrimp in olive oil helps lock in the natural juices and creates a beautiful texture. Once you've had a shrimp so delicately poached that it almost melts in your mouth, you'll have a whole new appreciation for the tiny delicacies.

12 jumbo (11 to15) shrimp count	1 pound asparagus, tough ends trimmed	8 ounces fresh shiitake mushrooms	2 green onions, whites and greens thinly sliced
2 garlic cloves, minced	⅓ cup plus 5 teaspoons olive oil	8 ounces soba noodles	2 tablespoons sesame seeds, toasted
2 tablespoons minced peeled fresh ginger	Salt	¼ cup soy sauce	
1 teaspoon sriracha (see Ingredient Spotlight, page 19)	Freshly ground black pepper	1 tablespoon honey	
		1½ teaspoons Dijon mustard	

1. Rub the shrimp with half of the garlic, half of the ginger, and the sriracha. Cover and let the shrimp marinate in the refrigerator for 1 hour.

2. Preheat the oven to 400°F.

3. Spread the asparagus on a baking sheet and brush with 2½ teaspoons of the olive oil. Roast just until the asparagus is tender, about 15 minutes. Remove, season with salt and pepper, and set aside to cool.

4. Reduce the oven temperature to 300°F. Toss the shiitakes with another 2½ teaspoons olive oil, spread them on a baking sheet, and transfer to the oven.

Continued . . .

Roast just until the mushrooms begin to shrivel, about 30 minutes. Season with salt and pepper and set aside to cool.

5. Put the shrimp in a small baking dish or ovenproof sauté pan, cover with the remaining ⅓ cup olive oil and season lightly with salt. Cover the dish with aluminum foil and poach the shrimp in the oven just until the exteriors are bright orange and if you slice into one, the interior is still opaque, about 15 minutes. (Don't worry that it doesn't look completely done as it will carry-over cook a bit.) Remove the shrimp from the oil and reserve the oil, allowing it to cool.

6. Meanwhile, bring a large pot of water to a boil. Cook the noodles according to the package directions. Rinse with cold water and set aside to cool.

7. Cut the asparagus into 1-inch pieces and the shiitakes into thin strips. Toss the vegetables with the cooled noodles.

8. Whisk together the remaining garlic and ginger with the soy sauce, honey, and mustard. Slowly whisk in the reserved poaching oil. Pour the dressing over the noodles and toss well to combine. Top with the shrimp, green onions, and sesame seeds before serving.

TECHNIQUE 101

Olive Oil Poaching : When I discovered that poaching seafood in olive oil turns the texture butter-smooth, I fell in love with this technique. What sets this method apart is that while pan-frying uses high heat to create a crisp outer layer that traps in the moisture, poaching at a low temperature in oil surrounds the protein with fat, allowing it to slowly steam on the inside. (Just think of it like barbecue—low and slow is the way to go.) Also, as opposed to frying, where the goal is not to have the flavor of the oil picked up by the food, in poaching you want that flavor to soak in, so it's very important to use high-quality oil. It's worth the extra money, and you can strain the oil after poaching to use in vinaigrettes, soup bases, or even to poach again (store the oil in the refrigerator). Beyond low and slow, other primary tips to remember with this technique are to always use an oven since you can regulate the temperature a bit more than on the stove, and always pull out the fish or shellfish just before it seems done, as it will continue to cook (carry over) because of the hot oil trapped within. The best news, though, is that this is a very forgiving method, so even a slightly overcooked piece of fish is still going to be very moist. (Of course, it's always better to aim for the right texture, but after a few tries, you'll probably nail it.)

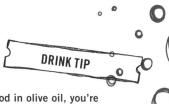

DRINK TIP

Anytime you poach rich seafood in olive oil, you're upping the richness quotient even more. To counter that, and to line up with our Asian noodles, go with a crisp lager. Even better if you can find it, try a Japanese rice-based lager.

ASPARAGUS LINGUINE WITH ALMOND BUTTER CRISP

SERVES 4 AS AN ENTRÉE, 8 AS AN APPETIZER

My love of asparagus comes up throughout this book in various forms: tempura battered and fried (see page 27), roasted and tossed with soba noodles (see page 122), and in this recipe, simply sautéed and taking on the lead role in a great spring pasta dish. Rather than blanching and shocking the spears, in this recipe we simply sauté bite-size pieces and let them cook to al dente in a bit of broth and soy so that they soak up some of that flavor while cooking.

Now if you're seeing the words "almond butter crisp" and thinking of a crunchy fruit dessert topping, go the opposite way. This is actually a completely savory compound butter, playing up the nutty almonds with salty grated Parmesan, a touch of heat from red pepper flakes, and fragrant roasted garlic. It's awesome served over a simple piece of fish or chicken with some grilled vegetables, or you can skip the protein and just liven up veggies with spiced garlic crunch. Along with taste, texture is the most important component in any dish, and here, the combination of bread crumbs and almonds gives you two for the price of one.

ALMOND BUTTER CRISP

1 head garlic, roasted, removed from skin (see Technique 101, page 127)

3 ounces butter, at room temperature

¼ cup dry bread crumbs

¼ cup grated Parmesan cheese

1 teaspoon salt

½ teaspoon red pepper flakes

1 cup toasted sliced almonds

PASTA

1 batch Basic Pasta Dough (page 230), cut into linguine noodles, or 1 pound dried linguine

1 tablespoon olive oil

1 pound asparagus, trimmed, cut on bias into 1-inch pieces

Salt

Freshly ground black pepper

½ cup chicken broth

2 tablespoons soy sauce

8 ounces baby arugula, stemmed

2 tablespoons julienned Preserved Lemon (page 241)

2 tablespoons chiffonade of fresh mint (see Technique 101, page 73)

Continued . . .

1. To make the crisp: In a small bowl, mix together the roasted garlic, butter, bread crumbs, Parmesan, salt, and red pepper flakes. Gently fold in the almonds, trying not to crush them. Cover and refrigerate until hardened.

2. To make the pasta: Bring a large pot of water to a boil. Drop the linguine in the boiling water and cook until al dente, 7 to 9 minutes, or according to the package directions. Reserve ⅓ cup of the cooking water before draining the pasta. Drain and rinse the pasta and reserve.

3. Heat a large sauté pan over medium-high heat. Add the olive oil, then the asparagus and sauté until the asparagus is bright green, 3 to 4 minutes. Season with salt and pepper, then add the broth, soy sauce, and the ⅓ cup reserved pasta water. Simmer to reduce the liquid by half. Add the pasta, arugula, lemon, and mint, tossing to coat them with the sauce. Season with salt and pepper.

4. Heat a medium sauté pan over medium-high heat. Add the almond crisp and cook until it has started to brown, 3 to 4 minutes. Pour half of the butter into the pasta, tossing to coat. Transfer the pasta to a platter or plates, and garnish with the remaining almond crisp before serving.

TECHNIQUE 101

Roasting Garlic: There are plenty of ways to roast garlic, but my favorite (and maybe the easiest) is to take a whole head, trim off the top quarter-inch to expose the cloves, place it on a sheet of aluminum foil, drizzle with olive oil, sprinkle with salt, fold up the foil like a little pouch, transfer to a 400°F oven, and roast until deep brown, 30 to 40 minutes. Once the garlic has cooled a bit, you can squeeze the cloves out from their skins. The sweet, caramelly garlic flavor is so good you can spread it directly onto crusty bread and eat it all by itself, but also feel free to mash it into potatoes, purée it into vinaigrettes, or use it anywhere you want a complex hit of garlic.

DRINK TIP

Sparkling wines have a certain nutty element that would be perfect to play up the almond crisp here. Also, a light and mild bubbly will do a nice job of letting the asparagus do its own thing without getting in the way.

LINGUINE IN CELERY ROOT CREAM WITH APPLES AND PANCETTA

SERVES 4 AS AN ENTRÉE, 8 AS AN APPETIZER

This recipe reminds me of a book I once came across that was supposed to help parents sneak vegetables into their kids' dinner, injecting a bit of nutrition into Billy or Suzy's favorite "sghetti." Likewise, this is a sneaky way to make an Alfredo-like sauce out of celery root. There's no cheese and just a bit of cream instead of a gallon, making it not only a healthier option but also a much more creative and memorable one. Still, the cream sauce tastes incredibly rich, which is exactly why the tart green apples are in the mix—to cut that richness. Ditto for the olives, which bring a briny saltiness to the picture. You won't get apple and olive with every bite, mainly because I didn't want to overpower the savoriness of the dish, but every now and then there'll be a nice surprise.

1 tablespoon olive oil	½ cup heavy cream	2 Granny Smith apples, peeled, quartered, and cut crosswise into wedges	1 cup manzanilla olives, pitted and roughly chopped (see Ingredient Spotlight, page 17), for garnishing
1 garlic clove, minced	1 batch Basic Pasta Dough (page 230), cut into linguine, or 1 pound dried linguine	½ red onion, thinly sliced	
3 cups diced celery root		2 cups peeled and thinly sliced celery, leaves reserved for garnishing	
¼ cup diced Yukon gold potato	1 tablespoon vegetable oil		
1½ cups vegetable broth	1 cup diced pancetta		

1. Heat the olive oil in a large stockpot over medium-low heat and add the garlic. Sweat the garlic by cooking for a couple of minutes until it is soft but not brown, then add the celery root and potato, increasing the heat to medium-high. Cook until the potato just begins to soften, about 5 minutes. Add the broth and cream. Fit the pot with a parchment paper lid (see Quick Tip, facing page) and reduce the heat to simmer until the celery root is very tender, about 35 minutes. Working with a tabletop or immersion blender, purée the sauce until smooth.

2. While the celery cream is cooking, bring a large pot of water to a boil. Drop the linguine in the boiling water and cook until al dente, 7 to 9 minutes, or according to the package directions. Drain and rinse the pasta and reserve.

3. Heat a medium to large sauté pan over medium-high heat. Add the vegetable oil and pancetta. Cook until the pancetta begins to brown and crisp, then remove them with a slotted spoon and set aside on a plate lined with paper towels.

4. Lower the heat to medium and add the apples. Cook until they caramelize in the pancetta fat, getting nice and browned on the edges and soft throughout. Add the onion and sweat it by cooking until the onion is translucent, about 3 minutes, then add the celery. Turn the heat to low.

5. Once the cream sauce is puréed, add it to the sauté pan with the apples, pancetta, and celery, stirring to coat. Toss the sauce with the pasta and garnish with the celery leaves and olives before serving.

QUICK TIP

- When you're draining the pasta, drain it over a bowl to reserve some of the pasta water. Pasta water has a lot of starch in it; this makes it great to add into the sauce as needed to help with the consistency as opposed to just plain old water, which, well, just waters down the sauce.

- In restaurants, we don't really have lids for our pots and pans like you do at home (that is if you didn't lose them like most people do). So when I want to simmer something for awhile without evaporating a lot of liquid, I cut a piece of parchment paper into a circle the size of the pot I'm using, and poke a tiny hole in the center to allow only a little steam to escape, locking in the moisture. You can essentially do the same thing by covering the pot or pan with a lid slightly ajar, but with the paper you can place it directly on top of what you're cooking to stunt the evaporation.

DRINK TIP

For a dish that evokes fall as much as this—with its pancetta and smoky fat-cooked apples—a *dunkel-weizen* would be ideal. These German-style dark wheat beers have more oomph than their summery counterparts, *hefeweizens*, and they're not overly sweet like American brown ales can be, which would make this dish cloyingly rich.

MANILA CLAM AND SAUSAGE LINGUINE WITH HORSERADISH CRÈME FRAÎCHE

SERVES 4 AS AN ENTRÉE, 8 AS AN APPETIZER

Horseradish crème fraîche has been a favorite sauce of mine for a long time. As a kid, my family would have it every year on my birthday with beef fondue. (Some kids want cake . . . I wanted beef with horseradish crème fraîche. Go figure.) These days I've found a way to use the same great flavor combination in a much lighter dish. The crème fraîche lightly coats the pasta without being overly heavy like a standard cream sauce.

½ cup crème fraîche

⅓ cup prepared horseradish

4 ounces sugar snap peas

1 tablespoon olive oil

8 ounces mild Italian pork sausage

1 cup minced fennel (about 1 baby bulb or ½ medium bulb)

1 small onion, minced

3 large garlic cloves, 1 minced and 2 sliced

½ teaspoon sambal paste (see Ingredient Spotlight, page 47)

1 batch Basic Pasta Dough (page 230), cut into linguine, or 1 pound dried linguine

1 tablespoon butter

1 medium shallot, minced

1 cup white wine

2 pounds (about 2 dozen) Manila clams (see Quick Tip, page 132)

Salt

Freshly ground black pepper

1. Combine the crème fraîche and horseradish in a small bowl and set aside.

2. Bring a large pot of salted water to a boil. Prepare a bowl of ice water. Drop the peas into the boiling water and blanch them, cooking for about 2 minutes. Lift them out of the water with a wide slotted spoon and drop them into the ice water to stop the cooking. Drain and set aside. Return the water to a boil for cooking the linguine later.

3. Meanwhile, coat the bottom of a large sauté pan with the olive oil and set over medium-high heat. When the pan is hot, squeeze the sausage out of the casings and into the pan, breaking it up into large chunks (discard the casings). Brown the sausage, cooking for about 5 minutes, stirring only occasionally.

4. Add the fennel, onion, and minced garlic, and reduce the heat to medium. Sweat the vegetables with the browned sausage until the onion and fennel are soft and fragrant, another 5 minutes. Stir in the sambal, remove the mixture from the heat, and set aside.

Continued . . .

5. Drop the linguine in the boiling water and cook until al dente, 7 to 9 minutes, or according to the package directions. Drain and rinse the pasta and reserve.

6. While the linguine is cooking, melt the butter in a Dutch oven or a large, wide saucepan over medium heat. Add the shallot and sliced garlic, sweating them by cooking until the shallot is translucent, about 1 minute. Add the wine, bring the liquid to a simmer, add the clams, and cover the pot with a tight-fitting lid. Steam the clams just until they have opened, about 5 minutes.

7. Pour the clams and their cooking liquid into the pan with the sausage.

8. Transfer the hot pasta to the pan with the other ingredients. Pour the horseradish crème fraîche on top, add the peas, and toss all of the ingredients together to combine. Season with salt and pepper and divide among the plates to serve.

 QUICK TIP ···

As with mussels, go through the clams before cooking them and discard any that aren't closed or don't close when lightly squeezed. That's a sign your clam is already in it's final resting place. Also, discard any clams that don't open during cooking—that's a sign that it had already kicked the bucket before hitting the water in the pot.

DRINK TIP

Not all bubblies are created equal, and not all should be relegated to just a meal-starting toast. A blanc de noir is a Champagne with a lot more weight than most, thanks to the red grapes it's made from, making it strong enough to stand up to sausage but clean and fizzy enough to cleanse your palate of the rich sauce in this pasta.

LINGUINE WITH MONKFISH AND ROMESCO

SERVES 4 AS AN ENTRÉE, 8 AS AN APPETIZER

Romesco sauce is a Spanish classic, typically made from almonds, pine nuts or hazelnuts, plenty of garlic, olive oil, and usually roasted tomatoes and dried peppers. In Catalonia, the region responsible for this delicious sauce, you can come across a dozen different versions of it all along the same block, some served on grilled fish, others with roasted lamb or even just a great charred pork chop. This variation is one that I use as my go-to sauce. Try this recipe as is, taste it, and start experimenting for yourself. It's incredibly versatile and since it does take a bit of time to make, I sometimes double the batch and keep the leftovers in the fridge to enjoy throughout the week or even freeze it so it will keep for a couple of weeks.

For this recipe, you want a meaty, sturdy-textured fish to stand up to the flavorful sauce, and if anything can, it's the ugly-as-hell monkfish. I still remember the first time I had monkfish, years ago in New York City with a friend from college. I remember biting into the monkfish and falling in love—the texture was meaty but light; the flavor was mild compared to oily fish like salmon, but it still had such a richness to it. It's often referred to as "poor man's lobster," but I'm going to have to disagree with that one, as lobster is infinitely sweeter. As much as I love the flavor of monkfish, the first time I saw a whole one as opposed to a cleaned and cooked slice on a pretty plate, I couldn't believe something so gnarly looking could taste so good. Just goes to show, you can't judge a book by its cover.

ROMESCO SAUCE

1½ pounds Roma tomatoes, halved lengthwise, seeded

12 garlic cloves, peeled

¾ cup extra-virgin olive oil plus 2 tablespoons

Salt

Freshly ground black pepper

½ cup cubed ciabatta bread

1 cup minced onion

½ cup white wine

2 cups chicken broth

¾ cup chopped fresh parsley

⅓ cup whole almonds, toasted

⅓ cup whole hazelnuts, toasted

2 dried ancho chiles, rehydrated in water, stemmed

1 ounce bittersweet chocolate

1 tablespoon brown sugar

1 teaspoon sherry vinegar

1 teaspoon soy sauce

1 teaspoon red pepper flakes

1 teaspoon smoked paprika (pimentón)

LINGUINE WITH MONKFISH

1 batch Basic Pasta Dough (page 230), cut into linguine, or 1 pound dried linguine

2 tablespoons butter

2 tablespoons olive oil

1 pound rapini, stems trimmed

4 tablespoons chicken broth

2 teaspoons soy sauce

½ teaspoon red pepper flakes

1½ pounds monkfish fillets, cleaned and cut into ½-inch slices (substitute halibut or cod if needed)

Salt

Freshly ground black pepper

¼ cup Wondra flour (see Ingredient Spotlight, page 135)

2 tablespoons blended vegetable oil (half vegetable, half olive oil)

2 ounces ricotta salata cheese, crumbled

1 tablespoon minced fresh parsley, for garnishing

Continued . . .

1. To make the romesco: Preheat the oven to 400°F. Line up the tomatoes, skin-sides up, in an 8-by-8-inch baking dish, tuck the garlic cloves in among the tomatoes, and drizzle with the ¾ cup extra-virgin olive oil. Season with salt and pepper. Roast until the tomatoes begin to brown and are very tender, about 35 minutes.

2. Meanwhile, toss the ciabatta with 1 tablespoon extra-virgin olive oil. Season with salt and pepper, spread on a baking sheet, and bake until golden brown, about 10 minutes.

3. In a large saucepan, heat the remaining 1 tablespoon extra-virgin olive oil over medium heat. Add the onion and sweat it by cooking until the onion is translucent, about 3 minutes. Add the wine and simmer until reduced by half.

4. Add the roasted tomato mixture, toasted bread, broth, parsley, almonds, hazelnuts, chiles, chocolate, brown sugar, vinegar, soy sauce, red pepper flakes, and paprika. Bring to near boiling, reduce the heat, and simmer for about 40 minutes for the flavors to come together. Working in a few batches, ladle the mixture into a blender and purée until nearly smooth. Season with salt and pepper. Cover and keep warm or refrigerate until needed.

5. To make the linguine and monkfish: Bring a large pot of water to a boil. Drop the linguine into the boiling water and cook until al dente, 7 to 9 minutes, or according to the package directions. Drain, rinse, and reserve.

6. Heat a large sauté pan over medium-high heat. Add 1 tablespoon each of the butter and olive oil and half of the rapini. Sauté until the rapini begins to wilt, about 3 minutes, then add 2 tablespoons of the broth, 1 teaspoon of the soy sauce, and ¼ teaspoon of the red pepper flakes. Continue to sauté until the rapini is almost tender and most of the liquid is absorbed, 3 to 4 minutes. Remove and set aside. Repeat with the other half of the butter, olive oil, rapini, broth, soy sauce, and red pepper flakes.

7. Wipe out the pan and return it to high heat. Season the monkfish with salt and pepper, then dust the fillets very lightly with the flour. Heat the blended oil in the pan. Add the monkfish and cook until nicely browned on all sides. Set aside, let cool slightly, and cut crosswise in ½-inch slices.

8. To serve, toss the pasta with the rapini, the monkfish slices, and about 2 cups of the romesco sauce (more or less to taste). Top with the cheese and garnish with the parsley.

DRINK TIP

Romesco is such a Spanish classic that you should stick to that country's wines for a great pairing. The Penedes region of Spain is *cava* country, home to a ton of sparkling wine producers. The light and refreshing bubbly is ideal because it won't overpower all of the complex flavors that go into a rich romesco.

INGREDIENT SPOTLIGHT

WONDRA FLOUR Wondra might look super old-school, with its '60s-era packaging, but it's a secret tool for many contemporary chefs. Essentially, Wondra is instant flour—granulated ultra fine and made to dissolve quickly, making it ideal for gravies or sauces. I actually use it for dusting fish because it's less likely to clump. It creates a nice even coating, and it gets super-crisp really quickly. I know of a few pastry chefs who swear by it for flaky pie crusts, but I'll leave the baking up to them.

ARTICHOKE FIDEOS WITH FRESH MOZZARELLA AND DILL

Fideos is a Spanish term for pasta, and in Spain, it refers to very thin vermicelli-like noodles that are cut short and used in dishes in place of rice. It sounds pretty simple, but what makes fideos so delicious is that the noodles are first toasted to bring on a nice nutty flavor, then slowly cooked in broth rather than boiled in water. In this method, they soak up the flavor of the broth and don't really need anything else.

At Scylla, we served a version of a very classic shrimp fideos, where we cooked the noodles in a light shrimp stock, then tossed the shrimp back into the dish and broiled it for a bit to get a bit of crispiness on the top just before sending it out to the table. For this recipe, I wanted to really celebrate the flavor of the artichoke by following the same method, but with a stock made from the scraps left over after cleaning the artichokes to their heart. It always feels so wasteful to me to discard the leaves after cleaning them. They're actually full of flavor, even though only the very bottom of them is edible when the artichoke is steamed or grilled whole. Plus, I figured after putting in all of the hard work to get to the heart, it's nice to really be able to enjoy the artichoke to its fullest.

4 artichokes, cleaned (see Technique 101, page 112)

½ cup olive oil plus 1 tablespoon

1 small onion, chopped

7 garlic cloves, 5 chopped and 2 minced

½ cup dry white wine

1 quart chicken broth

4 dried guajillo chiles

½ tablespoon black peppercorns

8 ounces dry angel hair pasta, broken into 2-inch pieces

1 shallot, minced

1 pound ground lamb

1 tablespoon Worcestershire sauce

1 tablespoon Dijon mustard

¼ teaspoon red pepper flakes

Salt

Freshly ground black pepper

2 tablespoons extra-virgin olive oil

4½ teaspoons fresh lemon juice

1 tablespoon chopped fresh parsley

1 tablespoon chopped fresh dill

4 ounces fresh mozzarella, sliced

1. Slice the artichokes hearts ¼ inch thick on a mandoline and set them aside, submerged in lemon water to prevent browning. Reserve the leaves.

2. Heat a large saucepan over medium-low heat. Add the ½ cup olive oil, then the onion and chopped garlic. Sweat them by cooking until the onion is translucent, about 3 to 5 minutes. Add the wine, increase the heat to medium-high, and simmer to reduce by half. Add the broth, artichoke leaves, chiles, and peppercorns and bring to a boil. Reduce the heat to low and simmer for about 45 minutes to combine the flavors. Strain the liquid through a fine-mesh sieve, discarding the solids.

3. Preheat the oven to 375°F. Spread the pieces of angel hair evenly onto a baking sheet and toast in the oven until golden brown, about 6 minutes.

4. Preheat the broiler. Heat the remaining 1 tablespoon olive oil in a Dutch oven over medium heat. Add the shallot and minced garlic and sweat by cooking until the shallot is translucent, about 3 minutes.

5. Meanwhile, in a medium bowl, combine the lamb, Worcestershire, mustard, red pepper flakes, and 1 teaspoon salt. Season with pepper. Increase the heat on the Dutch oven to medium-high and add the lamb mixture to brown, breaking up with a wooden spoon while cooking. Remove it with a slotted spoon and set aside to drain.

6. Strain the sliced artichokes from their water and dab them dry on paper towels. Heat the Dutch oven back over medium-high heat and add the extra-virgin olive oil. Add the artichokes and lightly brown them for 3 to 4 minutes. Season with salt and pepper. Add the strained artichoke stock and the pasta. As you stir the pasta, it will begin to cook, and it will submerge into the liquid. Continue to stir until the liquid is absorbed and both the pasta and the artichokes are tender. Return the lamb to the pot along with the lemon juice, parsley, and dill, stirring to combine. Transfer the mixture to a large oven-to-table baking dish. Place the mozzarella on the fideos, pressing it down into the pasta a bit while leaving some of the pasta exposed.

7. Broil until the cheese is lightly browned and bubbly and some of the pasta is crisped, about 4 minutes. Remove from the oven and serve.

DRINK TIP

We're working with difficult artichokes here, and we also have creaminess from the mozzarella and brightness from the dill. When you're dealing with tricky flavors, a good rule of thumb is to let the wine bow out of the flavor contest gracefully. A light and easy Pinot Grigio will do this well.

PAPPARDELLE IN BAGNA CAUDA
WITH CAULIFLOWER

SERVES 4 AS AN ENTRÉE, 8 AS AN APPETIZER

Bagna cauda is Italian for "warm bath," and the classic Italian dip is just about as comforting as its namesake. Usually served warm alongside crudités as an antipasti, bagna cauda at its core is all about anchovies, which are blended with a bit of olive oil, a good dose of garlic, and sometimes butter or even cream. You can use the bagna cauda traditionally as a dip for raw or roasted veggies (or you could even just slather it on good bread), but I actually think it's ideal as a sauce for pasta, which is how we often served it at Scylla. Just think of the same type of vegetables you usually dip into a bagna cauda—cauliflower, asparagus, and carrots— and it makes perfect sense to combine them into a pasta dish like this.

BAGNA CAUDA

½ cup minced white anchovies (see Ingredient Spotlight, facing page)

⅓ cup olive oil

⅓ cup butter

3 tablespoons fresh lemon juice

5 garlic cloves, sliced

1 teaspoon red pepper flakes

PASTA

1 batch Basic Pasta Dough (page 230), cut into pappardelle, or 1 pound dried pappardelle

1 large head cauliflower, cut into ¼-inch slices (see Technique 101, page 211)

Salt

Freshly ground black pepper

2 tablespoons julienned Preserved Lemon (page 241) or 1 lemon, zested

2 tablespoons chiffonade of fresh mint (see Technique 101, page 73)

2 tablespoons chiffonade of fresh basil

¾ cup sliced almonds, toasted, for garnishing

2 ounces crumbled feta cheese, for garnishing

1. To make the bagna cauda: Combine the anchovies, olive oil, butter, lemon juice, garlic, and red pepper flakes in a medium saucepan and bring to a low boil over medium heat. Reduce the heat and let the mixture simmer until the anchovies fall apart, about 30 minutes.

2. To make the pasta: Bring a large pot of water to a boil. Drop the pappardelle into the boiling water and cook until al dente, 7 to 9 minutes, or according to the package directions.

3. While the pasta is cooking, spoon 3 tablespoons of the bagna cauda into a large sauté pan over medium-high heat. Add the cauliflower and sauté until lightly brown and just softened, 5 to 7 minutes. Season with salt and pepper.

4. Drain the pasta and add it to the pan with the cauliflower along with the remaining bagna cauda, lemon, mint, and basil, stirring to thoroughly coat the pasta.

5. To serve, divide the pasta among bowls and garnish with the almonds and feta.

DRINK TIP

A really soft, full-bodied Chardonnay is perfect with the intense flavors in a bagna cauda, but try to go with a Columbia Valley Chard. These tend to be less buttery and oaky than California Chardonnays and more middle-of-the-road, easy drinkers.

INGREDIENT SPOTLIGHT

WHITE ANCHOVIES If you're wrinkling your nose at anchovies, I can understand why—I used to think that the very salty, hairy-looking canned anchovies were the only anchovies around, and I was never really a fan of them myself. But once you taste the delicate saltiness of the white anchovy, you'll change your mind about these little fish. Actually, white anchovies aren't a different type of fish; the difference is in how they're treated. Italians, specifically Sicilians, prefer to harvest the Mediterranean fish when they are smaller and milder, and, as opposed to curing them and instilling a strongly salty flavor, they fillet the fresh anchovies and package them in a light vinegar marinade. This method allows you to taste the delicate fish for what they are and not end up with a wallop of oily salt in your mouth. You'll usually find white anchovies in the refrigerated section of better grocery stores like Whole Foods, and keeping a package of them around is a good way to inject a bit of briny sea flavor into a dish.

APPLE-PORK RAGU WITH PAPPARDELLE

SERVES 4 AS AN ENTRÉE, 8 AS AN APPETIZER

This is an extremely simple recipe, but the number of flavors involved make it unique and a lot more fun than your average pasta with meat sauce. I really like to make this in early fall when apples are at their prime, and I specifically like to use the Honeycrisp variety. Their perfect sweet-to-tart ratio marries well with tomatoes, and the overall sweetness is offset by salty capers. This sauce is awesome with homemade pappardelle, but it would be great with any dried pastas as well. If you go the dried pasta route, a small shell-shaped pasta like orechiette would be ideal, capturing a few bits of pork in each bite. And if you're a cheese freak like me, top the whole thing off with a bit of freshly grated Parmesan.

1 teaspoon olive oil

12 ounces ground pork

2 strips thick-cut bacon, cut into ½-inch pieces

½ cup diced onion

3 garlic cloves, minced

2 Honeycrisp apples, peeled and cut into ¼-inch slices

½ cup dry white wine

One 15-ounce can whole peeled tomatoes, smashed by hand or chopped

1 cup chicken broth

1 batch Basic Pasta Dough (page 230), cut into pappardelle, or 1 pound dried pappardelle

2 tablespoons brined capers

2 tablespoons thinly sliced fresh basil

Coarse salt

Freshly ground black pepper

1. Heat the oil in a large sauté pan over medium-high heat. Add the pork and cook it until it browns, 5 to 7 minutes, breaking it into smaller pieces with a spoon. Set aside.

2. In a large saucepot or Dutch oven, lightly brown the bacon over medium heat. Add the onion and garlic and sweat them by cooking until the onion is translucent, about 2 minutes. Add the apples and wine and simmer until the wine is reduced by three-quarters.

3. Add the tomatoes, broth, and browned pork and bring to a boil. Reduce the heat and simmer, partially covered, until the sauce has thickened somewhat, about 15 minutes.

4. Meanwhile, bring a large pot of water to a boil. Drop the pappardelle in the boiling water and cook until al dente, about 3 minutes, or according to the package directions. Drain and rinse.

5. Add the capers and basil to the sauce just before serving. Season the ragu with salt and pepper. Serve over the pasta.

DRINK TIP

Apples work well in oatmeal, and likewise, this appley, pork-packed ragu goes hand-in-hand with oatmeal stouts. These yummy beers have enough body and plenty of creaminess to stand up to this rich dish, but being a stout, the slightly bitter malts will keep the pairing from being cloying.

FRENCH GNOCCHI WITH WATERCRESS SAUCE

SERVES 4 AS AN ENTRÉE, 8 AS AN APPETIZER

Recently I was discussing the difference between French gnocchi and Italian gnocchi at Girl & the Goat, expressing my love for these little morsels. One great thing about them is that they're very consistent compared to potato gnocchi, which are more likely to vary depending on who makes the dough. This dough is a bit less delicate and harder to mess up, so for a restaurant that sends out many orders a night, it's nice to have a consistent gnocchi.

I started making these back in my days at La Tache restaurant in Chicago with Dale Levitski, who turned me on to them. It was great for us as cooks because we were serving profiteroles at the bistro as well, and since French gnocchi is made from the same dough, we could make one big batch for both and kill two birds with one stone. The dough is technically a *pâte à choux*, and when it's baked, the egg yolks help create a rich and flaky pastry. When it's boiled, the yolks make for a puffy and airy gnocchi. Leave it to the French to create such a versatile dough.

So now that you know what they are, and you know that they're pretty easy to make, I expect you to make them all of the time! They're great tossed with veggies, added to soups as dumplings, or just crisped up in some butter and enjoyed as is. To keep things interesting, I've included a recipe for a very easy watercress sauce that came to be during a *Top Chef*–style cook-off demo I did in Ohio. One of our ingredients was frogs' legs, and I only had a few minutes to make a sauce, so I threw some watercress in the water, pulled it out, and blended it up with butter. It was perfect with those frog legs, but it turned out to be just as great with this equally-French gnocchi.

1 cup unsalted butter	Salt	2 large eggs	¼ teaspoon red pepper flakes
½ cup milk	½ cup plus 2 tablespoons all-purpose flour	2 tablespoons olive oil	
½ teaspoon freshly ground black pepper	8 egg yolks	8 ounces watercress	

1. Bring ½ cup of the butter, the milk, pepper, and ½ teaspoon salt to a boil in a medium saucepan over medium-high heat. Add the flour and stir with a wooden spoon until the mixture pulls away from the sides of the pot. Continue to cook for 30 seconds. Transfer the dough to a stand mixer fitted with the paddle attachment and beat on low speed until the dough has cooled to room temperature.

2. With the mixer running, add the egg yolks and eggs one at a time and mix until a tacky paste forms. Transfer the dough to a pastry bag with a ½-inch round tip (see Quick Tip, below). Line a baking sheet with parchment paper and pipe 1-inch dots onto the pan. Freeze the gnocchi until firm. Once they're firm, transfer the gnocchi to a resealable bag or plastic container with a lid and store in the freezer until you're ready to serve. They can hold for up to 2 weeks.

3. Bring a large pot of salted water to a boil. Add the frozen gnocchi and let them boil until they float, about 4 minutes. Remove them with a slotted spoon and transfer them to a large bowl, tossing them with the olive oil.

4. Add the watercress to the pasta water and blanch by simmering it until tender, 3 to 4 minutes. In a small pot, melt 6 tablespoons of the remaining butter. Remove and transfer the watercress to a blender (no need to strain; a little water will help the purée). Add the melted butter and red pepper flakes and blend until smooth. Season with salt.

5. Heat a large sauté pan over high heat. Add the remaining 2 tablespoons butter and cook until it browns slightly. Add the gnocchi and sauté until they are lightly golden brown. Add the sauce, stir to coat, and serve.

QUICK TIP

If you don't own a pastry bag, there's no reason to run out and buy one for just this recipe (although you might just take up cake decorating; you never know!). Instead, fill a large resealable plastic bag with the dough, pressing it into one corner to fully fill it out, then snip off the very tip of the corner about ⅓ inch up. Voila! Pastry bag.

DRINK TIP

If the only Chardonnays you've ever tried are from California, you won't even recognize French Chardonnays as siblings. Commonly called "White Burgundy," the Chardonnay from the Burgundy region can be beautifully rounded but still have good brightness, exactly like this watercress sauce.

GNOCCHI IN SIMPLE BROWN BUTTER–CAPER SAUCE

SERVES 4 AS AN ENTRÉE, 8 AS AN APPETIZER

Oh, gnocchi. It's one of the simplest foods to make as far as ingredients go, yet one of the hardest things to master. I've been making gnocchi for years, for many different chefs and for myself, and though this recipe can result in beautifully pillowy gnocchi, it's still not foolproof. Now, I'm not trying to scare you off from giving it a try; I'm just being honest in telling you that even chefs have trouble with gnocchi from time to time. For example, when I was working at Spring, every day I would get all of my other prep completed, put my potatoes in the oven, and go sit down with the crew for family meal, thinking about the gnocchi while I was eating, just hoping that it would be a good gnocchi day. One day I would create absolutely perfect little potato dumplings, and the next day they would fall apart in the water or be overly sticky.

Over time, I learned that Russet potatoes work better at producing the fluffy texture you want for gnocchi and that it's important to work with hot potatoes because they get really gummy as the starches cool. I also developed a method to cook them, ice them down, and then brown them in a pan with butter so they get nice, crisp edges. This recipe is the result of all of my trial and errors with this finicky little dumpling, but don't get down on yourself if you don't nail it the first time around—the brown butter–caper sauce is so good it should make up for a little flaw here and there.

GNOCCHI

2 pounds Russet potatoes

1½ cups all-purpose flour

½ cup ground Parmesan cheese

2 large eggs

3 teaspoons salt

Olive oil for tossing

BROWN BUTTER–CAPER SAUCE

1 cup unsalted cold butter, cubed

1 cup caper berries, thinly sliced

2 tablespoons finely julienned Preserved Lemon (page 241)

1 tablespoons fresh lemon juice

Salt

Freshly ground black pepper

⅓ cup grated Parmesan cheese

Continued . . .

1. To make the gnocchi: Preheat the oven to 350°F.

2. Using a fork, prick the potatoes generously to allow them to release steam. Bake the potatoes until they are tender, about 1 hour and 15 minutes. Peel the potatoes while still warm, and pass them immediately through a potato ricer into a large bowl. (Don't use a food processor, as that will make the potatoes gummy.)

3. While the potatoes are still warm, add 1 cup of the flour, the Parmesan, eggs, and salt. Mix gently with your hands until a soft dough begins to form. Move the dough to a floured work surface and lightly knead while gradually adding more of the flour until the dough is smooth and pliable. Think gentle, and do not overmix. You want it to be soft and pillowy but when you press your finger into the dough, the indentation shouldn't spring back.

4. Pull off a golf ball–size round of dough and gently form it into a log by rolling it back and forth. Starting from the left side, pinch about 1 inch in with your left forefinger and thumb and cut off the piece using a dough cutter or scissors with your right hand. The 1-inch piece will look a bit like a small bowtie. Be delicate with the dough and transfer each piece to a flour-dusted baking sheet. Repeat with the remaining dough.

5. Bring a large pot of salted water to a boil and then reduce the heat so that the water is slightly bubbling. Have a bowl of ice water ready to shock the gnocchi when they're removed from the boiling water.

Add the gnocchi to the pot in small batches, stirring the water slightly before adding them so that they don't stick to the bottom of the pot. Let each batch cook until the gnocchi have risen to the top and are floating for about 30 seconds, 4 to 5 minutes of cooking time. Remove them with a slotted spoon and transfer to the ice bath. Once the gnocchi are cool, remove them from the water, place them in a bowl, and toss with a drizzle of olive oil. Repeat with the remaining gnocchi, adding more ice to the water bath to keep it cold as you work. Set aside or refrigerate the gnocchi until almost ready to serve.

6. To make the sauce: Melt the butter in a large sauté pan over medium-high heat. Once the butter is thoroughly melted, add the gnocchi. Allow the butter to brown and the gnocchi to crisp up lightly around the edges, 3 to 4 minutes.

7. Add the caper berries, preserved lemon, and lemon juice. Season with salt and pepper. Transfer the gnocchi to plates or a serving platter and spoon any remaining brown butter over the top. Finish with the Parmesan and serve immediately.

DRINK TIP

Brown butter is about as earthy and rich as it gets, but the "brown" comes from the caramelizing of the fats, making it nutty but also somewhat sweet. Go for similar flavors in a beer, all of which can be found in *märzens* (a.k.a. Oktoberfest beers).

BAKED GOAT CHEESE POCHETTES WITH TOMATO-MELON SAUCE

SERVES 4 AS AN ENTRÉE, 8 AS AN APPETIZER

I'm sure we've all had goat cheese ravioli before (if not, you're in for a treat), so to switch things up a bit, I've taken a couple of different approaches with this dish. First, of course, is the sauce. Rather than sticking with a simple tomato sauce, I've added in some nice summer melon to lighten it up a bit. When the juices begin to release from the melon, they become the cooking liquid for the sauce to stew in, but for this to happen, the sauce has to cook very low and slow. This gives the juices enough time to extract, and it also allows the liquid to evaporate, leaving the sweet and sour notes behind while concentrating the flavors. I like to blend just half of the sauce to keep things a little rustic.

The *pochettes*, or "little pockets," are a very simple way to make a ravioli-style pasta. I learned this technique working an event in Chicago called "Girl Food Dinner," which raises money for the Chicago Food Depository. Just as the name suggests, it's a dinner cooked by all female chefs, and the year I participated, I was lucky enough to cook with Missy Robbins, who was then the chef of Spiaggia. These pochettes are something I picked up from her that night, and given that Missy went on to be named a *Food & Wine* "Best New Chef" in 2010, you can bet they're pretty good.

TOMATO-MELON SAUCE

¼ cup extra-virgin olive oil

1 cup diced yellow onion

3 garlic cloves, minced

Salt

Freshly ground black pepper

¾ cup dry white wine

5 vine-ripe tomatoes (just over 1 pound), seeded and julienned

2 cups cubed ripe cantaloupe

2 cups cubed ripe honeydew melon

2 tablespoons chiffonade of fresh basil (see Technique 101, page 73)

POCHETTES

6 ounces soft goat cheese

2 ounces cream cheese

¼ cup heavy cream

2 tablespoons grated Parmesan cheese

2 tablespoons extra-virgin olive oil

1 small shallot, minced

1 garlic clove, minced

Salt

Freshly ground black pepper

½ batch Basic Pasta Dough (page 230)

2 tablespoons Parmesan cheese

½ cup small dice cantaloupe, for garnishing

½ cup small dice honeydew melon, for garnishing

1 tablespoon chiffonade of fresh basil, for garnishing

1 tablespoon extra-virgin olive oil

Salt

Freshly ground black pepper

Continued . . .

1. To make the sauce: Heat a saucepan over medium-low heat. Add the olive oil, then add the onion and garlic and sweat them by cooking until the onion is translucent, 3 to 4 minutes. Season with a little salt and pepper, add the wine, increase the heat to medium-high, and simmer to reduce by about one-third. Add the tomatoes, cantalope, and honeydew and season with a bit more salt and pepper, tasting as you do. Reduce the heat to low and cook until the juices of the melons and tomatoes have been released fully and then evaporated some, reducing about halfway from the fullest point, about 35 minutes.

2. Carefully ladle half of the sauce into a blender and pulse until smooth. Add the purée back into the saucepan along with the basil. Stir and adjust the seasoning.

3. To make the pochettes: Put the goat cheese, cream cheese, cream, Parmesan, olive oil, shallot, and garlic in a stand mixer with a paddle attachment. Mix until smooth. Season with salt and pepper.

4. Using a pasta machine, roll out the pasta dough to number 9 (the thinnest setting—so if you're rolling by hand, go for paper thin). Cut the dough into 6-inch squares. You should have eight squares.

5. Bring a large pot of salted water to a boil. Boil a few sheets of pasta at a time until al dente, about 4 minutes. Remove them with a slotted spoon and place them on a baking sheet that's been rubbed with oil and topped with parchment paper. After each layer of cooked pasta dough, add another layer of parchment paper so that the layers of dough don't touch. Let the dough sit until cool enough to handle.

6. Place a square of pasta on a clean work surface and spoon about 2 tablespoons (just over 1 ounce) of filling into the middle. Fold the top side down until it is just covering the filling; then bring the left side over to the right of center, the right side just left of center, and the bottom toward the top. You should have a rectangular, envelope-like pouch shape. Flip the pochette over and place it on a parchment-lined baking sheet, seam-side down. Once all of the pockets are formed, they can sit in the refrigerator for a few hours or overnight, covered, until ready to serve.

7. Have four ovenproof serving bowls or cazuelas ready to go on a baking sheet. Heat the oven to 400°F. Divide the sauce among the four bowls. Place two pochettes in the middle of each bowl, leaning them up against each other (or one pochette for small servings). Transfer the bowls to the oven's top rack and bake for 10 minutes, until the cheese in the center is warmed through (to test, stick the edge of a knife or a skewer into a center, then carefully put it to your chin to see if it's hot). When it feels warm, pull out the oven rack a bit, sprinkle each dish with a bit of the Parmesan, and then increase the heat to broil. Broil until the tops begin to brown, about 3 minutes. Carefully remove the bowls and let them cool for a couple of minutes before serving.

8. In a small bowl, toss together the diced cantalope and honeydew, basil, and olive oil and season with salt and pepper, then divide them among the bowls as garnish before serving.

DRINK TIP

With beautiful, light fruit flavors from the tomato and melon in this sauce, you don't want a weighty or spicy wine to overpower it. Oregon Pinot Noirs are awesome at this: They offer a nice and simple red option when you are really just looking for a backup singer.

FOUR-CHEESE MACARONI WITH APPLES AND BACON

SERVES 4 AS AN ENTRÉE, 8 AS AN APPETIZER

Yes, I am putting a macaroni and cheese recipe in this book. You know why? Because I absolutely love it, and I think you will, too. For those fellow mac-and-cheese lovers out there (who will sometimes even settle for the stuff in the blue box to satisfy their cravings), consider this the gourmet version to make when you have more time than it takes to boil the mac and rip open the orange-powder packet.

This recipe is the result of a mac-and-cheese cook-off for a charity event in Chicago, and I had started out that day by visiting my friend Giles from the Great American Cheese Collection. (I like to call him the Santa of cheese since he is always bearing gifts of dairy delight and, well, since he's always cheery and has a big beard.) So Giles and I went down to his cheese cave and wandered around for a bit (tasting as we went, of course). I ended up finding some awesome cheeses, including a great smoky mozzarella and an aged Cheddar. Then I headed to another cheese shop to buy some tetilla cheese from Spain—a great melting cheese so named because of its shape (*tetilla* means "small breast," and, yes, it looks like a boob).

Now for this recipe, I used some cheeses that should be a bit easier for you to find, while still covering the same flavor and texture profiles. The goal is to have a bit of smoke, a nice sharpness from an aged Cheddar, and then a nice creamy cheese like tetilla or Havarti so your mac doesn't dry out. These are my suggestions, but feel free to improvise. The best part about making your own mac and cheese is just that—it's your own! Just be sure to use a nicely balanced cheese sauce that won't separate when cooked, and try to add some fun flavors and textures to really make it stand out. You may never go back to the blue box again. (Uh, unless you have a cold and live next to a 7-Eleven and wander in wearing your pajamas to pick up a box, only to be congratulated on *Top Chef* . . . while holding the box. Yes, that happened, and, yes, I felt like a bit of an ass.)

¼ cup unsalted butter plus 3 tablespoons

2 garlic cloves, minced

½ teaspoon red pepper flakes

4 cups cubed ciabatta bread

6 cups whole milk

1 small onion, halved

4 ounces bacon (3 to 4 slices), cut into ½-inch pieces

2 Fuji apples, peeled and diced

2 tablespoons apple cider vinegar

4 ounces sopressatta or other similarly spiced cured meat, diced

4 ounces cooked ham, shredded or chopped

1 pound dry conchiglie (shell) pasta

⅓ cup all-purpose flour

6 ounces whole-milk mozzarella cheese, grated

4 ounces aged Cheddar cheese, grated

4 ounces smoked Gouda cheese, grated

4 ounces Havarti cheese, grated

1. Preheat the oven to 375°F. Melt the 3 tablespoons butter in a large saucepan over medium heat. Add the garlic and red pepper flakes, steeping them in the butter until the garlic is soft and fragrant, about 1 minute. Remove from the heat and add the bread cubes to the pan, tossing to coat them in the garlic butter. Spread the butter-coated bread on a baking sheet. Bake until the bread is very crisp, about 15 minutes. Remove from the oven and let them cool completely. Preheat the broiler.

2. Meanwhile, combine the milk and onion in a medium saucepan over medium heat. Bring the milk just to a simmer, then reduce the heat to keep it at a low simmer. Cook, stirring occasionally to avoid scorching the bottom, 15 to 20 minutes.

3. Meanwhile, return the large saucepan to the stove over medium heat. When the pan is hot again, add the bacon and cook until crispy. Remove the bacon with a slotted spoon and set it aside with the cooling bread cubes. Add the apples to the hot fat in the pan, sautéing until the apples are just soft (not mushy), 1 to 2 minutes. Remove the apples with a slotted spoon to a large bowl. Add the vinegar and toss to coat. Add the sopressatta to the hot pan and sauté to crisp the meat, 1 to 2 minutes. Mix the sopressatta and the ham with the apples and set aside.

4. Put the cooled bread cubes and bacon in a food processor and pulse several times to form bread crumbs.

5. Bring a large pot of salted water to a boil. Drop the pasta into the boiling water and cook until al dente, 7 to 9 minutes, or according to the package directions.

6. As the pasta cooks, melt the ¼ cup butter in the saucepan over medium-high heat. Sprinkle the flour over the butter and whisk together, forming a thick paste (a roux). Let the roux cook until it begins to smell nutty, about 1 minute. Strain the milk and discard the onion. Slowly add the hot milk to the roux, about ½ cup at a time, whisking well to avoid lumps. Continue incorporating the milk. Bring it to a boil, reduce the heat to a simmer, and then cool until it thickens enough to coat the back of a spoon, about 5 minutes. Reserve ½ cup of the mozzarella and add the rest of the mozzarella, the Cheddar, Gouda, and Havarti to the sauce, stirring as they melt.

7. When the pasta is done, drain it and add it to the cheese sauce along with the apple mixture. Stir to combine all of the ingredients and pour them into a lightly greased 13-by-9-inch baking dish. Cover the macaroni and cheese with the bacon bread crumbs and scatter the reserved ½ cup mozzarella on top. Put the dish on a baking sheet and transfer it to the oven. Broil the top until the bread crumbs are golden and the cheese is bubbly, about 5 minutes. Serve immediately or hold in a barely warm (200°F) oven for up to 30 minutes.

DRINK TIP

When a dish is rich and smoky, you might tend to automatically think "brown beer," but in this case, not just any brown will do. When the dish is this rich and smoky, porter is the best dark beer for the job. It's lighter than stout but still has that bitterness to cut through the gooey cheese sauce here, and just a touch of smoke to line up nicely with the bacon.

CHA
FIVE

PTER

MAINS

WHEN I WAS GROWING UP, MY MOM DIDN'T MAKE COMPOSED ENTRÉES (WHOSE DID?)—IT WAS A PROTEIN, SIDE VEG, AND SALAD.

But these days, I'm a restaurant chef, so when it comes to mains, I think in terms of a fully composed dish of multiple elements, which I realize might seem a bit much for everyday cooking. That's exactly why I've given you two options with the more complicated recipes in this chapter: You can follow the "Plan of Attack" to help with the timing of nailing the full dish, or you can simplify by just making the parts of the dish you're most comfortable with, using the subrecipes. My hope is that you find a few

favorites, whether complete dishes or maybe just parts of them, and that you start to feel comfortable enough that you can mix and match components to create your own ideal meal. Start with executing a recipe in its entirety; it really is the best way to see how the flavors all come together to create a full picture and the best way to learn about balance of texture, acidity, sweetness, and so on. In other words, it's how to become a better cook. But when you do it is up to you.

CRISPY SOFT-SHELL CRAB SANDWICHES   SERVES 4 TO 8

This simple sandwich recipe came to be during a trip to North Carolina to hang with my friend Sean from Sea to Table and another friend, David, from Blue Ocean Market—a respected fish shop there in Morehead City. We were out on the boat early in the morning to pull up nets, and then we headed over to David's backyard to cook up some soft-shell crabs. David has been eating soft-shell crab sandwiches his whole life, and the "secret family recipe" is really just cocktail sauce and slaw from Kentucky Fried Chicken. I gotta admit that there is something about that slaw from KFC that really worked with the crab, so feel free to pick up some for this, but otherwise the simple slaw here will do.

Personally, I've always eaten soft-shells with a tasty aioli similar to a homemade tartar sauce, so David and I combined our traditions and this is what resulted. The tang and spice from the cocktail sauce and horseradish work great with the richness of the aioli, and a bit of fresh crunch from the slaw brings it all together. I do have to take credit for the hot dog buns (I think I may have changed David's mind on this one). The shape of the bun works perfectly with the crab, so you can enjoy all of the natural sweetness of the soft-shell without too much breading. Or you can leave the bun behind and serve the soft-shells over some greens with a bit of aioli if you want to get a little fancy, but I love the idea of a casual sandwich dinner.

SPICY COCKTAIL SAUCE

½ cup prepared cocktail sauce

1 tablespoon prepared horseradish

TARTAR SAUCE

1 egg yolk

2 teaspoons Dijon mustard

1 cup blended oil (half vegetable, half olive oil)

1 tablespoon chopped brined capers

1 tablespoon thinly sliced gherkins

2 teaspoons chopped pickled jalapeños

1 teaspoon hot sauce

Salt

Freshly ground black pepper

QUICK SLAW

1 very small cabbage or half of a medium cabbage (about 1 pound), cored and thinly shredded

1 large carrot, shredded

Salt

Freshly ground black pepper

CRISPY SOFT-SHELL CRABS

8 soft-shell crabs ("primes"), cleaned (see Technique 101, facing page)

Oil for frying

1 cup lager-style beer (Pabst works great)

¾ cup all-purpose flour

¾ cup cornstarch

Salt

8 hot dog rolls (brushed with butter and lightly toasted; optional)

1. To make the spicy cocktail sauce: In a small bowl, stir together the cocktail sauce and horseradish to combine. Cover and refrigerate.

2. To make the tartar sauce: In a medium bowl, whisk together the egg yolk and mustard. Slowly drizzle in the blended oil, continuing to whisk, to make an emulsified dressing. Stir in the capers, gherkins, jalapeños, and hot sauce, then season with salt and pepper. Cover and refrigerate.

3. To make the quick slaw: In a large bowl, mix together the cabbage and carrot with one-third of the tartar sauce to thoroughly coat the veggies to a slaw consistency. Season with salt and pepper. Cover and refrigerate.

4. To make the cripsy soft-shell crabs: Place the crabs in between paper towels to make sure any excess moisture is removed, then heat the oil to 375°F in a deep fryer or heavy-bottomed pan with high sides. The oil should be deep enough so that the crabs can fry without touching the bottom of the pan.

5. In a wide bowl, whisk together the beer, flour, cornstarch, and 1 teaspoon salt. Working in batches, dip two or three crabs into the batter, then carefully slide them into the fryer. Cook until they begin to brown, about 2 minutes, flip them over, and cook until they're evenly brown, about 2 minutes more. Remove them to a plate lined with paper towels to drain and season with salt. Fry the remaining crabs in one or two batches.

6. Spoon a bit of tartar sauce on the bottom half of each bun and cocktail sauce on the top half. Place a crab in each bun and top with a spoonful of slaw.

PLAN OF ATTACK
- A week in advance: Prepare the spicy cocktail sauce.
- Up to 3 days in advance: Prepare the tartar sauce.
- The day before: Prepare the quick slaw.
- Cook time: Remove the cocktail sauce, tartar sauce, and slaw from the refrigerator. Prepare the crabs.

TECHNIQUE 101

Cleaning Soft-Shell Crabs: There's a bit of prep involved when serving soft-shells, and it's not exactly the same as asking a fishmonger to clean a fish for you (although depending on your relationship with yours, you could possibly talk him or her into it). Still, it's a good technique to learn, and not very difficult to do. First, using a pair of sharp kitchen scissors, cut straight across the front end (the "head") of the crab, just behind the eyes so that you're removing the "face." Squeeze the shell just behind the cut you made to extract the contents of the sac located there. Next, turn the crab over and lift up the "apron"—the small flap that looks like it has a pull-tab—cutting at the base to remove it. Then lift each side of the shell from the pointy tips to remove the clear and fibrous gills. Dunk the crab under water to remove any bits of sand, then place it on a paper towel to dry.

DRINK TIP

A crisp, simple lager like Pabst Blue Ribbon (or PBR—yep, sometimes I like the cheap stuff) does a great job of cleaning the palate with the richness of fried seafood.

SEARED SCALLOPS WITH TOMATOES AND TRUFFLE-POBLANO VINAIGRETTE

SERVES 4

Chefs love scallops. They have a texture and taste that you just can't find in any other seafood—rich and buttery, with a natural sweetness and lingering saltiness from the ocean. But loving scallops and being able to cook them are two different things. I remember finally mastering this art when I worked the line at Spring, where I learned that the most important part of cooking a scallop is to get a beautiful brown sear on the exterior, which caramelizes the natural sugars to create a delicious crust and helps you avoid overcooking them. Once the outside is nice and brown, you're done; cook it any longer and you've got a scallop that will bounce off the floor (in fact, cooking any shellfish past medium will turn great texture into rubber).

Once you've nailed cooking the scallop, you can do a lot with it. This dish is one that comes from an event I did at the resort Sanctuary on Camelback Mountain, where I used to work with chef Beau MacMillan. He invited me to be part of "Lunch & Learn," an award-winning program where guest chefs are flown in from around the country to do a fun-filled demo during a four-course lunch. Mine was fun-filled indeed. We started out the morning with just enough bubbly to get everyone loosened up (including me) and by the end of the day, I was singing the "Happy Birthday" song from the Olive Garden. (You know I'm having a good, or rather buzzed, demo when the Olive Garden makes an appearance.) Somehow through the fun and the singing, I managed to execute the theme of the lunch: heirloom tomatoes. When they're at their prime, tomatoes are sweet enough to convince you they actually *are* a fruit and not a vegetable. I thought it would be interesting to pair tomatoes with similarly sweet scallops, then balance out all that sweetness with a slightly spicy and tart vinaigrette, making the dish refreshing enough to save you from a food coma—just so you can have seconds.

TRUFFLE-POBLANO VINAIGRETTE

2 poblano peppers

¼ cup white balsamic vinegar

1 egg yolk

1 teaspoon Dijon mustard

1 teaspoon honey

¾ cup extra-virgin olive oil

¼ cup white truffle oil

Salt

Freshly ground black pepper

SCALLOPS

2 cups diced heirloom tomatoes (about 1 pound; see Ingredient Spotlight, page 158)

2 tablespoons extra-virgin olive oil

1 tablespoon white balsamic vinegar

Salt

Freshly ground black pepper

12 large sea scallops, side muscles removed

2 teaspoons canola oil

2 tablespoons butter

1. To make the vinaigrette: Preheat a grill to medium-high, or turn on a gas-powered stovetop burner. Char the peppers until blackened on all sides, turning several times (see Technique 101, page 119). Transfer them to a bowl, cover with plastic wrap or a towel, and let cool. Remove the charred skins from the peppers. Cut off the stems and slice the peppers in half to scrape out and discard the seeds.

2. In a blender, combine the vinegar, egg yolk, mustard, and honey and pulse together. With the blender running, add the olive oil and truffle oil in a slow drizzle through the opening in the lid until a thick emulsion forms. Add the roasted peppers and blend until smooth. Season with salt and pepper. Refrigerate until needed.

3. To make the scallops: Toss the tomatoes with the olive oil and vinegar in a medium bowl. Season with salt and pepper. Set aside until ready to serve.

4. Pat the scallops dry and season both sides with salt and pepper. Heat the canola oil in a large sauté pan over high heat. Add the scallops to the hot pan. (Avoid overcrowding the scallops in the pan. If they are too close together, they will steam instead of sear. Sear them in batches if the pan is not big enough to hold them all at once.) Let the scallops brown for 1 minute,

then reduce the heat to medium. Continue to cook until a brown crust forms. Add the butter to the pan. Turn the scallops over to brown the other sides. While browning, spoon the melted butter over the tops of the scallops to baste them. Remove them from the pan once you've basted them well and all edges are nice and browned.

5. To serve, put a spoonful of the vinaigrette on each plate, offset from the center. Add 3 scallops to each plate and a few heaping teaspoons of the tomatoes next to the scallops.

PLAN OF ATTACK

- Up to 3 days ahead: Make the Truffle-Poblano Vinaigrette. Cover and refrigerate.
- Up to 1 hour ahead: Bring the vinaigrette up to room temperature while preparing the tomatoes.
- Cook time: Sear the scallops.

DRINK TIP

Ripe tomatoes always go great with rosé wines, but if you can find a French red Gamay and lightly chill it, you'll also get just enough soft texture to go with the rich scallops in this dish.

INGREDIENT SPOTLIGHT

HEIRLOOM TOMATOES No, an heirloom tomato isn't just an old tomato (that would be a rotten tomato—which is something entirely different). But its seed is old, or at least its seed's lineage is. Heirloom tomatoes are varieties that have been passed down through generations of "seed savers" who prize the particular types for their unique characteristics. Usually these are bumpy, misshapen, oddly colored fruits that look worlds apart from the uniformly smooth red tomatoes found in typical grocery stores, but the heirlooms pack more flavor in one bite than those guys do in a whole tomato. You can always find interesting varieties at farmers' markets in late summer, and some grocery stores are carrying them these days as well. I'm a fan of stripey, lightly tart 'Green Zebras'; big, fat, pinkish 'Brandywines'; fruity and fuzzy 'Garden Peaches'; and juicy maroon 'Cherokee Purples.' Slice up a few different types, sprinkle them with salt and pepper, and you have a beautiful plate of summer's finest.

SEARED SCALLOPS WITH GOAT CHEESE–YUKON PURÉE, ASPARAGUS, AND SORREL VINAIGRETTE

SERVES 4

About a year after being on *Top Chef*, I was invited to cook at the party that *Food & Wine* magazine throws each year to announce the annual "Best New Chefs." There were about ten chefs cooking for about five hundred people that night, all scattered throughout a cool space in Manhattan's Meatpacking District. Now, most chefs were smart enough to keep things simple: a chilled soup, a raw fish dish, or a mini custard. I, on the other hand, decided to not only sear five hundred scallops on portable burners that get nowhere near hot enough for a good sear but also to add a million components. Luckily I had the amazing Miss Lee Anne Wong cooking with me, but we still got our asses handed to us. Still, at the end of the day, the reception this tasty dish got was worth it. Just as I had hoped, people loved the tang of the goat cheese in the potatoes, as well as the bit of smoky and salty ham flavor the potatoes pick up while cooking. To counter good ol' pork and potatoes, the white and green asparagus lighten things up perfectly and just scream "spring." (Still, if you want to make this another time of year, just go with all green asparagus.)

2 smoked ham hocks (about 2 pounds)

GOAT CHEESE-YUKON PURÉE

1 pound Yukon gold potatoes, peeled and cut into large cubes

1¼ cups heavy cream

2 ounces plain, soft goat cheese

Coarse salt

Freshly ground black pepper

ASPARAGUS

8 ounces white asparagus, peeled

8 ounces green asparagus

2 tablespoons extra-virgin olive oil

Coarse salt

Freshly ground black pepper

SORREL VINAIGRETTE

8 to 10 sorrel leaves, washed

¼ cup white balsamic vinegar

1 egg yolk

2 teaspoons honey

1 teaspoon Dijon mustard

1 teaspoon yellow aji chile paste (see Ingredient Spotlight, page 162)

2 tablespoons vegetable oil

3 tablespoons olive oil

SCALLOPS

12 sea scallops, side muscles removed

Coarse salt

Freshly ground black pepper

2 tablespoons olive oil

1 tablespoon butter

¼ cup sliced almonds, toasted

Continued . . .

1. Put the ham hocks in a large stockpot and cover with 2 quarts cool water. Bring to a boil, then reduce the heat. Cover the pot and simmer the hocks until the meat is tender and can be peeled off the bone with a fork or by hand, about 2 hours.

2. To make the purée: Remove the hocks from the water and set them aside to cool. Add the potatoes to the pot and bring the water back to a boil. Cook the potatoes until fork-tender, 15 to 20 minutes.

3. Combine the cream and goat cheese in a small saucepan over low heat, letting the cheese melt into the cream, stirring occasionally.

4. Drain the potatoes and put them through a ricer into a clean bowl. Pour the cream and cheese mixture over the potatoes and stir to combine them into a thin purée. Pass the purée through a medium-mesh sieve (optional), season with salt and pepper, cover, and keep warm until ready to serve.

5. Pull the meat from the ham hocks and set it aside in a small bowl. Discard the skin and bones.

6. To make the asparagus: Slice the white and green asparagus into ⅓-inch pieces (reserving two or three green asparagus spears for garnish). Heat 1 tablespoon of the olive oil in a large sauté pan over medium-high heat. Add the ham and the sliced asparagus and sauté until the asparagus is just tender, 5 to 7 minutes. Toss with another 1 tablespoon olive oil and season with salt and pepper. Cover and keep warm.

7. To make the vinaigrette: Combine the sorrel, vinegar, egg yolk, honey, mustard, and chile paste in a blender and pulse several times to combine. Whisk the vegetable oil and olive oil together in a measuring cup with a spout. With the blender running, pour the oils through the opening in the lid in a slow steady stream and process until a smooth vinaigrette forms.

8. To make the scallops: Pat the scallops dry and season both sides with salt and pepper. Heat the olive oil in a large sauté pan over high heat. Add the scallops to the hot pan. (Avoid overcrowding the scallops in the pan. If they are too close together, they will steam instead of sear. Sear them in batches if the pan is not big enough to hold them all at once.) Let the scallops brown for 1 minute, then reduce the heat to medium. Continue to cook until a brown crust forms. Add the butter to the pan. Turn the scallops over to brown the other sides. While browning, spoon the melted butter over the tops of the scallops to baste them. Remove them from the pan once you've basted them well and all edges are nice and browned.

9. To serve, put a spoonful of potato purée on each of four plates. Top with a few spoonfuls of the sautéed ham and asparagus. Divide the scallops between the plates and drizzle with the vinaigrette. Slice the reserved raw green asparagus very thinly on a bias. Toss with the toasted almonds and sprinkle on top of each dish.

PLAN OF ATTACK

- Up to 5 days ahead: Make the Sorrel Vinaigrette. Cover and refrigerate.
- Up to 2 days ahead: Cook the ham hocks, let cool, pull the meat from the bones and store, covered, in the fridge. Prepare the Goat Cheese-Yukon Purée. Cover and refrigerate.
- Cook time: Bring the vinaigrette up to room temperature. Warm the purée while preparing the asparagus. Keep both warm while preparing the scallops.

DRINK TIP

Cheesy potato purée and rich scallops are pretty heavy, but luckily German Rieslings from the Mosel region are super zingy, with just the right acidity to cut through this dish as a contrasting pairing.

INGREDIENT SPOTLIGHT

AJI AMARILLO Literally translated "yellow pepper," this sun-colored chile grows like grass in Peru, where it's prized for its fruity heat. I became a fan of it a few years ago when I was asked to prepare Peruvian food for a world festival. After some research, it seemed that aji chiles showed up in more than half the recipes, so I decided to give them a try. While they are quite spicy, they have a great sweetness as well, and they don't have the burn of jalapeños. I use them all the time now, whisking the jarred paste into vinaigrettes or into mayo as a dip for fried foods and adding the dried chiles into braises and soups. The only drawback is that they're a bit tough to find in stores (although there are plenty of online sources), so if you want a quick substitution, go with sambal paste.

SEARED SKATE WING WITH MELTED FENNEL AND BROWN BUTTER–DATE SAUCE

SERVES 4

I can still clearly remember the first time I had skate. It was back when I first moved to Chicago, and I was at a restaurant in the Gold Coast (a very ritzy neighborhood), sitting on the patio on a beautiful night. Maybe I was caught up in the moment, but I saw skate on the menu and thought there was no time like the present to try this odd-sounding fish. Knowing nothing about it at the time, I just dug right in, feeling hard bones as I took a bite (insert image of very unpleasant facial expression here). I carefully spit the fish into my napkin without making a scene and decided to just focus on the veggies that it came with, swearing I would never try skate again. Turns out, the chef was simply serving the skate on the bone, and being a skate virgin, I ended up with a mouthful. A couple years later while working at Spring, I not only learned how to navigate the bones but also fell in love with this flat, thin, ugly member of the ray family.

Just as the name implies, skate wing is the wing of the skate fish. It's common to see them sold as deboned fillets at markets, but many restaurants get the fish on the bone and cook and serve it that way. The top side of the wing has a thicker fillet of meat, while the underside has a thinner piece. When served on the bone, it's easy to use your fork and simply scrape the top fillet right off the bones, remove the bones to set aside, and enjoy your two fillets (info that would have been useful to me ten years ago!). Now that you know what you're dealing with, let's just simplify and go with deboned fillets—you can flex your new skate-boning skills out at a restaurant.

BROWN BUTTER–DATE SAUCE

¼ cup butter

2 shallots, minced

2 garlic cloves, minced

½ cup red wine

6 dates, pitted

2 dried Thai chiles (see Ingredient Spotlight, page 61), stemmed

2 tablespoons balsamic vinegar

¾ cup chicken broth

MELTED FENNEL

2 ounces bacon, sliced into thin strips

2 fennel bulbs (about 1 pound), cored and thinly sliced

Salt

Freshly ground black pepper

SKATE

1 cup potato flakes (see Ingredient Spotlight, page 165)

Four 6-ounce deboned skate fillets

Salt

Freshly ground black pepper

2 tablespoons blended oil (half vegetable, half olive oil)

1 tablespoon butter

Continued . . .

1. To make the sauce: Melt the butter in a small sauce-pan over medium-high heat and let it brown just slightly, 2 to 3 minutes. Reduce the heat to medium-low, add the shallots and garlic, and sweat them by cooking until they are translucent, 3 to 4 minutes. Add the wine, dates, chiles, and vinegar and simmer to reduce by half. Add the broth. Bring it to a boil, reduce the heat to low, and simmer until the flavors come together, about 30 minutes. Transfer the ingredients to a blender and purée until smooth. Cover and keep warm.

2. To make the fennel: Heat a large sauté pan over medium-low heat. Add the bacon and slowly cook it until lightly browned but not crisped. Add the fennel, stir to coat it with bacon fat, and season with salt and pepper. Cook slowly, stirring often, until the fennel is tender and just barely caramelized, about 20 minutes. Set aside and cover to keep warm.

3. To make the skate: Pour the potato flakes onto a baking sheet and rub them through your fingers to break them into a finer powder. Season each skate fillet with salt and pepper and place it presentation-side down into the potato flakes, pressing it in to coat.

4. Heat the blended oil in a large sauté pan over high heat. Carefully add the skate, potato-side down, one piece at a time. Let the fish sear for about 1 minute, then reduce the heat to medium-high. Add the butter to the pan and let the fish lightly brown, 3 to 4 minutes. Flip for just a quick second to seal in the juices on the other side and then remove from the heat.

5. To serve, place a spoonful of date sauce just off center on each plate. Divide the fennel mixture into piles in the center of the plates and top each pile of fennel with a piece of skate.

PLAN OF ATTACK

- Up to 5 days ahead: Make the Brown Butter–Date Sauce. Cover and refrigerate.
- The day before: Make the Melted Fennel. Cover and refrigerate.
- Cook time: Warm the sauce and fennel, separately, while preparing the skate.

DRINK TIP

With rich brown butter and a skate wing, you need the good fruit and finesse of a Chardonnay from Australia's Margaret River. It's a really neat emerging wine, and the Chardonnay from there avoids the big, oaky pitfalls of California Chardonnays.

INGREDIENT SPOTLIGHT

POTATO FLAKES I'm sure at some point in my life, probably college, I've eaten mashed potatoes made from dried flakes, but I will say I've never actually made them myself. I do, however, love them for crusting fish. I've tried a few different brands of these instant potatoes, and I actually like Hungry Jack the best, mainly because they're nice and light flakes. (I still always run my fingers through them first to break them up just a bit so they stick to the fish better.) They might not make for the best mashed potatoes, but they produce a beautiful golden-brown crust with a delicate crunch. You can use them for all sorts of fish (I like them best on skate as a light counter to the rich fish), but regardless of what type you use, be sure you're only crusting the top of the fish. The flakes tend to get a bit soggy on a plate if you bread them on both sides.

SEARED HALIBUT WITH PEANUT-PORK RAGU

SERVES 4

I love the flavor profiles of Southeast Asian food—savory, sweet, salty, and sour all at once—and after I spent some time traveling there, I returned to Chicago and interpreted those flavors in my own style of cooking. The result included this ragu, which gets tartness from tamarind and lime juice and earthiness from miso and peanuts. It's actually really versatile—you can skip the fish and just serve it over polenta or pasta if you'd like. But no matter how you serve it, the vinaigrette really brings it all together, so a drizzle of that should always accompany the dish.

CILANTRO VINAIGRETTE

2 cups lightly packed fresh cilantro leaves

⅓ cup extra-virgin olive oil

2 tablespoons white balsamic vinegar

2 teaspoons Dijon mustard

¾ teaspoon honey

Salt

Freshly ground black pepper

PEANUT-PORK RAGU

¼ cup salted roasted peanuts

1 tablespoon peanut oil

1 medium shallot, minced

1 garlic clove, minced

8 ounces ground pork

1½ tablespoons sugar

1 tablespoon white miso paste (see Ingredient Spotlight, page 171)

1 teaspoon tamarind concentrate

1 teaspoon sambal (see Ingredient Spotlight, page 47)

Salt

Freshly ground black pepper

1½ teaspoons fresh lime juice

SEARED HALIBUT

1 tablespoon peanut oil

Four 6-ounce skinless halibut fillets

Salt

Freshly ground black pepper

1. To make the vinaigrette: In a blender, purée the cilantro, olive oil, vinegar, mustard, and honey. Season with salt and pepper. Set aside.

2. To make the ragu: Grind the peanuts in a mini food processor or grinder until fairly fine.

3. Heat the peanut oil in a medium saucepan over medium heat. Add the shallot and garlic and cook until softened, about 3 minutes, stirring occasionally. Add the pork and increase the heat to medium-high, breaking up the meat and cooking until browned, about 4 minutes.

4. Add ½ cup water, the sugar, miso, tamarind, sambal, and ground peanuts to the pork. Simmer over medium-low heat until thickened, about 2 minutes. Season with salt and pepper. Stir in the lime juice and keep warm.

5. To make the halibut: Heat the peanut oil over medium-high heat in a nonstick skillet large enough to hold the fillets without crowding.

6. Season the fish with salt and pepper, then cook until browned and just cooked through, about 4 minutes per side.

7. Divide the pork ragu among four plates, top each with a piece of fish, and drizzle with a bit of the vinaigrette.

PLAN OF ATTACK

- Up to 2 weeks ahead: Make the Cilantro Vinaigrette and store it in an airtight bottle or container in the fridge.
- Up to 2 days ahead: Make the Peanut-Pork Ragu. Cover and refrigerate.
- Cook time: Bring the vinaigrette up to room temperature and warm the ragu while searing the halibut.

DRINK TIP

Vouvrays are beautiful white wines named for the region in France from where they come, and their fruitiness will match well with this Asian-inspired peanut sauce, adding just a touch of sweetness to the spice of the sambal.

SEARED ARCTIC CHAR WITH LAMB-CHERRY HASH AND MINT YOGURT

SERVES 4

I made this dish for the first time in late spring/early summer for a charity dinner at my Aunt Marion's house. I was really excited, and a little nervous, to cook that night because the former mayor of Evanston, Illinois, Lorraine Morton, was coming to the dinner, and I've always considered her a very strong and inspiring woman. Luckily for me it was that perfect time of year in Chicago when we still have some goodies from spring (peas have reached their peak; big and plump and sweet enough to just pop in your mouth), while we're also starting to see the gorgeous stone fruits of summer. Sweet-tart Bing cherries are a natural pairing with lamb. Think about it: Sommeliers always serve Pinot Noir with lamb, and the main descriptor you hear with Pinot is "cherry." To give the meat a kick of salt but keep things interesting, I went with miso for seasoning.

As I've pointed out a couple of times, I'm a big fan of combining surf and turf on the same plate, and while this dish will work great with a few different fish, I love it with Arctic char. Not only is it a sustainable choice but char is also amazingly delicate yet rich at the same time, and it's becoming easier to find, so keep your eyes out for it. It's a close cousin to both salmon and trout, and either of those would work nicely here if you can't find char. All have really nice, thin skin that is delicious when crisped up. I always see people in restaurants push off the skin to the side of the plate, but if it's cooked right, it's the fish equivalent of bacon. Give it a try—you might just be a fish-skin fan after all.

MINT YOGURT

½ cup plain Greek-style yogurt

3 tablespoons half-and-half

1½ tablespoons finely chopped fresh mint

Salt

Freshly ground black pepper

LAMB-CHERRY HASH

1½ pounds English peas, shelled (about 3 cups)

2 teaspoons olive oil

1 shallot, minced

2 garlic cloves, minced

12 ounces ground lamb

2 teaspoons white miso paste (see Ingredient Spotlight, page 171)

½ teaspoon soy sauce

Salt

Freshly ground pepper

12 cherries, pitted and quartered

ARCTIC CHAR

Four 5- to 6-ounce skin-on Arctic char fillets

Salt

Freshly ground black pepper

1 tablespoon vegetable oil

2 tablespoons butter

Continued . . .

1. To make the yogurt: In a small bowl, whisk together the yogurt, half-and-half, and mint. Season with salt and pepper and refrigerate.

2. To make the hash: Bring a small pot of salted water to boil. Add the peas and blanch by simmering them until just tender, about 3 minutes. Drain and set aside.

3. Heat the olive oil in a large sauté pan over medium heat. Add the shallot and garlic and sweat them by cooking until they are translucent but not browned, about 2 minutes. Increase the heat to medium-high. Add the lamb, miso, and soy sauce and combine. Cook until the meat is browned, 5 to 7 minutes. Season with salt and pepper, then add the peas and cherries, stirring to heat them through. Turn the heat down to low and cover to keep warm.

4. To make the char: Season both sides of the fillets with salt and pepper. Heat the vegetable oil in a large sauté pan over high heat. Add the fish skin-side down the hot pan. Let the fish brown for 1 minute, then reduce the heat to medium. Continue to cook until a brown crust forms, then add the butter to the pan.

Turn the fish over to brown the other side. While browning, spoon the melted butter over the fillets to baste them.

5. To serve, divide the lamb and pea hash among four plates. Top each with a piece of fish and a drizzle of yogurt.

PLAN OF ATTACK

- Up to 3 days ahead: Make the yogurt. Cover and refrigerate.
- The night before: You can prepare the hash, but don't add the peas yet.
- Cook time: Let the yogurt stand at room temperature while you make the hash or, if you made the hash the night before, while you reheat it in a 350°F oven in a baking dish covered with aluminum foil, just until warm. Blanch the peas, add them to the hash, and then sear the fish.

DRINK TIP

This is a pretty specific pairing, but Santenay Burgundy would be awesome here. It's fairly light and feminine but just bold enough to keep up with the gamey lamb and funky miso. If you can't find it, an Oregon Pinot Noir would work almost as well.

INGREDIENT SPOTLIGHT

MISO PASTE I was introduced to miso back when I first started cooking at Sanctuary in Scottsdale, Arizona. I loved the saltiness and the slightly funky umami flavors from the fermentation process. Essentially, miso is a Japanese seasoning paste made from fermented soybeans, brown rice, barley, or a combination of grains. There are plenty of varieties out there, but what you're most likely to see at a specialty store like Whole Foods or at an Asian market are white (*shiro miso*) and red (*aka miso*) varieties. They're similar, but white miso uses more rice and less soybeans, it's less salty, and it's balanced by a natural sweetness that makes it more subtle and less over-powering in the recipes in which I use it.

JUNIPER-GRILLED SEA BASS STUFFED WITH FENNEL AND ONION

SERVES 4

I went through a gin phase back when I lived in Arizona. The only problem was that I was drinking whatever "well" gin the bartenders pour when you don't specify a better brand, so I never really got to appreciate the spirit for its subtle flavors. It wasn't until I was in Chicago and was introduced to Wisconsin's Death's Door gin that I realized what I was missing for all those years: the amazing juniper taste.

Fast forward to 2010, when I was recording a television segment celebrating juniper berries. These little, dusty-purple berries aren't something I cook with often, but I do love the subtle pine flavor they impart to fish. So I decided that with the evergreen thing going on from juniper and some good-quality gin, that the anise flavor of fennel would keep things moving in the clean, cool, crisp direction (think "winter" if it had a taste). This is the essence of the recipe and all you really need, but feel free to serve it with a little salsa verde and your favorite side.

1 tablespoon extra-virgin olive oil	3 garlic cloves, minced	Freshly ground black pepper	1 whole black sea bass (about 2 pounds), head and tail intact, bones and backbone removed to make a pocket (ask your fishmonger to do this)
1 medium fennel bulb, julienned	1 teaspoon juniper berries	2 tablespoons good-quality gin	
1 red onion, sliced	Salt		

1. Heat the olive oil in a medium sauté pan over medium heat. Add the fennel, onion, garlic, and juniper berries and sweat them by cooking slowly until the fennel is tender, 7 to 8 minutes. Season with salt and pepper. Add the gin to the pan and let it cook until it's soaked up by the vegetables, about 2 minutes. Remove the mixture from the heat and let it cool slightly.

2. Preheat a gas or charcoal grill to medium-high heat. Season the inside of the fish with salt and pepper and fill it with the fennel mixture. Season the outside with salt and pepper and transfer the fish to a well-oiled grate on the grill. Grill for about 5 minutes on each side, checking the inside for doneness. Serve whole, family-style, with utensils so people can cut off their own portion.

DRINK TIP

There's just enough spice in Belgian pale ales to complement the floral fennel that's at the core of this fish dish, but they're not heavy beers, so you won't run the risk of overpowering the delicate sea bass.

GRILLED WAHOO WITH TOFU-ASPARAGUS PURÉE AND SMASHED NEW POTATOES

SERVES 4

Wahooo-u-ooo! I wish you could press a little button on this page and hear me chanting for this delicious fish. Just use your imagination. (And also imagine that I have a beautiful chanting voice.) Now try to imagine a deep-sea fishing experience in the Bahamas and catching a 115-pound wahoo. Well, okay, almost catching a 115-pound wahoo. The story goes like this: I was invited down to a Club Med in the Bahamas to cook with a group of fellow chefs for the week. We each were to do a couple of cooking demos and a special dinner, then basically just enjoy the club. Upon arriving, I asked the resort's chef what type of fish I could order for my dinner that week and was told that we would all be fishing for our own fish. Sounded fun and all, but I was a little nervous. So 6 a.m. rolled around (and I'll remind you that ten chefs were together, so bedtime was around 3 a.m.), and we went out on this boat. Once we got out into the deep blue, I was first up to bat, err, to rod. I felt a tug and started reeling in, using all of my might, but it felt like a monster was on the other end of the line—I could barely reel at all. So a couple of other chefs joined in and we put all of our strength in for a good five minutes, all of us panting and sweating out booze from the night before. Finally, just as the fish was about to reach the surface and the end was near, I saw two sharks heading for the wahoo, clearly deciding that I'd caught their breakfast. I ended up pulling in a 35-pound head. The sharks got the rest, and I had to use frozen shrimp for my dinner. Sharks: 1. Stephanie: 0.

Alas, wahoo will always be one of my favorite fish, not just for that amazing memory, but because the nice meaty texture works perfectly for grilling, my favorite method of cooking fish. I always like to pair a meaty fish with something light, and I have to give credit for this springy purée to Lee Anne Wong, who I once saw blanch peas, then blend them with tofu for a beautifully creamy purée with less fat. Try the technique yourself with various vegetables and have some fun without the guilt of heavy cream.

ASPARAGUS PURÉE

5 or 6 asparagus spears (about 3 ounces), bottoms trimmed

3 ounces medium-firm tofu, drained and cubed

1 tablespoon fresh lemon juice

Coarse salt

Freshly ground black pepper

ASPARAGUS SALAD

8 asparagus spears (about 4 ounces), sliced very thin on the bias (diagonally)

4 large basil leaves, cut into chiffonade (see Technique 101, page 73)

8 mint leaves, cut into chiffonade

2 teaspoons fresh lemon juice

2 teaspoons olive oil

SMASHED POTATOES

1½ pounds small red potatoes

2 tablespoons olive oil

1 tablespoon butter

Salt

Freshly ground black pepper

GRILLED WAHOO

Four 5-ounce wahoo or halibut fillets

Salt

Freshly ground black pepper

1. To make the purée: Prepare an ice water bath in a medium bowl. Bring a large stockpot of salted water to a boil and blanch the asparagus by simmering it until very tender, about 5 minutes. Strain the asparagus from the water with tongs and transfer it to the ice water bath to shock. Strain again and chop the asparagus into small pieces.

2. Combine the asparagus, tofu, and lemon juice in a blender and purée until smooth. Season with salt and pepper. Set aside or refrigerate until ready to use.

3. To make the salad: In a medium bowl, combine the asparagus, basil, and mint. Drizzle them with the lemon juice and olive oil and toss to coat. Set aside.

4. To make the potatoes: Put the potatoes in a large stockpot of salted water and bring them to a boil. Boil until tender, about 15 minutes. Strain and then smash the potatoes with a fork, working in the olive oil and butter. Season with salt and pepper. Cover and keep warm until ready to serve.

5. To make the wahoo: Heat a grill to high and oil the grill grate. Season both sides of the wahoo with salt and pepper. Place the fish presentation-side down on the grill. Let the fish cook until the flesh easily removes from the grate, about 5 minutes. Turn the fish over and continue grilling until just medium-rare, an additional minute or two.

6. Place a spoonful of asparagus purée on each plate, just off center. Add a scoop of potatoes, just touching the purée. Slice each wahoo fillet once on the bias, exposing the medium-rare center. Stack the pieces in the center of the plate and garnish with the asparagus salad.

PLAN OF ATTACK

- Up to 5 days ahead: Prepare the asparagus purée and refrigerate, covered.
- Day before: Prepare the asparagus salad. Cover and refrigerate.
- Cook time: Remove the purée and the salad from the refrigerator to bring them to room temperature. Prepare the potatoes, and then grill the fish.

DRINK TIP

They say asparagus is one of the toughest ingredients to pair with wine, but New Zealand Sauvignon Blancs aren't afraid. They're grassy enough to mimic that freshly sprouted flavor at the core of this spring vegetable, with enough solid acidity for the bit of oil in the fish.

BALSAMIC BARBECUE QUAIL WITH PISTACHIO-CILANTRO BUTTER AND DAIKON SLAW

SERVES 4

A few years back, I made my first trip to the American Culinary Foundation (ACF) conference in Orlando as a representative of my alma mater, Le Cordon Bleu. It was a really interesting experience, being part of a completely different realm of the culinary field—one filled with certified master chefs who compete in competitions and cook at huge hotels and resorts with international clout. At first I felt a little out of place as the only chef not walking around in a tall white toque, but I should have known that no matter what place people have in the industry, they're bound to like having a good time. Turns out, even the most professional chefs still like to tear it up—something I'm pretty good at myself.

So aside from having a great time with a bunch of fellow chefs, I also held a simple demo. I had a 1½-hour time slot to kill, so I decided to do a dish with a number of different elements, countering the rich bacony barbecue sauce with the acid of quick-pickled daikon. The finished dish is awesome, but feel free to simplify by using only some of the components. The barbecue sauce is great on any roasted or grilled meat, and the slaw is a simple and refreshing side you can throw together in a pinch to bring to a cookout.

BALSAMIC BARBECUE SAUCE

3 slices bacon, cut into ½-inch pieces

1 cup diced onion

3 garlic cloves, roughly chopped

¼ cup balsamic vinegar

3 tablespoons dry sherry

One 28-ounce can crushed tomatoes

¼ cup packed brown sugar

1 fresh Thai chile, minced (see Ingredient Spotlight, page 61)

1 tablespoon Dijon mustard

1 tablespoon Worcestershire sauce

Coarse salt

Freshly ground black pepper

8 semi-boneless quail, wing tips trimmed off

DAIKON SLAW

1 medium daikon radish (about 12 ounces), peeled and thinly sliced on a mandoline

1 cup loosely packed fresh cilantro leaves, roughly chopped

3 tablespoons rice wine vinegar

2 teaspoons granulated sugar

Salt

Freshly ground black pepper

½ cup Pistachio-Cilantro Butter (page 238), at room temperature

Continued . . .

1. To make the sauce: Place a heavy-bottomed pot over medium heat. When the pot is hot, add the bacon and cook it until crisp, 5 to 7 minutes. Add the onion and garlic and sweat them by cooking until the onion is translucent, about 5 minutes. Pour in the vinegar and sherry, increase the heat to medium-high, and simmer until the liquid has reduced by more than half. Add the tomatoes, brown sugar, chile, mustard, and Worcestershire sauce and stir to combine. Simmer, uncovered, about 30 minutes. Let the sauce cool slightly and then transfer it to a food processor or blender and purée until smooth. Season with salt and pepper.

2. Arrange the quail in a glass baking dish or bowl and brush them with about 1 cup of the barbecue sauce. Set aside to marinate for at least 1 hour and up to 3 hours.

3. To make the slaw: Toss the daikon slices with the cilantro in a large bowl. In a separate bowl, whisk together the vinegar and granulated sugar so the sugar dissolves a little. Pour the mixture over the daikon and cilantro and toss to combine. Season with a pinch of salt and pepper. Set aside.

4. Preheat a gas or charcoal grill to medium-high. Place the marinated quail on hot, well-greased grates, breast-side down. Grill for 5 minutes, turn the quail over, and then grill until just cooked through, about 5 more minutes.

5. To serve, spread about 2 tablespoons of pistachio butter on each plate and top with two grilled quail and a few spoonfuls of the daikon slaw.

PLAN OF ATTACK

- Up to 2 weeks ahead: Make the Balsamic Barbecue Sauce and Pistachio-Cilantro Butter; cover tightly and refrigerate.
- Up to 12 hours head: Marinate the quail and make the Daikon Slaw.
- Cook time: Bring the slaw up to room temperature while grilling the quail.

DRINK TIP

Tart Belgian lambics aren't for everyone, but give them a try, specifically the *kriek* style, which are lambics fermented with sour cherries. The puckery flavor mimics the balsamic in this dish's barbecue sauce but has a notch more acid to cut through the sweetness of the brown sugar.

INGREDIENT SPOTLIGHT

DAIKON A Japanese or Korean meal is really not complete without some sort of daikon. This long, tubular, white radish's name translates to "large root," and its porous texture makes it great for soaking up vinegar for a quick pickle. Its size makes it really versatile, as you can cut it into matchsticks, thin rounds, or even slice it into one long continuous sheet by paring it as you would skin an apple. When I worked at Vong, that was the method we used to get the paper-thin sheets of daikon that we used to roll around hunks of steamed lobster, almost like a spring-roll wrapper. That can take a bit of knife skills though, so if you want to keep it simple, try dicing up some daikon, soaking it in a bowl of salted brown rice vinegar for an hour, and then serving it alongside any Asian-style grilled meats or stir-fries. You can also shave it or use a mandoline to create matchsticks, then toss the bits of daikon into a slaw to add interest or over a salad for a refreshing crunch.

ROASTED POUSSIN WITH FINGERLING POTATO–BEET SALAD

SERVES 4

Beets seem to be one of those ingredients that people either love or they hate. I've always fallen into the first group. I think beets have such a beautiful natural sweetness and just enough earthiness for perfect balance. I love the rich magenta color of red beets, but the flavor is generally the same regardless of color, so if you're in the mood for golden, go for it. If you can find them, striped Chioggia beets are fun for shaving raw into salads, as the white and pink rings look somewhat like swirled peppermints. Whatever type you use, remember that because beets are naturally sweet, you need to balance them out with a bit of salt and a little acid. For this recipe, I do this with niçoise olives and a simple vinaigrette. And although I really like poussin (young chicken that's more tender), this recipe works great with any poultry, other than maybe whole turkey. Just try to stick with bird on the bone to ensure the meat will stay nice and juicy.

Two 1¼- to 1½-pound poussins	1 teaspoon black peppercorns	12 ounces fingerling potatoes	Freshly ground black pepper
MARINADE	3 cups hot water	2 teaspoons olive oil	½ cup niçoise olives, pitted and chopped
½ cup salt	3 cups cold water	Salt	½ cup baby arugula, stemmed and chopped
½ cup sugar	1 teaspoon canola oil	¼ cup Basic Honey-Dijon Vinaigrette (page 234)	1 teaspoon extra-virgin olive oil
6 garlic cloves, sliced	**FINGERLING POTATO–BEET SALAD**	1 teaspoon canola oil	
5 sprigs fresh oregano	1 pound medium red beets, greens removed	1 tablespoon butter	

1. Place the poussins on a cutting board breast-side up and cut each in half lengthwise, slicing along each side of the spine. Cut off the wing tips (save for future use in a stock or for a snack).

2. To make the marinade: Combine the salt, sugar, garlic, oregano, and peppercorns in a very large bowl and add the hot water, stirring until the sugar and salt dissolve. Add the cold water. Let cool until the liquid is at least at room temperature so the birds don't cook. Add the poussins to the marinade, cover, and refrigerate for 2 hours.

3. Pull the poussins from the marinade and lay them skin-side up on a clean kitchen towel or paper towels to air-dry to ensure they will crisp in the oven. Meanwhile, preheat the oven to 375°F. Heat either one large ovenproof sauté pan or two medium ovenproof sauté pans over medium-high heat (you don't want to overcrowd the pan, and the cooking time means this isn't really something you want to cook in batches). Add the canola oil to the pan(s) and then the poussins, skin-side down. Cook until the skin begins to brown, about 5 minutes, then transfer the pan(s) to the oven to cook until the skin is fully browned and crisped, about 7 minutes more. Flip the poussins skin-side up and continue to cook until the juices run clear when you press the flesh, 4 to 5 minutes more.

4. To make the salad: Lower the oven to 350°F. Toss the beets and potatoes in the olive oil, season with salt, and wrap each beet in aluminum foil (see Quick Tip, below). Place them on a baking sheet along with the unwrapped potatoes and roast until a knife can easily be inserted in a beet, about 15 minutes. You can pull them out when they're still slightly underdone because they'll continue to cook for a bit (carryover cook). Let them cool until easy to handle, then use a paper towel to rub the skins off the beets. (It's easier to get the skin off when they're slightly warm.) Cut the beets into ¼-inch dice, toss them in the vinaigrette, and set aside. Slice the potatoes into ¼-inch rounds and set aside.

5. Heat the canola oil and butter in a large sauté pan over high heat. Once the butter melts, add the sliced potatoes, toss them to coat, and let them sit to get a little color. Once they've browned a bit, turn them and let them brown some more. Once they're nice and browned, turn off the heat, season with salt and pepper, and add the olives.

6. In a small bowl, toss the arugula in the extra-virgin olive oil and season with salt and pepper.

7. Divide the potatoes evenly among four plates. Place one poussin half over each pile of potatoes, top with beets, and divide the remaining vinaigrette among the plates. Garnish with the dressed arugula to serve.

PLAN OF ATTACK

- Up to 2 days ahead: Make the marinade and Basic Honey-Dijon vinaigrette.
- About 2 hours ahead: Marinate the poussins.
- Cook time: Start by roasting the fingerling potatoes and beets. Cook the poussins and while they are cooking, finish the potato-beet salad.

 QUICK TIP ···

To save time and oven space, you can roast beets and potatoes at the same time, but you need to consider two factors: One, if you roast the vegetables together loose, your beets will bleed and color your potatoes; and two, the beets generally need more time to reach doneness. A good way to solve both problems is to wrap each beet individually in foil after tossing it in olive oil, and leave the skins on to act as a natural steamer, helping the beets cook faster in the same amount of time it takes to cook the potatoes.

DRINK TIP

With both olives and balsamic in this dish, you have a lot of acid going on, so you need to reach for a beer that's good and malty as opposed to tart. *Altbiers* fit the bill perfectly, as medium-bodied workhorse beers that are incredibly balanced and versatile. Germans invented them, but you can find plenty of American examples these days.

CRISPY BRAISED CHICKEN THIGHS
WITH BLACK BEAN TAPENADE

Chicken thighs have recently become quite popular on restaurant menus as people have (finally!) come to realize that it's the dark meat that holds all of the delicious flavor. Like so many people, I used to avoid dark meat, often buying boneless, skinless breasts to be a bit more health conscious. But the truth is, there are only two more grams of fat in six ounces of chicken thigh than there are in the same amount of chicken breast. And for the extra flavor you get, that's two grams of fat well spent.

So while I could be perfectly happy with these braised chicken thighs on their own (or even just nibbling the crispy skin), the fun part about this recipe is the olive and fermented black bean tapenade. I had a container of these beans sitting in my house for over a year, just getting pushed around in the cupboard from time to time when I was searching for ingredients. We used to make a sauce with the salty fermented soybeans (a Chinese product) back during my days at Spring, but I think I subconsciously blocked it out because it came with a potato-wrapped salmon dish that was quite the pain in the ass to prep and cook properly. But back to those beans in my pantry: They sat there until a trip to Yosemite a couple years back, when I saw another chef do a demo in which he talked up fermented black beans, explaining how they can add the same earthy, pungent kick to American dishes that they do for Chinese classics. Inspired, I went back home and made this tapenade from them. Keep in mind that on their own, they're extremely intense, so you might not want to pop them in your mouth to snack on while cooking, or else your palate will be shot for a few hours at least.

MARINATED CHICKEN

½ cup salt

½ cup sugar

1 orange, sliced

4 or 5 sprigs fresh thyme

½ onion, chopped

5 garlic cloves, peeled and smashed with the back of a knife

1 tablespoon black peppercorns, toasted

1 tablespoon coriander seeds, toasted

1 teaspoon red pepper flakes

3 pounds chicken thighs with skin (about 8), bone in

BLACK BEAN TAPENADE

½ cup niçoise olives, pitted and roughly chopped

¼ cup extra-virgin olive oil

1 tablespoon fresh lemon juice

1 tablespoon fermented black beans

1 tablespoon chiffonade of fresh mint (see Technique 101, page 73)

½ teaspoon sambal (see Ingredient Spotlight, page 47)

½ teaspoon honey

SAUCE

1 tablespoon blended oil (half vegetable, half olive oil)

½ onion, chopped

4 garlic cloves, chopped

1 quart chicken broth

½ cup white wine

2 tablespoons butter

1 tablespoon blended oil (half vegetable, half olive oil)

Continued . . .

1. To make the marinated chicken: In a medium saucepan over medium-high heat, combine 6 cups water, the salt, sugar, orange slices, thyme, onion, garlic, peppercorns, coriander, and red pepper flakes. Bring to a boil, then remove the pan from the heat. Transfer the marinade to a container with a lid that's large enough to fit all of the chicken and let it cool to room temperature, then refrigerate until chilled. Add the chicken, cover, and marinate overnight.

2. To make the tapenade: In a small bowl, mix together the olives, olive oil, lemon juice, black beans, mint, sambal, and honey. Set aside.

3. To make the sauce: Pull the chicken out of the marinade and discard the marinade. Place the chicken, skin-side down, on a baking sheet lined with a kitchen towel or paper towels, to let it dry a bit. Heat a large sauté pan over medium-high heat. Add ½ tablespoon of the blended oil, then half of the thighs, skin-side down. (Be careful, as chicken may splatter a bit.) Turn the heat down to medium and let the thighs brown for 4 to 5 minutes. Turn them over and let them brown a couple of minutes more. Transfer the chicken, skin-side up, to a 4-inch-deep baking dish or pot large enough to fit all the thighs in one layer (4 by 8 inch works well). Repeat with another ½ tablespoon oil and the remaining thighs.

4. Once all of the thighs are browned and are in the baking dish, discard all but about 1 tablespoon of fat from the sauté pan. Add the onion and garlic and brown for 4 to 5 minutes. Transfer them into the baking dish with the thighs.

5. Bring the broth to a boil in a separate saucepan.

6. Preheat the oven to 275°F. Return the sauté pan to the heat and add the wine. Simmer to reduce by half, using a wooden spoon to loosen the browned bits that are left from cooking the chicken. Add it all to the baking dish along with the hot broth.

Cover the baking dish with a lid or aluminum foil and place it in the oven to braise until very tender, about 2 hours. Remove it from the oven, uncover, and let the chicken cool in the liquid for 30 minutes to finish up cooking.

7. Carefully remove the thighs and transfer them to a rack, skin-side still up. Strain the liquid from the dish through a fine-mesh sieve into a saucepan. Let it sit long enough for the fat to separate, about 10 minutes, then use a ladle to skim off most of the fat. Place the pan on high heat and simmer the sauce to reduce until it coats the back of a spoon. Reduce the heat to low and whisk in the butter.

8. Preheat the oven to 375°F. Heat a large nonstick ovenproof sauté pan over medium-high heat. Add the 1 tablespoon blended oil. Add the chicken thighs, skin-side down, and let them begin to crisp. Transfer them to the oven to heat through, about 8 minutes.

9. Serve the chicken topped with sauce and tapenade.

PLAN OF ATTACK

- Up to 3 days ahead: Make the Black Bean Tapenade. Cover and refrigerate.
- Day before: Make the marinade and marinate the chicken.
- Cook time: Brown the chicken, make the pan sauce, and braise the chicken in the oven. While the final sauce is reducing, crisp the chicken, rewarm in the oven, and bring the tapenade to room temperature.

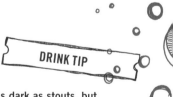

DRINK TIP

German *schwarzbiers* can be as dark as stouts, but they are as crisp and punchy as stouts are rich and creamy. Those coffee-like roasted malts are still heavily present though, with enough bitterness to cut through the salty, funky, fermented black beans used here and a good zing to counter the rich, dark-meat chicken.

SEARED DUCK BREASTS À L'ORANGE WITH BRAISED DUCK SPRING ROLLS

SERVES 4

This recipe is based on the duck that I made to win the first challenge on *Top Chef*, which I believe really gave me the confidence to go all the way. The challenge was to cook a classic dish, going head-to-head against one of the other chefs. Fellow contestant Mark Simmons chose me to cook against, and I chose duck à l'orange.

There's a lot going on in this dish, but if you want to make it a bit simpler, go with just the spring rolls and orange sauce as a great hors d'oeuvre or cook some delicious duck breasts to star with your favorite sides. I have to thank Dale Levitski for teaching me the cooking method. I'd always slowly rendered the excess fat out in a very low-heat pan. When I started working at La Tache with Dale, I was a little taken aback when he put the duck in a smoking hot pan. But when I tasted how crisp and amazing the skin had become and saw the beautiful rich caramel color, I was hooked, and I haven't looked back since.

BRAISED DUCK SPRING ROLLS

2 duck legs
(6 to 8 ounces each)

Salt

Freshly ground black pepper

3 medium shallots, minced

4 garlic cloves, minced

¾ cup white wine

1 tablespoon Worcestershire sauce

1 teaspoon Dijon mustard

1¼ teaspoons soy sauce

1 teaspoon fish sauce (see Ingredient Spotlight, page 187)

1¼ teaspoons sambal (see Ingredient Spotlight, page 47)

1-inch piece fresh ginger, peeled and thinly sliced, plus ¼ teaspoon minced peeled fresh ginger

4 cups chicken broth

3 cups canola oil

1 egg yolk

Four 6-inch egg roll wrappers (wonton skins)

6 fresh shiitake mushrooms, stemmed and thinly sliced

1 head baby bok choy, leaves removed and thinly sliced

ORANGE SAUCE

1 cup fresh orange juice

¼ cup packed brown sugar

½ teaspoon soy sauce

½ teaspoon sambal

SHIITAKE MUSHROOMS

1 pound fresh shiitake mushrooms, stemmed

Olive oil

Salt

Freshly ground black pepper

BABY BOK CHOY

1 head baby bok choy, quartered

1 tablespoon butter

Salt

Freshly ground black pepper

DUCK BREASTS

2 boneless duck breasts with skin (10 to 12 ounces each)

Salt

Freshly ground black pepper

1. To make the spring rolls: Season the duck legs with salt and pepper. Heat a large stockpot over high heat and add the duck legs. Brown on both sides, about 5 to 7 minutes total; remove and set aside.

2. In the same pot, reduce the heat to medium-low and add two-thirds of the shallots and three-fourths of the garlic. Sweat by cooking them until the shallots are translucent, about 3 minutes. Add the wine,

Worcestershire sauce, mustard, 1 teaspoon of the soy sauce, the fish sauce, 1 teaspoon of the sambal, and the sliced ginger. Increase the heat to medium-high and simmer to let the sauce reduce by half, about 5 minutes.

3. Add the broth and the browned duck legs and bring to a boil. Cover, reduce the heat, and simmer over very low heat until the meat is falling off the bones,

Continued . . .

about 1½ hours. Remove the legs and let them cool to room temperature. Meanwhile, simmer the sauce over medium heat to reduce to a thick glaze, about ¼ cup. Strain the sauce over medium heat, and season with salt and pepper.

4. Remove the meat from the duck legs and cut it into 1-inch pieces. In a medium sauté pan, heat 1 teaspoon of the canola oil over medium heat. Add the remaining shallot, garlic, and the minced ginger and sweat by cooking until the shallot is translucent, about 3 minutes. Remove from the heat and let cool slightly. Add the duck meat and season with the remaining ¼ teaspoon soy sauce and ¼ teaspoon sambal (more if you like it spicier).

5. In a small cup, beat the egg yolk with 1 teaspoon water. Lightly brush the edges of one egg roll wrapper with a bit of the beaten egg. Turn the wrapper with a point down, and lay one-fourth of the duck mixture, one-fourth of the mushrooms, and one-fourth of the bok choy across the third of the wrapper closest to you. Take the corner of the wrapper closest to you, tightly wrap it around the mixture, and roll it over one full rotation. Tightly fold the sides in toward the center and continue to roll up to the end of the wrapper, making sure the end is tightly sealed. (You can use a little more egg yolk to help glue it, if necessary.) Set the roll seam-side down on a plate. Repeat with the remaining three wrappers. Cover and refrigerate or freeze until ready to fry.

6. To fry, heat the remaining canola oil in a heavy-bottomed 2-quart pot. When the oil reaches 365°F, fry two spring rolls at a time until golden and crisp, about 2 minutes on each side. Remove them to paper towels to drain. Slice each roll in half on the diagonal.

7. To make the orange sauce: Combine the orange juice, brown sugar, soy sauce, and sambal in a small saucepan. Bring to a boil, lower to a simmer, and reduce to a syrup (about ¼ cup total), about 40 minutes. Set aside.

8. To make the mushrooms: Preheat the oven to 325°F. Toss the mushrooms in olive oil and season with salt and pepper. Transfer them to a baking sheet and roast until they just begin to crisp, about 25 minutes. Set aside until ready to serve. Increase the oven to 400°F.

9. To make the bok choy: Bring a large pot of salted water to a boil. Prepare a bowl of ice water. Blanch the bok choy by simmering until it just begins to soften.

Remove and shock the bok choy in the ice water. Drain. Heat the butter in a sauté pan, add the bok choy to warm through, and season with salt and pepper.

10. To make the duck breasts: Score the skin side of the duck breasts with hatch marks, ¼ inch apart, and set aside.

11. Heat a dry skillet or ovenproof sauté pan over high heat until smoking hot. Season the breasts with salt and pepper and add them to the pan skin-side down. Let the skin brown for a few minutes, then transfer the pan to the oven, letting the duck roast until the center is cooked to your desired doneness (pink is good; red is not), 8 to 10 minutes. Remove from the oven and quickly turn over the breasts to sear the other sides of the meat. Remove the breasts from the pan and let them rest for 5 minutes before cutting into ¼-inch slices crosswise on a bias.

12. Place one piece of bok choy and an equal amount of shiitakes on each of four plates. Place two spring roll halves around the vegetables, one half standing and one lying down. Fan half of a duck breast over each plate. Spoon the reduced duck sauce over the meat. Drizzle the plates with the orange sauce.

PLAN OF ATTACK

- Up to 5 days ahead: Prepare the Braised Duck Spring Rolls, wrap tightly, and freeze. (Or you can prepare them the day ahead and they can rest in the refrigerator.) Refrigerate the reduced duck sauce from the legs. Make the Orange Sauce and refrigerate it.
- Cook time: First, roast the shiitakes. While they're roasting, fry the spring rolls. Next, prepare the duck breasts. While the duck is in the oven, prepare the bok choy and reheat both the reduced duck sauce and the orange sauce.

DRINK TIP

You might have been programmed to automatically think Pinot Noir with duck, but actually Alsatian Gewürztraminers have a really beautiful orange-blossom note to them. Let them warm up a bit, almost to room temp, and they have just the right weight to stand up to fatty duck.

INGREDIENT SPOTLIGHT

FISH SAUCE One of my favorite things to do at demos is to ask people to smell the fish sauce straight from the bottle. Every time, they wrinkle their noses, but the "a-ha!" moment comes when they taste the finished dish and just love the earthy, slightly funky flavor that a spoonful of the stuff can add. Fish sauce is exactly what its name would imply: a seasoning made from extracting the liquid from fish via a salting and fermentation process. The best advice I can give you on buying fish sauce requires an extra trip to the Asian market, but it's worth it. The stuff you'll find at most regular grocery stores is processed junk. High-quality brands include Golden Boy, Tra Chang, and King Crab, but if you don't see any of those, just be sure to look for fish sauce that's reddish brown and fairly clear. The darker and cloudier it is, the lower the quality. Once you have a bottle of the stuff in the pantry, reach for it in place of salt to add a little extra depth to dishes. I love it in vinaigrettes, soups, and braising liquids, but my favorite use is blending it with fresh garlic and rosemary to make a paste to rub on meats before roasting or grilling them.

GRILLED PORK TENDERLOIN WITH APPLE BUTTER, RAPINI, AND ROSEMARY VINAIGRETTE

SERVES 4

The first time I had rapini (a.k.a. broccoli raab) was when I was working with Shawn McClain, a James Beard winner for Best Chef Midwest, at his restaurant Spring. I remember biting into the rapini expecting the sweet taste of broccoli, but, boy, was I wrong. Rapini has a very intense bitterness that, for a first timer, is pretty strong. After a few bites though, I was able to appreciate the flavor, mainly because Shawn was serving it with a nice, rich, meaty oxtail broth, which taught me that rapini can stand up to intense flavors and still shine through. For this dish, I've added a bit of sweetness from the apples and a rich rosemary flavor from the vinaigrette, elements taken from Shawn's lesson that balance is key.

PORK TENDERLOIN

3 garlic cloves, minced

4 sprigs fresh thyme, stemmed

1 tablespoon olive oil

1 teaspoon sambal (see Ingredient Spotlight, page 47)

2 pork tenderloins (about 1½ pounds total)

Salt

Freshly ground black pepper

APPLE BUTTER

2 Gala apples, peeled and thinly sliced

2 tablespoons cider vinegar

2 tablespoons sugar

Salt

Freshly ground black pepper

RAPINI

1 pound rapini, stemmed

3 slices bacon, cut into thin strips

Salt

Freshly ground black pepper

ROSEMARY VINAIGRETTE

¼ cup sherry vinegar

2 egg yolks

1 tablespoon Dijon mustard

1 cup canola or grapeseed oil

¼ cup ground fresh rosemary (use a spice grinder)

1 tablespoon honey

Salt

Freshly ground black pepper

1. To prepare the tenderloin: In a small bowl, combine the garlic, thyme, olive oil, and sambal and rub them on the pork. Season with salt and pepper. Seal the pork in a plastic bag and refrigerate overnight.

2. To make the apple butter: In a medium nonreactive saucepan, combine the apples, vinegar, and sugar. Add enough water to cover the apples by about ½ inch. Bring it to a boil, then reduce the heat. Simmer until most of the liquid is gone and the apples are very tender.

3. Transfer the apple butter ingredients to a blender and purée until smooth. Season with salt and pepper.

4. To make the vinaigrette: Combine the vinegar, egg yolks, and mustard in a blender. On low speed, slowly drizzle in the canola oil until thickened. Add the rosemary and honey. Season with salt and pepper. Cover and refrigerate until needed. (This will make more vinaigrette than you'll need for this recipe, but it can be held for up to 5 days, refrigerated, and used on salads or other grilled proteins.)

5. Preheat a gas or charcoal grill for direct cooking on medium heat. Remove the pork from the refrigerator and let it come up to room temperature.

Continued . . .

6. Grill the pork, covered, for 8 to 10 minutes over direct heat on a gas grill or over coals that are no longer on fire but are glowing white (you should be able to hold your hand over the fire for 4 seconds). Rotate the tenderloins every couple of minutes until they're evenly browned on the edges, light pink in the interior, and have an internal temperature of 145°F (the temperature will rise up to 150°F while they rest). Transfer them to a plate to let the meat rest for 5 to 10 minutes. Cut it in ½-inch-thick slices just before serving.

7. To make the rapini: Bring a large stockpot of salted water to boil. Prepare a bowl of ice water. Blanch the rapini by simmering until it's just tender. Transfer to an ice bath to stop the cooking and then drain.

8. Cook the bacon in a large skillet or sauté pan over medium heat until just crisp. Add in the rapini and toss to combine and warm. Season with salt and pepper.

9. Rewarm the apple butter over low heat, if necessary. Then place a heaping spoonful of apple butter on each of four plates. Top with the rapini. Divide the pork tenderloins among the plates, fanning them over the rapini. Drizzle with the rosemary vinaigrette and serve.

PLAN OF ATTACK

- Up to 5 days ahead: Make the vinaigrette and apple butter.
- Night before: Marinate the pork tenderloin.
- Cook time: Grill the tenderloin. While the meat is resting, warm the apple butter in a small saucepan and prepare the rapini.

DRINK TIP

India Pale Ales are a favorite of "hop heads," beer drinkers who gravitate toward the citrusy herbal bitterness of hops. Many American IPAs go to extremes, using an intense amount of hops, both fresh and dry, and the result is often an almost piney plant-like flavor—one that not only matches up perfectly with rosemary but has just enough bitterness to help keep the fattiness of pork in check.

CRISPY OR ROASTED PORK LOIN WITH LEMONY FAVA BEANS AND DILL YOGURT

About a year after my first trip to Madison, Wisconsin, to take part in a pig kill with my chef friends Dan and Jason, I headed back up again with my good friend Lee Anne Wong to work through the process again. I think the first time around I was a little too overwhelmed by the whole experience to be able to focus on the details, but the second time I was much more comfortable and able to pay attention to what was happening and why. I'm not sure it's a process I'll master any time soon, but I'll certainly continue to learn and bring fellow chefs along to learn as well, as I think that the experience really increases the respect for the animal and the farmers who raise them.

After breaking down our half of the pig into cuts to cure for prosciutto, speck, and pancetta, we took half of the loin back to Dan and Jason's house and cooked up a storm, moving from tempura mushrooms from Washington state to Lee Anne's fried rice and pork *tonkatsu*. Later, I took the other half of the loin home and decided to play around a bit, crisping up part of it for my own version of *tonkatsu*, but subbing a nice springy fava salad and dill yogurt for the classic Japanese *tonkatsu* sauce. I roasted the other part of the loin with a simple dill rub. Both are simple and delicious ways to prepare loin, and I provide the method for both preparations here. Regardless of which preparation you choose to make, remember that the most important thing with this cut of meat is not to overcook it. We no longer live in an age where we need to cook our pork to well done to avoid getting sick. Pork loin is meant to be enjoyed closer to medium, so the meat remains tender and juicy. For the fried pork, where the color is impossible to keep an eye on, just lightly brown each side, remove it, and you should end up with pork that is perfectly crisp on the outside, yet juicy and tender on the inside.

DILL YOGURT

6 ounces Greek-style yogurt

2 tablespoons finely chopped fresh dill

2 tablespoons buttermilk

1 tablespoon fresh lemon juice

Salt

Freshly ground black pepper

LEMONY FAVA BEAN SALAD

2 pounds whole fava beans

2 tablespoons olive oil

1½ tablespoons finely julienned Preserved Lemon (page 241)

1 tablespoon roughly chopped fresh dill

1 tablespoon fresh lemon juice

¼ teaspoon red pepper flakes

Salt

Freshly ground black pepper

ROASTED PORK LOIN

½ cup salt

2 tablespoons chopped fresh rosemary

1 tablespoon sugar

1 tablespoon freshly ground black pepper

1 tablespoon mustard seeds

1 tablespoon cider vinegar

3 garlic cloves

1 tablespoon finely chopped fresh dill

1½ pounds pork loin

CRISPY PORK LOIN

1½ pounds pork loin

½ cup all-purpose flour

2 eggs, whisked

1 cup panko bread crumbs (see Ingredient Spotlight, page 193)

6 tablespoons olive oil

Continued . . .

1. To make the yogurt: In a small bowl, whisk together the yogurt, dill, buttermilk, and lemon juice. Season with salt and pepper. Cover and refrigerate.

2. To make the salad: Remove the fava beans from their pods, discarding the pods.

3. Bring a medium stockpot of salted water to a boil. Prepare a bowl of ice water. Blanch the beans by boiling them for 5 to 6 minutes (test by pulling one from the water and tasting; it should be al dente in texture). Drain, then place the beans in the ice bath to shock. Once chilled, peel off the outer protective layer of the beans (see Technique 101, page 22). Roughly chop the favas and place them in a bowl. Combine them with the olive oil, lemon, dill, lemon juice, and red pepper flakes and season with salt and pepper. Cover and refrigerate.

4. To make the roasted pork loin: Preheat the oven to 400°F. Combine the salt, rosemary, sugar, pepper, mustard seeds, vinegar, garlic, and dill in a food processor and process to make a rub. Place the pork in a baking dish and thoroughly coat the outside with the rub. Roast until the internal temperature reaches 150 to 155°F, 35 to 40 minutes. Remove from the oven and let the meat rest for 10 minutes before slicing.

To make the crispy pork loin: Slice the pork loin into ½-inch slices (you should be able to get twelve slices). Place each piece, one at a time, in between plastic wrap or deli paper. Pound the loin slices ¼ inch thick with the flat side of a meat tenderizer. Set them aside on a baking sheet lined with parchment. Get three bowls large enough to each fit a slice of pork. Place the flour in the first one, eggs in the second, and panko in the third. Season both sides of the pork with salt and pepper. One piece at a time, place the pork in the flour, coating each side but shaking off the excess. Transfer the pork to the egg, coating both sides, and then into the panko, making sure to fully coat with the bread crumbs. Return each slice to the parchment. Once all of the pork is breaded, heat a large sauté pan over medium-high heat. You'll be working in three batches, four pieces at a time. Heat 2 tablespoons of the oil, add four slices of the pork, and lightly brown them on both sides until just crisp. Remove with a slotted spoon and set the slices on a clean kitchen towel or paper towels to drain. Repeat with the remaining oil and pork.

5. To serve, fan three pieces of pork on each of four plates and top with a large spoonful of fava salad. Garnish with a spoonful of dill yogurt on the side.

PLAN OF ATTACK

- Up to a week ahead: Prepare the dill yogurt and store covered in the refrigerator.
- Up to 3 days ahead: Prepare the fava bean salad and store covered in the refrigerator.
- Cook time: Roast one pork loin. Prepare the other loin for crispy pork.

DRINK TIP

Whether you go fried or roasted with this dish, a tart hard cider will be a fantastic pairing. Pork and apples go hand-in-hand (pork chops and applesauce, anyone?), plus the dry tartness of cider mimics the lemon that dominates this dish.

INGREDIENT SPOTLIGHT

PANKO The Japanese should win some kind of award for creating the crunchiest bread crumbs out there. Once panko hit American restaurants in the early 1990s, there was no turning back. Now chefs use it to coat everything from shrimp to green tomatoes, and the crunch is so intense you can hear it across the room. Panko really more like flakes than crumbs, so the large surface area absorbs less grease, making them infinitely crunchier when fried. If you want that big crunch, use them as is, but I often pulse them in a food processor for just a few seconds or crumble them up with my hands a bit before using to make them a bit finer. Use them as you would any bread crumbs; you can find them at any Japanese market and better grocery stores like Whole Foods.

VEAL OSSO BUCO WITH MASHED NEW POTATOES AND MAPLE APPLES

I know that there are plenty of ethical issues over veal, but over the past couple of years I've been traveling around the Midwest, primarily southern Illinois, to find the best locally raised meats I can. It's important to me to see how the animals are raised before bringing them to my guests, and with veal, it's extra important. Because veal is a young cow that is meant to be very tender, it's sometimes not able to roam freely, the main point of many people's aversion to eating it. (I always wonder what those same people would think if they knew about the quality, or lack thereof, of conditions in which most supermarket chickens are raised, but that's a whole other can of worms.) Luckily, I found Kilgus Farm, where two teenage farmers, brothers Justin and Trent Kilgus, raise veal the most ethical way around—on the milk of their mothers and in their own small pasture area, where they roam freely.

The only downside to finding a conscientious local supplier of veal is that you will pay quite a bit more for the product, but I assure you it will be worth it. The tender meat of the shank nearly falls apart when slowly braised, and the pure beef flavor is unbeatable. Still, if you prefer, you can sub lamb shanks for this recipe, and it will turn out just as delicious. Just be sure to serve it with some crusty bread that you eat with the marrow. Don't be squeamish; that's one of the best parts!

MAPLE APPLES

1 tablespoon olive oil

1 apple, peeled and cut into ¼-inch cubes

1 teaspoon white balsamic vinegar

1 teaspoon maple syrup

Salt

Freshly ground black pepper

MASHED NEW POTATOES

1½ pounds new (baby) potatoes

Salt

4 tablespoons butter

1 teaspoon extra-virgin olive oil

Freshly ground black pepper

OSSO BUCO

2 teaspoons blended oil (half vegetable, half olive oil)

4 veal shanks (about 2½ pounds total)

2 teaspoons fennel seeds

2 teaspoons mustard seeds

4 slices bacon, diced

2 apples, peeled and sliced

1 small onion, diced

1 fennel bulb, diced

1 cup red wine

½ cup dry sherry

¼ cup maple syrup

¼ cup balsamic vinegar

4 dried Thai chiles (see Ingredient Spotlight, page 61)

2 tablespoons Worcestershire sauce

2½ cups chicken broth, plus more if needed

One 14-ounce can whole plum tomatoes

1. To make the maple apples: Heat the olive oil in a small sauté pan over medium heat. Add the apples and sauté for 3 to 4 minutes. Add the vinegar and maple syrup and continue cooking until tender, about 6 minutes more. Season with salt and pepper. Set aside.

2. To make the potatoes: Place the potatoes in a large pot and cover with cold water. Add 2 teaspoons salt, bring the water to a boil, and cook until very tender, about 25 minutes.

3. Strain out the water, leaving the potatoes in the pot. Add the butter and olive oil and smash with a potato masher. Season with salt and pepper.

4. To make the osso buco: Preheat the oven to 300°F. In a large Dutch oven, heat the blended oil over medium-high heat. Season the veal shanks well with salt and pepper, then brown them on all sides, using tongs to turn. Remove them from the pan and set aside.

5. In a small, dry sauté pan, toast the fennel and mustard seeds and set aside.

6. In a large, deep sauté pan or skillet, cook the bacon over medium heat to render the fat. Once the bacon pieces have just started to brown, add the apples, onion, and fennel and sweat by cooking them until the onion is translucent, about 4 minutes. Add the toasted seeds along with the wine, sherry, maple syrup, vinegar, chiles, and Worcestershire sauce. Simmer to reduce by half. Add the broth, tomatoes,

and 1 teaspoon salt. Add the veal shanks. The liquid should just cover the shanks; if not, add just enough more broth to cover them. Bring them to a boil, cover with a lid or tightly with aluminum foil, and place in the oven. Braise until the meat is very tender, about 1 hour and 45 minutes.

7. Remove the pan from the oven and carefully pull out the shanks, being careful not to pull the meat off the bones. Place the shanks in a separate baking dish and cover with foil to keep warm until ready to serve.

8. Strain the solids from the liquid left in the Dutch oven and simmer to reduce the liquid in a small pot over medium heat until it's thick enough to coat the back of a spoon.

9. To serve, place a small mound of potatoes on each of four plates. Top each with a veal shank. Spoon sauce over the veal and top with a spoonful of maple apples.

PLAN OF ATTACK

- Up to 3 days ahead: Make the maple apples. Store covered in the refrigerator.
- Day before: Make the potatoes. Store covered in the refrigerator. (Alternately, start the potatoes with about half an hour to go on the osso buco during cook time).
- Cook time: Make the osso buco. After it's pulled from the oven and the pan sauce is reducing, warm the maple apples and potatoes.

 QUICK TIP ·

With braised items, there tends to be some leftover sauce. Save it in the refrigerator for up to 1 week and serve over any other meats or even with scallops or meaty fish. Alternatively, you can freeze it and add it to your next braising liquid for an additional boost of flavor.

DRINK TIP

Osso buco is undoubtedly rich, and the tannins (those things that make the back of your throat pucker) in Mendoza Malbecs will grab right onto the fat of these shanks to become a pretty great marriage.

PAN-ROASTED NEW YORK STEAKS WITH SAUTÉED CUCUMBERS AND SALTED GOAT MILK CARAMEL

SERVES 4

While working on some "goat" ideas for my new restaurant, Girl & the Goat, I played around with goat meat, as well as goat's milk. My old pastry chef from Scylla, Jessie Oloroso, makes an awesome ice cream with goat's milk caramel, known as *cajeta* in Mexico. She added cashews for crunch and a bit of salt, convincing me that salted caramel is the only way to go; otherwise, the caramel is just too sweet. Inspired by Jessie's ice cream (which she now sells at her shop Black Dog Gelato in Chicago), I decided to try a salted goat's milk caramel as a sauce for a savory dish. The interesting thing with cajeta is that it's not a classic caramel sauce, as the sugar is not actually what caramelizes. The liquid never reaches a high enough temperature for the added sugar to caramelize; instead, the fats of the milk caramelize with the help of the added baking soda, which neutralizes the natural acids and also helps the milk solids to turn a rich brown color.

So now that you know everything you'd ever want to know about caramelizing goat's milk, let me explain why I added fish sauce to it. It might seem strange, but that's the salty element, with just enough earthy funk to pair perfectly with the equally earthy "browned" flavor of the caramel. Sounds weird, but trust me, you'll love it.

And finally, because the beef and the sauce are so rich, we need to cut through it a bit with some lightly sautéed cucumbers. I realize it also sounds strange to cook cucumbers, but doing so releases some of their natural juices and allows them to quickly soak up the salt, taking on a great flavor and texture while keeping things perfectly refreshing.

SALTED GOAT MILK CARAMEL

1 quart goat milk

½ cup sugar

¼ teaspoon baking soda

1 tablespoon fish sauce

2 teaspoons sambal (see Ingredient Spotlight, page 47)

1 teaspoon balsamic vinegar

1 teaspoon soy sauce

1 teaspoon Dijon mustard

Salt

Freshly ground black pepper

PAN-ROASTED NEW YORK STRIP STEAK

3 tablespoons olive oil

3 garlic cloves, minced

1 tablespoon grainy mustard

1½ teaspoons sambal

4 New York strip steaks (about 12 ounces each)

Salt

Freshly ground black pepper

1 tablespoon canola oil

1 tablespoon butter

SAUTÉED CUCUMBERS

2 tablespoons olive oil

One 12-inch English cucumber, sliced into ⅛-inch rounds

Salt

Freshly ground black pepper

1 tablespoon thinly sliced fresh basil

Continued . . .

1. To make the caramel: In a heavy-bottomed saucepan, combine the goat milk and sugar and slowly bring to a boil over medium-high heat. Dissolve the baking soda in ½ teaspoon warm water. Whisk it into the milk mixture, reduce the heat to medium, and let it simmer. Whisk often until the mixture reduces and begins to thicken and turn a light caramel color, about 1 hour and 10 minutes. As the caramel begins to darken, reduce the heat and continue to stir constantly with a whisk, making sure the caramel doesn't stick to the bottom of the pot and burn. Continue to cook and whisk constantly, until the caramel darkens and is thick enough to coat the back of a spoon, about 20 minutes more. It will have reduced to about ½ cup when finished. Strain the caramel through a fine-mesh sieve into a small pot. Add the fish sauce, sambal, vinegar, soy sauce, and mustard and season with salt and pepper. Cover and keep warm.

2. To make the steak: Whisk together the olive oil, garlic, mustard, and sambal for a marinade, then rub it into the steaks. Refrigerate, preferably overnight but for at least 3 hours. Take the steaks out of the fridge about 30 minutes before getting started so they cook more evenly.

3. Salt and pepper both sides of the steaks. Heat a large skillet or sauté pan over high heat until it's almost smoking. Add the canola oil, then the steaks. (Don't overcrowd the pan; cook in two batches if you must.) Once the steaks brown on one side, flip them over and add the butter to the pan. Tilt the pan and spoon the melted butter over the steaks to baste. Once the edges of the steak are nice and brown, make a small slit to the center of the steak to check for doneness.

You're aiming for medium-rare, so the very center should still be red because the meat will continue to "carry-over cook" as it rests. Remove the steaks from the pan and let them rest on a plate for 5 to 10 minutes to allow the steak to retain its juices and to even out the doneness.

4. To make the cucumbers: While the meat rests, heat a large sauté pan over medium heat. Add the olive oil, then the cucumbers, and cook until the cucumbers just begins to soften, about 3 minutes. Remove from heat and season with salt and pepper. When ready to serve, toss with the basil.

5. To serve, spoon a couple tablespoons of the caramel onto each plate, top with a steak, and place the sautéed cucumbers alongside.

PLAN OF ATTACK

- Up to 3 days ahead: Make the goat milk caramel. Refrigerate.
- The night before: Marinate the steaks.
- Cook time: Prepare the steaks. While the meat is resting, sauté the cucumbers and reheat the caramel over low heat in a saucepan.

DRINK TIP

Who doesn't love Shiraz with steak? Big, bold, and peppery, it's a classic pairing, but try to seek out Shiraz from Australia's Barossa Valley for added interest.

BRAISED LAMB SHANKS WITH CURRIED CAULIFLOWER AND GRAPE GREMOLATA

SERVES 4

Growing up, I was not a fan of lamb. At all. That's not to say my mom didn't make some great food, but come lamb-chop night I looked to our dog, Dr. Pepper, under the table for a little help. I always thought of lamb as very gamey (even though I didn't know that terminology at the time). So what did I do? The worst thing possible: I doused it with mint jelly—something my dad still does to this day. Whoever decided that bright green and overly sweet mint jelly should exist at all, much less cover up perfectly good lamb, must have had a broken palate. But the idea is based on the fact that mint does complement lamb, something I pulled from for this recipe.

Gremolata is a classic Italian condiment for roasted and grilled meats, traditionally made from chopped herbs, garlic, and lemon zest, and I decided to adjust that to include mint and roasted grapes to better pair with the lamb. And because so many cultures, especially Indian, use curry when cooking with lamb, I thought that a little hot and yellow curry powder in the cauliflower would help pull everything together. Both the gremolata and the curried cauliflower are versatile enough that I hope you start working them into your favorite dishes—especially if you have a lamb phobia like I once did.

GRAPE GREMOLATA

1 pound red grapes, stemmed

⅓ cup loosely packed mint, cut into chiffonade

⅓ cup loosely packed basil, cut into chiffonade (see Technique 101, page 73)

1 lemon, zested

½ orange, zested

2 tablespoons olive oil

Salt

Freshly ground black pepper

LAMB

2 tablespoons olive oil

4 lamb shanks (about 4 pounds total)

Salt

Freshly ground black pepper

1 large onion, medium diced

3 garlic cloves, roughly chopped

1 cup dry red wine

¼ cup dry sherry

2 tablespoons balsamic vinegar

2 tablespoons Worcestershire sauce

2 tablespoons tomato paste

5 cups dark chicken stock or veal or beef stock

2 teaspoons fennel seeds, toasted

2 teaspoons yellow mustard seeds, toasted

CURRIED CAULIFLOWER

1 head cauliflower (about 1 pound)

3 tablespoons butter

1 teaspoon olive oil

2 shallots, thinly sliced

2 garlic cloves, thinly sliced

1 teaspoon hot curry powder

½ teaspoon yellow curry powder

Salt

Freshly ground black pepper

Continued . . .

1. To make the gremolata: Preheat the oven to 350°F.

2. Place the grapes on a silicone baking sheet or wax paper–lined baking sheet. Roast until the grapes are shriveled but not completely dry, about 20 minutes. Remove from the oven and let cool. Leave the oven on.

3. Toss the grapes with the mint, basil, lemon zest, orange zest, and olive oil and season with salt and pepper. Cover the surface directly with plastic wrap to prevent browning and set aside.

4. To make the lamb: Heat the olive oil in a large roasting pan over high heat. Season the lamb with salt and pepper. When the oil is very hot, add the shanks and brown on all sides, using tongs to turn. Remove the shanks to a plate and set aside.

5. Reduce the heat under the pan to medium. Add the onion and sweat by cooking until translucent, 2 to 3 minutes. Add the garlic, sautéing for about 30 seconds. Pour in a little of the wine to deglaze the pan, scraping the browned bits from the bottom with a wooden spoon as the liquid evaporates. Add the rest of the wine, the sherry, vinegar, and Worcestershire sauce, and simmer to reduce by half. Add the tomato paste, stirring as it melts into the liquid.

6. Return the shanks to the pan, add the stock and toasted fennel and mustard seeds, and cover the pan. Braise the lamb until very tender, 1½ to 2 hours. Remove the shanks from the braising liquid and set aside.

7. While the shanks are cooking, make the cauliflower. Cut the head of cauliflower in half and cut out most of the stem. Cut the florets into ¼-inch slices.

8. Heat the butter and olive oil in a large sauté pan over medium-low heat. Add the shallots and garlic and sweat by cooking them until the shallots are translucent, 1 to 2 minutes. Add the cauliflower and toss to coat with the butter and oil. Sauté until the cauliflower releases much of its liquid and begins to brown, 5 to 10 minutes. Reduce the heat to medium-low and continue to sauté until the florets are just tender, an additional 10 minutes, tossing often.

9. Add both curry powders, tossing to coat the florets, and season with salt and pepper. Set aside and cover to keep warm.

10. Strain the braising liquid and simmer to reduce it by a little more than half for a rich sauce. Season with salt.

11. Divide the cauliflower among the plates. Top with the lamb shanks, spoon the pan sauce over the top of each, and garnish with a generous sprinkling of gremolata.

PLAN OF ATTACK

- Day before: Make the gremolata. Cover and refrigerate (bring up to room temperature before using).
- Cook time: Start the lamb shanks. With about 20 minutes left to cook the lamb, prepare the cauliflower.

DRINK TIP

One of the most classic pairings ever is Bordeaux with lamb, although you could just as well go with a subtle American Cabernet as well. The robustness and the black currant notes go great with the braised meat gravy.

CHA
SIX

SIDES

SIDES GET A BAD RAP. SIDES. EVEN THE NAME SAYS, "HEY, YOU'RE NOT THE MAIN EVENT." THANKSGIVING, WHERE THE TURKEY GETS TO BE THE STAR OF THE SHOW, IS A PERFECT EXAMPLE OF SIDE PREJUDICE. BUT IN MY OPINION, THE SIDES ARE WHERE THE MAGIC REALLY HAPPENS.

(Speaking of Thanksgiving, I love classic green bean casserole so much, I even put a version of it in this chapter.) And here's the thing about sides: They're easy. If you don't cook a single main dish out of this cookbook, at least try a few of the sides. That way you can carry on with the same roasted chicken, pot roast, or broiled fish you've been making for years, but by adding a couple new sides to the table, you've created a completely different meal.

Actually, some of the sides in this chapter might even replace your go-to main course—the Wilted Spinach with Roasted Tomatoes and Sausage (page 213) a perfect example of a side that can be tossed with pasta or scooped onto good bread for a quick dinner. Or make a few different sides, serve them family-style, start passing plates, and no one will even notice what's missing.

TOMATO AND CASHEW SOUBISE

SERVES 4

Soubise (pronounced soo-BEEZ) is a very classic French dish that's sort of like an onion-heavy take on risotto. The onions are combined with rice and cooked very low and slow, allowing the juices from the onion to cook the rice. In this version, I've added a bit of tomato to bring in a little acidity to help balance the natural sweetness of the onions. If tomatoes are in season, grab a nice ripe one and chop it up. If not, some canned San Marzanos will do the trick (just be sure to drain off most of the liquid so the onion juice can do its job). And the cashews in this bring in just a bit of crunch, which I love in rice—maybe because it always reminds me a little of the cashew chicken that I used to order from the Chinese place near my house growing up. Now that I think about it, a little grilled or roasted chicken would be perfect with this side. And keep the leftovers to do what we often did at Scylla—purée it to make a nice thick onion sauce to serve under fish or poultry.

2 tablespoons salt	1 cup diced tomato (canned is fine; just drain)	Freshly ground black pepper	2 tablespoons chiffonade of fresh basil (see Technique 101, page 73)
½ cup basmati rice (see Ingredient Spotlight, page 206)	3 tablespoons butter, cubed	¾ cup salted, toasted cashews, roughly chopped	
1½ pounds yellow onions, thinly sliced			

1. Preheat the oven to 325°F.

2. Bring a small pot of water to a boil with 1½ teaspoons of the salt. Add the rice, boil for 3 minutes, and then strain (you're just par-cooking it).

3. In a medium bowl, combine the rice, onions, tomato, and butter. Season with the remaining 1½ tablespoons salt and some pepper. Transfer the mixture to a Dutch oven (or baking dish with tight fitting lid or aluminum foil) and bake for 1½ hours, removing to stir every 30 minutes. You can tell it's done when the rice is nice and fluffy and the liquid is absorbed. Remove from the oven and stir in the cashews and basil before serving.

INGREDIENT SPOTLIGHT

RICE By now we've all read enough health magazines (or women's magazines trying to guilt the pounds off) that we know brown is the healthiest option when it comes to rice. Those nutty grains are good with an earthy mushroom stir-fry, but they won't really work for soubise, just as short-grain, high-starch jasmine rice wouldn't because it's likely to clump during a long cooking time. Basmati is pretty much made for a dish like soubise, as the grains are long enough that they won't get fat and sticky. Likewise, basmati is the ideal rice for Indian *biryani*, each grain remaining intact while soaking up all of the spices. Clearly, specific dishes call for specific rice types, like Arborio or Carnaroli for risotto, as the high starch content helps fuse the dish for creamy pasta-like results. And plain old white rice? Let's just say that beyond late-night Chinese takeout, you won't see it in my kitchen that often.

SWEET-AND-SOUR CIPOLLINI ONIONS

SERVES 4 TO 6

I'm pretty much obsessed with all things onion, and cipollinis are no exception. These Italian onions may look a little funny—like a small yellow onion that's been run over by a car and flattened like a cartoon coyote—but they have a great delicate flavor that's naturally sweet with just the right amount of kick, something like a cross between a red onion and a Vidalia onion. Here I've given them a nice balance of sweet and sour, along with the salty and spiced element of pancetta and a floral note from my go-to favorite, fennel. This is great alongside roasted chicken or under a beautifully grilled piece of fish.

1 tablespoon butter	1 large fennel bulb (about 8 ounces)	¼ cup red wine	Salt
2 ounces pancetta, finely diced	1 pound cipollini onions, halved	1 tablespoon sugar	Freshly ground black pepper
		2 teaspoons balsamic vinegar	

1. Heat the butter in a large sauté pan over medium heat. Add the pancetta and let it brown.

2. While the pancetta is browning, cut off the stalks of the fennel (reserving a few fronds for garnish and storing them in a damp paper towel until ready to serve). Thinly slice the fennel bulb, cutting around and removing the core. Once the pancetta has browned and sautéed for about 2 minutes, add the sliced fennel and the onions to the pan. Stir in the wine, sugar, and vinegar and season with salt and pepper. Continue to cook until the liquid is almost gone and the vegetables are just tender. Serve immediately.

EGGPLANT AND NECTARINE CAPONATA

SERVES 4

I'm hoping that by the time you read this book, I've found the time to make it to Italy and try authentic *caponata* firsthand. (The reality is, I probably won't have found the time to get a haircut.) Caponata is a Sicilian eggplant-based dish, served both cold and warm, either with crusty bread for slathering or as a side for grilled fish or other main events. I may not have eaten the real deal yet, but this is my interpretation of it, created from plenty of reading and tasting. In late summer when eggplants are popping up at farmers' markets, you'll also come across nectarines, which is exactly why I thought to combine the two. It might not get past the authenticity police in Sicily, but I've never been one for coloring inside the lines anyway.

5½ tablespoons olive oil

1 Vidalia or other sweet onion, thinly sliced

2 garlic cloves, minced

5 tablespoons white balsamic vinegar

5 tablespoons sugar

Salt

Freshly ground black pepper

1 red bell pepper, thinly sliced

1 medium to large fennel bulb, quartered, cored, and thinly sliced

3 medium Japanese (long, purple) eggplants (see Ingredient Spotlight, facing page), cut into ¼-inch rounds

2 large nectarines (slightly underripe), peeled and cubed

½ cup pine nuts, toasted

½ cup brined capers

8 leaves fresh basil, cut into chiffonade (see Technique 101, page 73)

1. Heat 1½ teaspoons of the olive oil in a large skillet or sauté pan over medium heat and add the onion. Sweat by cooking until the onion is almost translucent.

2. Add the garlic and cook for another 2 minutes.

3. Add 1 tablespoon each of vinegar and sugar, plus ½ teaspoon salt and a grind of pepper. Once the moisture has evaporated and the onion is soft, transfer to a baking sheet, making a small pile.

4. Now you'll start the process over with the red bell pepper. First wipe the skillet clean with a paper towel. Then heat 1 tablespoon of the oil in the skillet or sauté pan over medium heat and cook for a couple of minutes until the pepper is bright red.

5. Once again, add 1 tablespoon each of vinegar and sugar, plus ½ teaspoon salt and a grind of pepper. Once the moisture has evaporated and the pepper is soft, transfer it to the baking sheet, making a separate small pile.

6. Continue the same process with the fennel, then the eggplant (although use 2 tablespoons oil with this batch) and finally, the nectarines, remembering to wipe the pan between batches and avoiding stacking the vegetables on the baking sheet to prevent overcooking.

7. Once all the ingredients have cooled to room temperature, mix them together in a large bowl, add the pine nuts, capers, and basil, and gently toss together. Season with salt and pepper before serving.

INGREDIENT SPOTLIGHT

EGGPLANT Take one trip to the farmers' market in late summer, and you'll quickly see how many different varieties of eggplant are out there. The most common eggplants you'll find year-round at grocery stores are large globe eggplants, with a deep purple color and smooth skin. These are fine for eggplant Parmesan or as a play on the veggie burger, but I don't cook with them that often, mainly because I think the skin is tough and the flesh is bitter. I actually prefer Japanese eggplants, which are almost as easy to find in regular grocery stores. They're also purple, but they're smaller and thinner and seem to have a nice natural sweetness. (Chinese eggplant looks similar, but I skip it because I think it has too many seeds.) If you come across small, globe-shaped, green eggplants, those are a Thai variety that are awesome in stir-fries and curries—just halve or quarter them and toss them into the mix, cooking until they're tender.

ROASTED RADISHES WITH BLUE CHEESE, PEANUTS, AND CILANTRO

SERVES 4 TO 6

I love the slightly spicy and refreshing crunch of radishes, but most people don't think of cooking them. When roasted, the heat of the radish really mellows out and the sweetness shines through. Just remember, though, that you're not looking to turn them into mush. You just want to get some nice color on the radishes, then cook them a couple minutes more with the garlic and shallots so they can pick up those flavors but retain a bit of crunch.

Now, I have to say that this recipe is not for those who don't have a love for the tangy taste of a nice blue cheese, a flavor that goes surprisingly well with salty peanuts and fresh cilantro. Ideally, you would make the recipe as is to get a feel for the flavor combo, but if you'd rather leave out the blue cheese, I won't hold it against you (well, maybe just a little).

1 tablespoon olive oil

1 tablespoon butter

1 pound radishes, trimmed and quartered

1 head endive

1 garlic clove, minced

1 shallot, thinly sliced

Salt

Freshly ground black pepper

½ cup roasted, salted peanuts, chopped

1 ounce Gorgonzola cheese

2 tablespoons chopped fresh cilantro

1. In a large sauté pan over medium-high heat, melt the olive oil and butter together. Add the radishes, toss to coat, and let them sit in the pan to brown, about 5 minutes.

2. While the radishes are browning, quarter and core the endive. Slice it into ¼-inch pieces and set aside.

3. Add the garlic and shallot to the pan, reduce the heat to medium, and cook until the radishes are fork-tender, 3 to 4 minutes longer.

4. Add the endive and toss to coat. Season with salt and pepper.

5. Remove the pan from the heat. Add the peanuts, cheese, and cilantro. Toss to combine and serve hot.

ROASTED CAULIFLOWER WITH CRANBERRY SAÒR (ITALIAN SWEET AND SOUR)

SERVES 6 TO 8

Don't be scared off by the fancy name *saòr*. It literally means "sour," but it's also a culinary term that refers to an Italian sweet-and-sour preparation, one that's often used on fish, especially oily, briny types like sardines. I like using saòr on seafood as well, but I've found that it's even better on simple roasted vegetables. When I was growing up, my mom used to roast a whole head of cauliflower, then pour goopy cheese sauce over it. We'd devour it (but honestly, we probably would have devoured anything smothered in cheese sauce back then). This is my more "adult" version of a super-tasty vegetable side.

2 tablespoons butter	1 head cauliflower (about 1 pound), cut into ¼-inch slices (see Technique 101, below)	1 cup white balsamic vinegar	¼ cup sugar
2 teaspoons olive oil		¾ cup diced onion	1 garlic clove, minced
		½ cup dried cranberries	¼ teaspoon salt
			½ cup pine nuts, toasted

1. Melt 1 tablespoon of the butter and 1 teaspoon of the oil in a large skillet or sauté pan over high heat.

2. Add half of the cauliflower (you'll be cooking in two batches) and cook until the edges brown. Then turn the heat down to medium and continue to cook until just tender, 6 to 8 minutes. Remove the cauliflower and set it aside. Raise the heat to high and repeat the process with the remaining butter, oil, and cauliflower. Set it aside with the first batch.

3. In a small nonreactive pot, combine the vinegar, onion, cranberries, sugar, garlic, and salt and bring them to a boil. Reduce the heat and simmer until almost all of the liquid is absorbed (you're looking to keep a little syrup), about 20 minutes. Just before serving, stir in the pine nuts, then toss the saòr with the cauliflower in a large serving bowl or deep platter.

TECHNIQUE 101

Sautéing Cauliflower: The problem with sautéing cauliflower florets is that you'll never be able to get a uniform size, so some will cook fast while others are still hard. And if you try to cut mini florets off the head, you'll wind up with a bunch of tiny cauliflower crumbs that will burn before the rest of your batch is ready. The secret to cooking cauliflower evenly is to cut it into slices so that you have more surface area that will brown more easily. The best way to do this is to cut off the base of the cauliflower, cut it in half (top to bottom), quarter it, and then cut each quarter it into ¼-inch-thick slices. Sauté as directed above.

BACON-BRAISED SWISS CHARD

This is a very simple recipe for one of my favorite greens, Swiss chard. I firmly believe that chard leaves are best when cooked until they're just wilted. I remember doing a dinner with another chef one night, and just as my chard was ready to go, he asked if I was going to cook it for another half hour! Not a chance. I like my greens to have a bit of texture left in them, even spinach, which some people insist on cooking until it's complete mush. Not only is it an unpleasant texture, but you're cooking away all of the nutrients.

For this recipe, I remove the chard stems completely, as I think they can be a bit bitter and I prefer the flavor of the leaves. But if you come across some beautiful rainbow Swiss chard with vibrant stems, you can either save them to sauté in a little olive oil for your next meal or thinly slice and sauté a few as garnish for this dish. Just don't use too many, as they'll overpower the more delicate flavor of the leaves.

One final note: If you don't eat pork, the recipe is still great without it. Just start off with a little olive oil to sub in for the bacon fat. Of course, if you really want the great layer of salty and smoky flavor bacon adds to, well, everything, you may want to reconsider not eating pork. Just a thought.

---

4 slices bacon, cut crosswise into ¼-inch strips

½ cup diced red onion

3 garlic cloves, minced

4 Roma tomatoes, seeded, and finely diced

Salt

Freshly ground black pepper

3 pounds Swiss chard, stemmed, leaves torn into large pieces

3 tablespoons soy sauce

1 tablespoon balsamic vinegar

½ teaspoon red pepper flakes

---

1. Heat a Dutch oven or a large sauté pan with high sides or a over medium heat. Add the bacon and render the fat.

2. When most of the fat is rendered from the bacon and it begins to crisp, add the onion and garlic and cook until the onion is translucent, 2 to 3 minutes.

3. Stir in the tomatoes and cook 2 minutes longer. Season lightly with salt and pepper.

4. Add the chard, soy sauce, vinegar, and red pepper flakes. Stir until the chard wilts, 3 to 4 minutes.

5. Remove from the heat, adjust the seasoning, and serve hot.

WILTED SPINACH WITH
ROASTED TOMATOES AND SAUSAGE

SERVES 4

Spinach just doesn't get that much love anymore in contemporary restaurants. Somehow, it's gotten lost in the shuffle as chefs have started getting access to a whole other world of greens. But I'm starting a campaign to return dignity to spinach—a movement inspired by a delicious dish of roasted pork chop with sautéed spinach at my friend Roger Herring's restaurant Socca, right here in Chicago. It made me realize that it had been way too long since I had simple sautéed spinach, something I only began to appreciate later in life (as a kid, the only way I would spinach was in frozen spinach soufflés that my mom would pop into the oven every once in a while).

So, inspired by Roger's reminder of the full flavor of this green, I put together this recipe that enhances the earthiness of spinach with a nice rich sausage and the sweet tartness of roasted tomatoes. You can flip to the Extras chapter to make my sausage (see page 243) for this, but you can also just pick up some fresh sausage from your butcher or market and remove the casing so you have nice chunks of ground pork in every bite.

1 pint (about 10 ounces) grape tomatoes	1 tablespoon Worcestershire sauce	8 ounces Italian pork sausage, removed from casing	8 ounces fresh spinach, stemmed
2 tablespoons olive oil plus 1 teaspoon	Salt	½ small onion, thinly sliced	1 teaspoon balsamic vinegar
	Freshly ground black pepper		

1. Preheat the oven to 400°F.

2. In a medium bowl, combine the tomatoes, the 2 tablespoons olive oil, and the Worcestershire sauce. Season with salt and pepper and then transfer to a baking sheet covered with a silicone baking sheet or parchment paper. Roast until the tomatoes are blistered and begining to brown, about 12 minutes.

3. While the tomatoes are roasting, heat the remaining 1 teaspoon olive oil in a large sauté pan over medium-high heat. Add the sausage and brown while breaking it into small pieces with a wooden spoon. Once the sausage begins to brown and is almost cooked through, add the onion, reduce the heat to low, and sweat until the onion is translucent, about 3 minutes. Add the spinach and vinegar, stirring to coat and cooking until the spinach is just wilted. Season with salt and pepper.

4. Remove the tomatoes from the oven, toss them with the wilted spinach, and serve.

ROASTED MORELS WITH FAVAS AND WHITE ASPARAGUS

SERVES 4 TO 6

This side dish just shouts "Spring!" For starters, it features morels, perhaps the most prized mushrooms out there (after truffles, of course), and probably the hardest to find as well. Foragers throughout the Midwest and Pacific Northwest are so secretive about where they harvest their stash that they rarely take anyone not related to them on a hunt. Not only are morels unique in their perforated texture and meaty taste, but they're shaped almost like little Christmas trees, with small holes that I call hotel rooms, mainly because the holes tend to house bits of dirt and, from time to time, little worms that need to be removed before cooking. Even if the mushrooms look nice and clean, there's sure to be a bit of crunchy dirt hiding in them, so clean them well.

Coming in at Numbers Two and Three for veggies that epitomize spring are favas and white asparagus, a great addition of both texture and color. So now that we have earthy and crisp, we need creamy and sweet, done here with a bit of fresh ricotta cheese and a little drizzle of honey.

1 pound fresh morel mushrooms	1½ pounds fava beans, shelled	1 lemon, zested	1 pound white asparagus, peeled and cut into ¾-inch lengths
4 tablespoons olive oil	¼ cup honey	1½ teaspoons finely minced peeled fresh ginger	3 ounces fresh ricotta cheese
Salt	2 tablespoons chopped fresh oregano	½ teaspoon red pepper flakes	
Freshly ground black pepper	1 tablespoon fresh lemon juice		

1. Preheat the oven to 400°F.

2. Cut the morels in half lengthwise and dunk them under water a few times to remove any dirt (see Quick Tip, below). Lay them out on a kitchen towel for 15 minutes to dry. Then toss them in a bowl with 2 tablespoons of the olive oil. Season with salt and pepper. Transfer to a baking sheet and roast until they start to brown and shrivel, 12 to 15 minutes. Remove and let them cool to room temperature.

3. Bring a large pot of salted water to a boil. Prepare a bowl of ice water. Blanch the favas by simmering them until bright green, 3 to 4 minutes. Drain and transfer them to the ice bath to chill. Remove the thin outer shells (see Technique 101, page 22) and set aside.

4. Combine the honey, oregano, lemon juice, lemon zest, ginger, and red pepper flakes in a small saucepan over medium-low heat, stirring until the honey melts. Season with salt and pepper and set aside.

5. Heat a large sauté pan over medium-high heat with the remaining 2 tablespoons olive oil. Add the asparagus and sauté until just tender, 3 to 4 minutes. Add the mushrooms and favas and heat through. Transfer the vegetables to a serving platter, top with dollops of the ricotta, and drizzle with the melted honey mixture, and serve.

QUICK TIP

The easiest, and most thorough, method I've found for cleaning morels is to fill a clean sink full of cold water and then dunk the morels around a few times. The dirt settles to the bottom, so you can just pull the morels out with your hands and set aside. Then drain the sink and repeat one more time to make sure you get all the sediment and any pests. After rinsing the final time, lay the morels out on paper towels so they can air dry and avoid getting mushy. If you don't use them all after cleaning them, wrap them in a dry paper towel and store in the refrigerator for up to 2 days.

GREEN BEAN CASSEROLE

Make fun of me all you want, but I just had to put this recipe in the book. It's been my long-time favorite at holidays (I know I'm not alone here), and it's what I always bring to any pot-luck Thanksgiving. Growing up, my mom was like most of yours and, of course, made this classic with Campbell's canned mushroom soup, frozen beans, and Durkee onions . . . and it was delicious. I remember when I had just started culinary school in Arizona and my parents came out to visit for Thanksgiving. It was my first time hosting a big holiday meal, and I was ready to show off my new Le Cordon Bleu skills. My parents headed to the store to pick up some last-minute items, and my mom asked if she should pick up some cream of mush-room soup. I assured her that I had just learned the basics of the béchamel mother sauce, and how to turn it into the perfect mushroom soup, so I had it covered. About 30 minutes later, in walk my parents with, yes, two cans of mushroom soup. Thanks for the vote of con-fidence. Let's hope by now they trust my skills a bit more.

So this recipe is essentially what I made for my parents that holiday to prove to them their tuition money wasn't going to waste. It's simple to do, but the addition of maitake and shiitake mushrooms give it a bit of a gourmet boost and the extra earthiness the dish deserves. Feel free to add in other varieties, whatever you come across, and honestly, if you don't want to do the step of frying the shallots, those Durkee onions have a crisp like no other. I promise not to tell anyone.

MUSHROOM SOUP

5 tablespoons unsalted butter

2 shallots, minced

1 garlic clove, minced

1 pint (about 8 ounces) button mushrooms, sliced

¼ cup all-purpose flour

2 cups milk, at room temperature

1 to 2 teaspoons sambal (see Ingredient Spotlight, page 47)

Salt

Freshly ground black pepper

CASSEROLE

2 tablespoons unsalted butter

1 pound fresh maitake mushrooms, broken into small pieces

1 pound fresh shiitake mushrooms, stemmed and halved

1 shallot, sliced

2 garlic cloves, minced

Salt

Freshly ground black pepper

2 pounds fresh haricots verts (green beans), trimmed

CRISPY SHALLOTS

Oil for frying

¾ cup rice flour

¼ cup cornstarch

4 shallots, very thinly sliced into rounds

Salt

Freshly ground black pepper

1. To make the soup: In a large saucepan, melt the butter over medium-low heat. Add the shallots and garlic and sweat by cooking until the shallots are translucent, about 5 minutes, being watchful not to brown them. Add the button mushrooms and sweat them for 5 minutes more. Add the flour and stir to coat the mushrooms. Whisk in the milk and continue to whisk for a minute or so to avoid lumps. Over medium heat, slowly bring the mixture to a boil, whisking often. Simmer until it reaches the thickness of canned mushroom soup, about 10 minutes. Season with the sambal, salt, and pepper. (A thick soup is best for the casserole; however, if it becomes too thick, thin with additional milk).

2. To make the casserole: In a large sauté pan over high heat, melt the butter. Add the maitake and shiitake mushrooms, shallots, and garlic and sauté until lightly browned, 4 to 5 minutes. Season with salt and pepper and set aside.

3. Bring a large stockpot of salted water to a boil. Prepare a bowl of ice water. Add the haricots verts and blanch by boiling them until bright green and barely tender, about 2 minutes. Transfer the beans to the ice bath. (The beans will continue to cook in the casserole.) Drain and lay them on paper towels to remove excess water.

4. In a large bowl, combine the haricots verts, mushroom casserole, and soup. Mix well and transfer to a 9-by-13-inch baking dish. Bake, covered with aluminum foil, until heated through, about 35 minutes.

5. Meanwhile, make the crispy shallots: Heat the oil in a fryer or heavy-bottomed pan with high sides to 375°F.

6. In a medium bowl, mix together the rice flour and cornstarch. Toss the shallots in the mixture, then shake well in a sieve to remove excess flour. Add half of the shallots to the fryer and move them around with tongs while frying to avoid clumping. When just light brown, 4 to 5 minutes, strain them out, drain on paper towels, and sprinkle with salt and pepper. Repeat with the remaining shallots.

7. Top the casserole with the crispy shallots and serve.

ORANGE-GLAZED ACORN SQUASH WITH ROASTED MUSHROOMS AND PUMPKIN SEEDS

SERVES 4

I used to use acorn squash only in purées and soups. Their odd, ribbed shape makes them difficult to peel and almost impossible to achieve a nice uniform dice cut. But over time I realized that the outer skin isn't as tough as other squash like butternut and pumpkin, and when roasted, the skin is tender enough that you can actually munch on it along with the flesh.

Squash and oranges are natural partners, and not just because they tend to be the same color. Both have a good amount of sweetness and a slight touch of bitterness, although you still need to add a little vinegar to an orange glaze for enough acid to balance the sugar. And because squash are so synonymous with autumn, I wanted to boost that fall feeling with the season's other star ingredient: mushrooms. Finally, don't forget about texture. The crunch you get from the pumpkin seeds helps keep your palate from falling asleep in the soft roasted squash and mushrooms, and nobody wants to fall asleep at the table.

ORANGE GLAZE

1 cup fresh orange juice

4 dried Thai chiles (see Ingredient Spotlight, page 61), broken into pieces

2 tablespoons sugar

1 tablespoon sherry vinegar

1 acorn squash (about 1½ pounds)

5 tablespoons extra-virgin olive oil

Salt

Freshly ground black pepper

8 ounces trumpet royale mushrooms (see Ingredient Spotlight; page 221)

⅔ cup pepitas (hulled pumpkin seeds; see Ingredient Spotlight, page 78)

1. To make the glaze: Combine the orange juice, chiles, sugar, and vinegar in a nonreactive pot over medium-high heat. Bring to a simmer to reduce by two-thirds, or until it resembles a light syrup. Remove from the heat and strain, discarding the solids. Set aside.

2. Preheat the oven to 400°F.

3. Trim off the top and bottom of the squash and cut it into four wedges (leaving the skin on). Scoop out the seeds and "guts" of the squash and discard. Slice each quarter of the squash into ¼-inch half moons. Combine the squash with 2 tablespoons of the olive oil in a large bowl. Season with salt and pepper and spread evenly onto a baking sheet. Roast the squash until just tender, about 20 minutes uncovered.

Continued . . .

4. Meanwhile, trim ¼ inch off the end of each mushroom. Slice them lengthwise ¼ inch thick. Toss the mushrooms with 2 tablespoons of the olive oil in a medium bowl. Season with salt and pepper and set aside.

5. Toss the pepitas with the remaining 1 tablespoon olive oil. Place them on a separate baking sheet and bake until lightly browned, about 8 minutes. As soon as you remove the seeds from the oven, toss them with a good amount of salt.

6. After the squash has roasted for 20 minutes, remove the pan from the oven and immediately spread the mushrooms over the top. Return to the oven and continue baking until the mushrooms have wilted, another 5 minutes.

7. Toss the squash and mushrooms with the orange glaze and roasted pepitas and serve.

INGREDIENT SPOTLIGHT

TRUMPET ROYALE MUSHROOMS As the name would imply, these 'shrooms look a bit like trumpets when on their side, with a cap that just barely curves out beyond the thick stem. Chefs love this variety, mainly because the mushrooms have a long shelf life but also because the stems are just as meaty as the caps, meaning you can get a lot of yield out of each mushroom. Their firm texture means they hold up really well to roasting or sautéing without turning to mush, but they're still pliable enough that they'll soak up whatever sauce you want. They can be a bit pricy, but a good tip is to look for them at Asian markets, where they're often sold as king oyster mushrooms for half the price.

SAUTÉED BRUSSELS SPROUTS AND SUNCHOKES WITH CANDIED PECANS

SERVES 4

I do not have fond memories of Brussels sprouts from my childhood. Not to throw my mom under the bus, but she used to serve frozen Brussels sprouts that were boiled until they were as tender as baby food and then coated with margarine. I tried to pass them off to my dog, Dr. Pepper, who was always hanging out under the dinner table waiting for tasty scraps. But even he knew better than to eat them, and since he'd just roll them around under there and get me in trouble, I was stuck with them.

I'm not sure if fresh Brussels sprouts just weren't as readily available back in the day, but nowadays they're everywhere. You can even find them in basic grocery stores still on their tall stalk, which actually makes a great dining table centerpiece in a vase. The flavor of the fresh sprouts versus the frozen (or, God forbid, canned) is immensely better, enough that they even made a convert out of me. In fact, I like the flavor so much now that my preferred method of cooking Brussels sprouts is simply to brown them in a bit of butter and oil, then pop them in the oven for just a couple of minutes, serving them while they still have a little crunch left. A lot of times I'll add in another one of my earthy favorites—the sunchoke. The two vegetables complement each other nicely, and they cook at about the same rate, making the dish quite simple to make. Sage brings in a nice aromatic element that adds depth without overpowering, while the pecans add a nice texture as well as a little sweet spice. And if you're like me and just can't get enough bacon, feel free to brown some pieces along with the butter to add a smoky element to the mix.

CANDIED PECANS

2 tablespoons confectioners' sugar

Rice bran oil for frying (see Technique 101, facing page)

¾ cup raw pecans

⅛ teaspoon cayenne pepper

Salt

BRUSSELS SPROUTS AND SUNCHOKES

3 tablespoons butter

1 tablespoon extra-virgin olive oil

12 fresh sage leaves

1 pound Brussels sprouts, bottoms trimmed, sliced in half

8 ounces sunchokes, peeled and cut into ¼-inch slices

Salt

Freshly ground black pepper

1. To make the candied pecans: Put the confectioners' sugar in a small stainless-steel bowl.

2. Heat the rice bran oil to 375°F in a fryer or heavy-bottomed pan with high sides.

3. In a medium pot, bring 1 quart water to a boil. Put the pecans into the boiling water and cook for 2 to 3 minutes. Drain the pecans and transfer them to the bowl of confectioners' sugar, evenly coating them. Transfer the pecans to the fryer and fry until they are a deep brown, 1 to 1½ minutes. Be careful not to burn the nuts. Remove the nuts from the oil and place them on a plate or cooling rack lined with waxed paper. Sprinkle with the cayenne and salt. Let cool.

4. To make the Brussels sprouts and sunchokes: Preheat the oven to 375°F.

5. Heat a large ovenproof sauté pan over medium heat. Add the butter and olive oil to warm. Add the sage leaves and let them cook for 2 minutes. Increase the heat to high and add the Brussels sprouts and sunchokes. Toss to coat, let them brown, and toss again. Season with salt and pepper and then transfer to the oven, cooking until the vegetables are just tender, about 5 minutes. Stir in the pecans, adjust the seasoning, and serve.

TECHNIQUE 101

Candying Nuts: There are many different ways to candy nuts, but I've found over the years that I get the best results from frying them. Some people prefer to make a caramel to coat the nuts and then bake them, but I think that frying makes for a thinner, crunchier candy coating, as the nuts aren't just sitting in goo while they cook. The trick to frying nuts is to quickly boil them first, which makes the sugar stick and really penetrate. You can do this with virtually any nut, but I find that I use this technique more with pecans, hazelnuts, and walnuts. One thing I am specific about though is the frying oil. Rice bran oil has a delicious flavor and a high smoke point, making it ideal for frying. (If you can't find it, substitute peanut oil.) Feel free to get creative by adding spices to the sugar—cayenne, cinnamon, and nutmeg are a nice combo. Beyond the common use as a salad topper, try candied nuts tossed into pastas or chopped up as a garnish for sautéed fish.

CHESTNUT CONFIT WITH ROASTED POTATOES, BACON, AND KUMQUATS

SERVES 4 TO 6

I was never a big fan of chestnuts growing up—chestnuts roasting on an open fire was just not appealing in the least to me, as warm and merry as it sounded. The texture is just so different from all other nuts out there that I couldn't really get with it. But later, when I was working with my friend (and fellow *Top Chef* contestant) Dale Levitski at the Chicago bistro La Tache, he made a version of a chestnut confit to serve with a duck dish in winter. It totally changed my opinion of the chestnut and I eventually made my own version of it to serve at Scylla. To any other non-chesnut believers out there: Give it a try. I think it'll change your mind, too.

4 slices thick-cut bacon, cut into ¼-inch pieces	Freshly ground black pepper	12 kumquats (see Ingredient Spotlight, page 226), quartered, flesh removed and discarded (reserve the skins)	1 tablespoon sherry vinegar
2 pounds new (baby) potatoes, quartered	2 cups fresh orange juice		8 ounces fresh chestnuts (about 12), shelled and peeled (see Technique 101, page 226)
Salt	½ cup sugar		

1. Preheat the oven to 425°F.

2. Heat a large skillet or sauté pan over medium heat. Add the bacon and cook until crisp, about 5 minutes. Remove the bacon with a slotted spatula, drain on a paper towel, and reserve the rendered fat.

3. Add the potatoes to the pan with the bacon fat, toss to coat, and season with salt and pepper. Transfer the potatoes to a nonstick baking sheet and bake until tender, about 30 minutes.

4. Meanwhile, combine the orange juice, sugar, kumquat skins, and vinegar in a medium nonreactive saucepan. Bring the mixture to a boil, reduce the heat

to medium, and let it simmer until the skins are tender, about 10 minutes. Remove the skins with a slotted spoon and set aside.

5. Add the chestnuts to the liquid and bring them to a boil. Reduce the heat to medium and cook until the liquid has reduced by three-fourths into a thick syrup, about 1 hour. The nuts should be tender enough to break into bits with the nudge of a wooden spoon. Season with salt and pepper.

6. Toss the roasted potatoes with the reserved bacon and kumquat peels. Place them on a platter and top with the chestnut confit to serve.

INGREDIENT SPOTLIGHT

KUMQUATS This tiny citrus fruit—which looks like a miniature, oval tangerine—is primarily cultivated in East Asia, but you should be able to find it in local grocery stores in winter. Almost the opposite of an orange, the skin of a kumquat is actually sweet while the flesh is bitter, which is why people often just pop them in their mouth and eat them whole. Otherwise, either just the skin is used in cooking or the whole kumquats are made into preserves or candied. If you can't find kumquats or they're not in season and you still want to make this recipe, use the peel of another citrus such as a tangerine, Clementine, or Mandarin orange. Just try to remove as much bitter white pith from the peel as possible, then cut the skins into small strips.

TECHNIQUE 101

Peeling Chestnuts Fresh chestnuts have a much better flavor than pre-peeled, but most people go for the packaged stuff anyway out of the fear that peeling them is a total pain. It can be—but not if you know what you're doing. There are many methods, but I found that this one is easiest. With the tip of a sharp knife, score an "X" on the flat side of each shell. Place the chestnuts in a large saucepan and fully cover them with cold water. Bring them to a boil for 1 minute. Turn off the heat. Remove a chestnut from the water (working one at a time) with a slotted spoon and peel away the shell, beginning at the score mark. If you have trouble getting the inner peel to come off with the outer peel, toss the peeled chestnuts back into the water, bring them up to a boil again, drain them, toss them onto a towel, and rub back and forth—any remaining skin should slide right off.

ROASTED FINGERLINGS
WITH PISTACHIO PICADA

SERVES 6 TO 8

I included this recipe in the book to introduce one of my favorite condiments or sauce enhancers: *picada*. (Not to be confused with a very different dish, the classic Italian piccata.) Picada is a Catalan staple used to thicken and flavor soups, stews, and sauces, and while it usually always includes nuts (primarily almonds), bread, and some sort of liquid, recipes vary dramatically and can include any combination of crackers, nuts, wine, saffron, game livers, chocolate . . . the list goes on. Think of it as a finishing flourish to add an extra dose of complex flavor while also enhancing the texture of the dish.

My take on picada combines one of my favorite nuts, the pistachio, with just a bit of heat and a great deal of garlic (feel free to cut back if you're not a garlic lover). This recipe will yield more than necessary for this side dish, so hold on to it to use in sauces and soups. It will hold in the fridge for up to a week and in the freezer for a month or so, and it's a nice flavor enhancer to have on hand for a last-minute dish. One I like is to cook up some pasta and toss it in picada warmed in a splash of cream or stock. Quick and easy . . . and oh so good.

PISTACHIO PICADA

1 cup toasted pistachios

1 cup fresh parsley

¼ cup cubed ciabatta bread, toasted

4 garlic cloves

1 teaspoon red pepper flakes

1 teaspoon salt

½ teaspoon paprika

½ cup extra-virgin olive oil

POTATOES

1½ pounds fingerling potatoes

¼ cup olive oil

Salt

Freshly ground black pepper

¼ cup white wine

1 cup vegetable or chicken broth

1. To make the picada: Combine the pistachios, parsley, bread, garlic, red pepper flakes, salt, and paprika in a food processor and purée. With the motor running, drizzle in the olive oil and ¼ cup water until a paste forms. Transfer the picada to a small bowl, cover the surface directly with plastic wrap, and set aside.

2. To make the potatoes: Preheat the oven to 400°F.

3. Toss the potatoes in the olive oil and season with salt and pepper. Spread them on a baking sheet. Bake for 35 minutes, shaking the pan to move around the potatoes every 10 to 12 minutes. After 35 minutes, increase the heat to 450°F to brown the potatoes for 10 minutes more.

4. Meanwhile, in a large sauté pan (large enough to fit the potatoes), simmer the wine to reduce by half. Add the broth and reduce by half. Whisk in ½ cup of the picada and set aside.

5. When the potatoes are ready, add them to the sauté pan with the picada mixture and toss well to coat. Serve immediately.

CHA
SEVEN

EXTRAS

I KNOW MOST OF YOU AREN'T LOOKING TO BECOME PROFESSIONAL CHEFS, BUT EVEN IF YOU'RE JUST LOOKING TO BECOME A BETTER HOME COOK, IT'S GREAT TO HAVE AN ARSENAL

of recipes that make that extra difference between store-bought and a step above. I created this chapter with that in mind passing along simple recipes for doughs, dressings, stocks, nut butters, and even a fresh sausage (easy enough that it might just kick-start a whole new hobby). There's no shame in buying these things when you're short on time, but it's nice to know you can make them when you're in the mood to take a few extra minutes. I promise it's worth it.

BASIC PASTA DOUGH

There are a number of basic pasta recipes out there. The variables include the amount of egg, the type of flour, the ratio of olive oil to water . . . there are many adjustments that can be made to get just the right texture. At the restaurant, we do often use "00" flour, an Italian type used for pizzas and pastas that is finer than all-purpose flour. The problem is that it can be tricky to find and you may not always have it readily available, so I wanted to give you a great recipe made from ingredients you likely have on hand all of the time. I played around with this recipe for awhile, but in the end I picked this version that's high in egg yolks because I love the richness the yolks give the noodles and the texture that results.

| 2 cups all-purpose flour | 5 egg yolks | 1 tablespoon extra-virgin olive oil |

1. Start by placing ¼ cup of the flour off to the side on a workspace. Put the remaining flour onto a clean, flat workspace. Using your hands, create a well in the middle of the flour, approximately 6 inches across. Put the egg yolks, ¼ cup cold water, and the olive oil into the well. Use a fork to start incorporating the flour into the egg mixture a little at a time. When the dough begins to form, discontinue using the fork and begin working the flour into the dough with your hands. When most of the flour is combined, move the dough to a clean workspace and knead it, pulling from the reserved flour if needed, until the dough is firm and smooth, 5 to 7 minutes. Wrap it with plastic wrap and refrigerate it for 20 minutes to rest.

2. Divide the dough into four pieces. Take one piece at a time and roll it out with a rolling pin on a floured surface until ¼ inch thick. Transfer it to a pasta machine and roll it out to the desired thicknesses and/or shapes (see Technique 101, below).

3. If you're not using the pasta immediately, sprinkle a bit of semolina flour on a sheet of wax paper, then top with a single layer of pasta. Continue with layers of flour and wax paper. Seal in a freezer-safe plastic bag or airtight container and store in the freezer for up to 2 weeks. Once ready to use, the pasta will cook up in boiling water in 3 to 4 minutes, as opposed to the 10 minutes or so it takes to cook dry pasta.

TECHNIQUE 101

Rolling Pasta: These days, you can find all kinds of pasta machines, but I'm a big fan of the old-school hand-crank variety, mainly because you can control the speed, which is nice when you're first learning. You'll want to start out your dough on the thickest setting, roll it through a couple of times, and then keep going down in thickness, one number at a time. I like my linguine a little thicker, so I roll it out to a 6. For pappardelle, I go to a 7, and I like to hand-cut the strips 1½ to 2 inches wide with a pizza cutter. For raviolis, go thinner, to an 8 if your filling is hearty (e.g. ground meats) and to a 9 if your filling is light (e.g. purées). Try working with smaller pieces at first so you don't have to manage a long sheet of dough. After a bit of practice, it becomes easy as pie . . . er, pasta.

BASIC PIZZA DOUGH

This is a great pizza dough, although I can't really take the credit. My friend Karen, who's a personal chef, invited me and some other friends over for Valentine's Day dinner one year (as usual, I did not have a hot Valentine's date), and she and her girlfriend made the most amazing flatbreads. I had to get the recipe from her to share it with you. Top it with whatever you are in the mood for. I, of course, can't do flatbread without cheese, but any array of veggies and meats will do.

¼ cup mild white wine

2½ teaspoons dry yeast

1 tablespoon honey

1 tablespoon olive oil, plus extra to coat dough

1 teaspoon salt

3½ cups all-purpose flour

1. Combine ¾ cup warm water, the wine, and yeast in a large bowl and stir well, until the yeast is dissolved. Add the honey, the 1 tablespoon olive oil, and the salt and stir well to combine. Add 1 cup of the flour and mix with a wooden spoon until it becomes a loose batter. Add 2 more cups of the flour and stir for 2 to 3 minutes, incorporating as much flour as you can with the wooden spoon. Bring the dough together by hand and turn it out onto a clean work surface dusted with the remaining flour. Knead the dough for 6 to 8 minutes, until it is smooth and firm. Place it in a clean, lightly oiled bowl, and cover with a kitchen towel. Let it rise in the warmest part of the kitchen until doubled in volume, about 45 minutes.

2. For individual pizzas or calzones, cut the dough into four equal pieces and knead them into rounds. For a large pizza, knead the dough into a large round. For both sizes, cover and let them rest for 15 minutes after shaping.

3. The next step is crucial: proofing. Place the dough on an oiled sheet of parchment paper and let it sit for 1 to 2 hours (depending on how hot your kitchen is), or until it has puffed up and nearly doubled in size. Roll it very thin on a floured workspace and bake at the hottest temperature your oven allows—450 to 500°F, if possible. If you have a pizza stone, preheat it for at least 30 minutes in the oven. The pizza should take no longer than 10 minutes to cook in this environment.

CHICKEN STOCK

Stock is one of the true basics of cooking. Back in culinary school, we very carefully weighed out our vegetables, or *mirepoix*, to make sure we had two parts onion to one part celery and one part carrot. I remember at my first restaurant job when I was asked to make the stock, I started weighing the vegetables as I had learned. The other cooks looked at me like I was nuts, telling me, "Just estimate, Steph. Eyeball it. It's stock, not an exact science."

They were right. Although you do want to have more onions than carrots, little else about stock recipes needs to be exact. This is a basic stock recipe to use as your base, but you should really feel free to alter it after you get more confident. At many restaurants where I've worked, we had a couple of different chicken stocks. One "white" stock, where the bones were simply rinsed and cooked down, with no tomato product used, and another "dark" stock, where the bones were roasted and both red wine and tomato product were used for a richer broth. I like to make one base stock; a bit of a compromise, with roasted bones, a little tomato, and white wine. I also decided years ago that I much prefer the flavor of fresh fennel to celery in my stocks; it's a great way to use up the fennel stalks and fronds, and I just love the floral notes. I also decided a while ago that I just don't like the taste of bay leaves, as traditional as they may be, so I use just a bit of fresh thyme and peppercorns in my stocks instead. One thing to remember is that although stocks are a great way to use up vegetable scraps—corncobs, mushroom stems, tomato cores—it is not a place for peels of vegetables or other inedible scraps. Any parts of the chicken carcass, including chicken wings, are great for stock. But you don't want to use bones that have already been cooked. As tempting as it may be, the leftovers from a whole roasted chicken dinner aren't really good for much at that point. All of the great flavors that we suck out of bones to flavor the stock have already seeped out to flavor the meat while you roasted it. You want to make sure you're putting nothing but quality flavors in there that will shine in the end.

5 pounds chicken backs (see Quick Tip, facing page)

2 tablespoons blended oil (half vegetable, half olive oil)

2 carrots, rough chopped

2 yellow onions, peeled and rough chopped

1 fennel bulb (stems included), rough chopped

8 garlic cloves

1 pound canned plum tomatoes

1 pound chicken feet

6 to 8 sprigs fresh thyme

1 tablespoon black peppercorns

1 cup dry white wine

1. Preheat the oven to 400°F.

2. Put the chicken backs in a roasting pan and roast until they're nice and browned, about 1 hour.

3. Meanwhile, heat a large stockpot over medium heat. Add the blended oil, carrots, onions, fennel, and garlic and sweat by cooking them until the onions are translucent, about 5 minutes. Turn off the heat and add the tomatoes, chicken feet, peppercorns, and thyme.

4. Once the chicken backs are browned, transfer them to the stockpot. Skim off the chicken fat from the roasting pan, discard it, and then place the pan on the stovetop over medium heat. Add the wine and use a wooden spoon to loosen the bits of skin and meat that stuck to the pan. Once the liquid is reduced by half, transfer it all to the stockpot and add 6 quarts cool water. Bring it to a boil, then reduce to low and simmer until the stock is fragrant and flavorful, about 8 hours. Strain, discarding the solids, and cool the stock completely. After an hour or so in the refrigerator, the fat will separate, so you can skim it off and discard or save for other use. Store in an airtight container in the refrigerator for up to 1 week or in the freezer for up to 3 months.

QUICK TIP ···

I don't expect the average home cook to just have 5 pounds of chicken backs lying around, but you can easily go to any butcher and ask to purchase them. You'll find good prices on chicken backs at Latino grocery stores, where they usually get in whole birds and break them down themselves to sell by the piece. Plus, you'll definitely find chicken feet there, which I require in all of my stocks. Why? Chicken feet contain a lot of gelatin, which adds a great viscosity to stock. If you take a batch of stock made with feet and one without and reduce both down to make a sauce, the one with feet will reach a beautiful thickness much faster.

FAVORITE VINAIGRETTES

Vinaigrettes are one of my favorite flavoring agents to have on hand, and not just for salads. A splash of vinaigrette can add flavor to anything, from roasted veggies to grilled fish to pan-roasted meats. You might be tempted to make a big batch of vinaigrette and keep it in the fridge, but be a bit careful. Any vinaigrette you make using raw egg yolks (which are great for adding the thick texture of an emulsion) is probably best to hold on to for only about three days. If you substitute pasteurized egg yolks, which you can buy in a carton, you can hang on to the vinaigrette for about a week. Still, it also depends on what else is going into your vinaigrettes. If you're using fresh herbs, they're likely to turn color after a few days and can get a bit slimy. Or if you're using lemon in the vinaigrette, it will turn after about four days. Vinegar seems to give the longest shelf life, although the flavor can change a bit over time, so just be sure to taste it and adjust seasonings before using.

BASIC HONEY-DIJON VINAIGRETTE

MAKES ABOUT ½ CUP

This is about as simple as it gets; a great base to which you can add various herbs or spices, or even chopped-up olives. I use this one most often on salads or to dip fries.

2 tablespoons balsamic vinegar

1 tablespoon honey

1 teaspoon Dijon mustard

1 teaspoon chopped fresh oregano

¼ teaspoon sambal
(see Ingredient Spotlight, page 47)

2 tablespoons extra-virgin olive oil

Salt

Freshly ground black pepper

In a medium bowl, whisk together the vinegar, honey, mustard, oregano, and sambal. Add the olive oil while whisking and continue to whisk until blended. Season with salt and pepper. Store in an airtight container in the refrigerator.

LEMON-MAPLE VINAIGRETTE

MAKES ABOUT ¾ CUP

A delicate, simple vinaigrette like this needs to go with something mild. Try it on steamed green beans, a nice piece of grilled fish, or a fresh tomato salad.

¼ cup fresh lemon juice

2 tablespoons maple syrup

½ teaspoon sambal
(see Ingredient Spotlight, page 47)

¼ teaspoon coarse salt

Freshly ground black pepper

½ cup extra-virgin olive oil

In a small bowl, whisk together the lemon juice, maple syrup, sambal, salt, and pepper. Add the olive oil in a slow drizzle, whisking constantly until emulsified. Store in an airtight container in the refrigerator.

CAPER VINAIGRETTE

MAKES ABOUT 1¼ CUPS

This is my go-to Caesar dressing substitution for people who don't like anchovies. You get a similar flavor profile without the fishiness. Simply toss it with romaine and croutons.

¼ cup white balsamic vinegar

2 tablespoons Dijon mustard

1 egg yolk

1 cup blended oil (half vegetable, half olive oil)

¼ cup capers, drained

1 teaspoon honey

1 teaspoon sambal
(see Ingredient Spotlight, page 47)

Freshly ground black pepper

Put the vinegar, mustard, and egg yolk in a blender. Blend on low speed and slowly drizzle in the blended oil with the motor running. Add the capers, honey, and sambal and blend until smooth. Season with pepper. Store in an airtight container in the refrigerator.

ROSEMARY VINAIGRETTE

MAKES ABOUT 1¼ CUPS

Think Italian. This is an ideal drizzle for roasted pork loin or lamb chops, or even tossed with leftover pasta for a quick, cool pasta salad.

¼ cup sherry vinegar

1 tablespoon Dijon mustard

1 egg yolk

1 cup blended oil (half vegetable, half olive oil)

1 tablespoon ground fresh rosemary
(use a spice grinder)

2 teaspoons soy sauce

1 teaspoon sriracha (see Ingredient Spotlight, page 19)

Salt

Freshly ground black pepper

Put the vinegar, mustard, and egg yolk in a blender. Blend on low speed and slowly drizzle in the blended oil with the motor running. Add the rosemary, soy sauce, and sriracha and blend until smooth. Season with salt and pepper. Store in an airtight container in the refrigerator.

SHERRY-THYME VINAIGRETTE

MAKES ½ CUP

I love using thyme, but sometimes its flavor can be overpowering. Rather than adding thyme directly to a dish, I prefer to work it into this really simple vinaigrette and then control exactly how much of the flavor I add by adjusting how much I drizzle over the dish. This viniagrette is great over roasted chicken or grilled beef.

2 tablespoons sherry vinegar

1 tablespoon soy sauce

1 tablespoon honey

1 chopped fresh thyme leaves

1 teaspoons Dijon mustard

2 tablespoons extra-virgin olive oil

Freshly ground black pepper

In a small bowl. whisk together the vinegar, soy sauce, honey, thyme, and mustard. Add the olive oil while whisking and continue to whisk until blended. Season with pepper. Store in an airtight container in the refrigerator.

CILANTRO VINAIGRETTE

MAKES ABOUT 1¼ CUPS

Use this just as you would cilantro, leaning toward Mexican or Asian foods. I like it as a nice topper for grilled skirt steak or as a dip for grilled shrimp.

¼ cup white balsamic vinegar

1½ tablespoons Dijon mustard

1 egg yolk

1 garlic clove, sliced

1 cup blended oil (half vegetable, half olive oil)

1½ cups tightly packed fresh cilantro (some stem is okay)

2 teaspoons honey

½ teaspoon red pepper flakes

Salt

Freshly ground black pepper

Put the vinegar, mustard, egg yolk, and garlic in a blender. Blend on low speed and slowly drizzle in the blended oil with the motor running. Add the cilantro, honey, and red pepper flakes and blend until smooth. Season with salt and pepper. Store in an airtight container in the refrigerator.

PISTACHIO-LEMON VINAIGRETTE

MAKES ABOUT 1¼ CUPS

I just love this over grilled meats, tossed with grilled calamari, or on salads tossed with fresh cheese like ricotta salata.

1 cup chopped roasted, salted pistachios

2 lemons, juiced

2 tablespoons honey

1 teaspoon sambal
(see Ingredient Spotlight, page 47)

¾ cup extra-virgin olive oil

Salt

Freshly ground black pepper

In a medium bowl, whisk together the pistachios, lemon juice, honey, and sambal. Add the olive oil while whisking and whisk until blended. Season with salt and pepper. Store in an airtight container in the refrigerator.

THE ULTIMATE CAESAR DRESSING

MAKES ABOUT 2 CUPS

I just had to throw in my version of Caesar dressing. It's a classic that I've always had a love/hate relationship with. When it's done right, with the perfect amount of anchovy and layers of flavors from Worcestershire and hot sauce, I could skip the romaine and just dip fresh bread in it all day. Done wrong, and it just makes me sad.

12 to 15 white anchovy fillets
(see Ingredient Spotlight, page 139)

¼ cup balsamic vinegar

2 tablespoons Dijon mustard

1 egg yolk

¾ cup extra-virgin olive oil

¾ cup canola oil

¼ cup grated Parmesan

1 teaspoon hot sauce

1 teaspoon fresh lemon juice

¾ teaspoon Worcestershire sauce

½ teaspoon salt

¼ teaspoon honey

¼ teaspoon freshly ground black pepper

1. In a blender, combine the anchovies, vinegar, mustard, and egg yolk and blend until the anchovies are puréed.

2. Slowly drizzle in the olive oil and canola oil with the motor on, until thickened. Add the Parmesan, hot sauce, lemon juice, Worcestershire sauce, salt, honey, and pepper and blend until smooth. Check the seasoning and adjust if necessary. Store in an airtight container in the refrigerator.

PISTACHIO-CILANTRO BUTTER

MAKES ¾ CUP

I am a big fan of using nuts other than peanuts to make butters. The color of this butter—made with pistachios—adds a much prettier color to the plate than the average nut butter. In addition to the quail that it's paired with in Balsamic Barbecue Quail with Pistachio-Cilantro Butter and Daikon Slaw (page 176), this is great with scallops, shrimp, grilled beef, and roasted chicken. If you're not a fan of cilantro, try a mix of basil and parsley, or even some fresh oregano.

1 cup shelled, salted, pistachios, toasted

½ cup packed fresh cilantro leaves

3 tablespoons blended vegetable oil
(half vegetable, half olive oil)

1 tablespoon fresh lemon juice

1 tablespoon honey

2 teaspoons soy sauce

2 teaspoons Dijon mustard

1 teaspoon sriracha (see Ingredient Spotlight, page 19)

1 teaspoon white miso
(see Ingredient Spotlight, page 171)

½ teaspoon lemon zest

½ teaspoon salt

¼ teaspoon freshly ground black pepper

Put the pistachios, cilantro, blended oil, lemon juice, honey, soy sauce, mustard, sriracha, miso, lemon zest, salt, pepper, and ½ cup water in food processor. Process until the mixture forms a thick paste (slightly thicker then peanut butter). Scrape down the sides with a spatula once or twice and process again. Use immediately or refrigerate, well covered, for several weeks.

MISO–MARCONA ALMOND BUTTER

MAKES ABOUT 1½ CUPS

Marcona almonds are a bit dangerous because there's no way you can eat just one. The best solution I found is to turn them into a nut butter and then you have no idea how many you're eating! You really don't need to add much to almond butter to make it delicious, but for this recipe I decided to add a bit of depth through miso and a little spice from sambal. It makes a great sauce for grilled shrimp, sautéed scallops, or lamb meatballs, and feel free to thin it a bit with water to your desired consistency for other uses—it's intense enough to handle being spread a bit thin.

¾ cup (about 6 ounces) Marcona almonds

3 tablespoons extra-virgin olive oil

2 tablespoons white miso paste
(see Ingredient Spotlight, page 171)

1 tablespoon soy sauce

1 tablespoon honey

½ teaspoon sambal
(see Ingredient Spotlight, page 47)

Coarse salt

Freshly ground black pepper

Combine the almonds, olive oil, 3 tablespoons water, the miso, soy sauce, honey, and sambal in a blender or food processor and process into a thick-textured sauce. Scrape down the sides with a spatula once or twice and process again. Season with salt and pepper. Use immediately or refrigerate, well covered, for several weeks.

INGREDIENT SPOTLIGHT

MARCONA ALMONDS Marcona almonds are like the front-row seats of the nut world—more expensive, but worth every penny. Rounder and sweeter than traditional almonds, these Spanish exports have a higher fat content as well, making them great for purées or soups to add extra richness. Typically you'll find them in stores already toasted, tossed in oil, and seasoned (usually with salt and sometimes also rosemary), so seek out plain Marconas if you can. But if the seasoned are all you can find, just taste them to judge their saltiness and adjust accordingly when cooking with them.

SALSA VERDE

MAKES ABOUT 2 CUPS

It's funny how sauce names in other languages sound so fancy (this one simply means "green sauce"). It is, in fact, a simple green sauce, but it's packed with flavor, and it's quite different from the green tomatillo-based *salsa verde* you get at your favorite taqueria. The freshness from the variety of herbs, along with the salty notes of anchovy, make for a great topping for grilled meats and fish, roasted potatoes, or even just some chips.

2 cups tightly packed fresh parsley

1 cup tightly packed fresh basil

1 cup tightly packed fresh cilantro

6 white anchovy fillets
(see Ingredient Spotlight, page 139)

½ cup olive oil

2 tablespoons yellow mustard

1 tablespoon white balsamic vinegar

2 teaspoons honey

2 teaspoons sambal
(see Ingredient Spotlight, page 47)

½ teaspoon salt

½ teaspoon freshly ground black pepper

Combine all the ingredients in a blender or food processor and blend until smooth. Cover and store in the refrigerator for 2 or 3 days (if you store it longer, you'll lose the bright color).

SHERRY VINEGAR REDUCTION

MAKES ABOUT ¼ CUP

Vinegar reductions, or gastriques, are one of my favorite ways to add extra acidity to dishes, which is so important to highlight the natural flavors of anything. See how I use them in Sautéed Shrimp with Butternut Purée and Cider Gastrique (page 45) and Brown Butter–Delicata Squash Soup with Sherry Vinegar Reduction (page 68). You can infuse this basic reduction with any number of other flavors, including various herbs or even berries that are about to bite the dust. Just be sure to strain out any solids before serving.

½ cup sherry vinegar

2 tablespoons sugar

1 sprig fresh thyme

1 teaspoon black peppercorns

1. Combine the vinegar, sugar, thyme, and peppercorns in a small heavy-bottomed, nonreactive pot. Bring to a boil, then reduce the heat to medium-low. Simmer the liquid to reduce until syrupy, 8 to 10 minutes.

2. Cool the liquid and strain out the thyme and peppercorns. Store in a tightly sealed container (no need to refrigerate) for up to 1 month.

PRESERVED LEMON

I recommend having preserved lemons in the fridge all the time. I just love using them to add an intense bit of lemon tartness to dishes, savory or sweet. In many recipes where I call for these, you can substitute lemon zest, but it's just not the same. Just remember that when you are using lemon rinds, it's important to remove all of the pith before using, as that's where the lemon's bitterness hides and your end result will overpower a dish very easily. Also, you want to cut the lemon peels as thinly as possible. They're very intense and a little goes a long way!

2¼ cups coarse salt	1½ cups vodka	1 teaspoon black peppercorns	1 teaspoon mustard seeds
9 lemons	1 teaspoon fennel seeds	1 teaspoon red pepper flakes	
2 cups sugar			

1. Bring a large pot of water to a boil with ¼ cup of the salt. Boil four of the lemons, whole, until they begin to soften, 5 minutes. Remove them with tongs and set them aside to cool. Add the remaining five lemons to the boiling water for 5 minutes, and then remove them and set them aside to cool with the others.

2. In a small pot, combine the remaining 2 cups salt, the sugar, vodka, fennel seeds, peppercorns, red pepper flakes, and mustard seeds. Set the pot over low heat and simmer until the sugar and salt have dissolved, about 15 minutes.

3. Meanwhile, cut the cooled lemons, running your knife lengthwise from just below the top of the lemon to just above the bottom tip, so as to cut it into quarters without cutting all the way through the fruit. Stuff the lemons into a large glass jar with a lid (at least ½-gallon size). Pour the salt liquid over the lemons, pushing the fruit down to make sure it's submerged. Let the liquid come to room temperature and close the lid tightly. Let the lemons sit at cool room temperature for 2 weeks (make sure they are submerged in the liquid; use a piece of parchment paper and then a plate to weigh them down if needed), then they are ready to use. Once you open them, the preserved lemons can be refrigerated for up to 6 months.

HOT-SMOKED FISH

When I was growing up, my mom loved smoked salmon, so every year at Christmas my Uncle Ron would send Mom a big smoked salmon, and we'd eat it for days. To this day, he still does that, but when I got out of culinary school I decided to make Mom my own smoked fish creation, an hors d'oeuvre of smoked trout and mascarpone cheese inside puff pastry with strawberry chutney on top. Not to one-up Uncle Ron, but I'd say Mom liked my donation to the holidays even better.

Now that I finally live in a Chicago apartment with a patio, I've been playing around a lot with my new favorite toy, a Bradley smoker. I like to use maple wood chips because they're not super-intense, but feel free to experiment with mesquite or hickory for a deeper, smokier flavor. Whatever you do, try to avoid frozen fish, and stick with fish with a high fat content and oily skin, like trout or salmon. With the slow-and-low method of smoking, anything leaner will likely dry out. I've included a very basic brine to get you started, but once you try it and taste the flavor, feel free to adjust with a handful of fresh herbs, a couple cloves of garlic, a minced shallot, and/or some lemon zest. When it comes to spices, I like to keep it simple, and a go-to combo of mine is just a bit of fennel seed, coriander, and mustard seed.

½ cup sugar

½ cup kosher salt

Choice of flavoring (herbs, garlic, shallot, etc.)

1 to 4 pounds high-fat fish, such as trout or salmon, with skin on (brine can be doubled for larger amounts)

1. In a large saucepan, combine 1 quart water, the sugar, salt, and any flavorings and cook over medium heat, stirring until the salt and sugar are dissolved. Turn off the heat and let the brine cool completely.

2. Put the fish in a large baking dish, pour the brine over the fish, and cover it tightly with plastic wrap. Refrigerate for a minimum of 8 hours, and a maximum of 24 (more than that will start to break down the fish and turn it to mush). Remove the fish from the brine, pat it dry, and place it uncovered on a platter in the refrigerator for 1 hour to dry out a bit.

3. Prepare a grill or smoker for indirect heat and a temperature of 165 to 175°F. Smoke the fish until it reaches an internal temperature of 140°F. Smoking times are approximately as follows:

½ to 1 pound: 1½ to 2 hours
1 to 2 pounds: 2 to 2½ hours
2 to 3 pounds: 2½ to 3 hours
3 to 4 pounds: 3½ to 4 hours

4. Transfer the fish to a cooling rack. Once the fish has cooled to room temperature, it's ready to serve or can be held in the fridge, well wrapped, for up to 5 days.

CLASSIC PORK SAUSAGE

MAKES ABOUT 3 POUNDS

It might take a few tries to get the hang of sausage making, but once you do, you can really have fun with it and make good use out of scraps like fatback. The basic formula is a 5-to-1 ratio of meat to fat. With pork, there is some natural fat in nearly all cuts, but I still do the 5-to-1 ratio when using fatback. With leaner meats like lamb and goat, I often add just a little more fat. The most important thing is to make sure that the equipment, meat, and fat are all very cold when grinding, as this prevents the sausage from "breaking" when cooked. I'm sure we have all had some sausage that seems dry inside and crumbly, which results when the fat and meat are unable to emulsify and they "break," or come apart. The final step of whipping in some liquid helps bind the fat and meat as well. Feel free to sub in other liquids, as beer, red wine, or even water will work just fine. In fact, I often cut the wine with water so that the flavor is not overpowering. Finally, if you're going to make the sausage into links, be sure to cook a little of the loose sausage to taste before going through all the hard work of casing the meat so that you can make sure the flavor is right on.

2½ pounds boneless pork shoulder, cubed	1½ teaspoons fennel seeds	1 teaspoon black peppercorns	1 tablespoon Dijon mustard
8 ounces pork fatback, cubed	1½ teaspoons cumin seeds	1 teaspoon red pepper flakes	
1½ teaspoons mustard seeds	1½ teaspoons coriander seeds	2 tablespoons kosher salt	
		¼ cup white wine	

1. Put the attachments for your grinder in the freezer along with the pork shoulder and fatback until all are well chilled, at least 30 minutes.

2. Meanwhile, toast the mustard, fennel, cumin, and corriander seeds; peppercorns; and red pepper flakes in a dry pan over low heat until fragrant, then grind them very finely in a spice grinder.

3. Set up the meat grinder. In a large container, season the pork and fat with the spice mixture and salt. Grind them to a moderately fine grind (using the 8-mm attachment or comparable) and put the mixture into the bowl of a stand mixer fitted with the paddle attachment. Turn it on medium-low and drizzle in the wine and ¼ cup cold water, along with the mustard. Mix for 3 minutes, or until it become sticky. Form the sausage into patties, use loose, or use a sausage stuffer to form links. If you make links, let them sit on a rack, uncovered, in the refrigerator overnight before using; this will help keep the casings from bursting when cooking. Regardless of form, fresh sausage should be used within a couple of days of making. You can also wrap and freeze it for up to 2 weeks.

INDEX

Wilted Spinach with Roasted Tomatoes and
Sausage, 213
Trout
Hot-Smoked Fish, 242
Smoked Trout, Fingerling, and Bacon Salad, 116
Truffle oil
Truffled White Asparagus Soup, 70
Truffle-Poblano Vinaigrette, 156–57
Tuna, Seared, with Blueberries and Snap Peas,
115
Turbinado sugar, 35

U
The Ultimate Caesar Dressing, 237

V
Veal
stock, 53
Veal Osso Buco with Mashed New Potatoes and
Maple Apples, 194–95
Vichyssoise, Sweet Garlic, 58
Vinaigrettes. *See* Salad dressings

W
Wahoo, Grilled, with Tofu-Asparagus Purée and
Smashed New Potatoes, 174–75
Walnuts, candied, 223
Warm Marinated Olives, 16
Watercress Sauce, French Gnocchi with, 142–43
Watermelon, Arugula Salad with Feta and, 103
Wilted Spinach with Roasted Tomatoes and
Sausage, 213
Wines
Blanc de Blanc, 44
Blanc de Noir, 132
Bordeaux, 201
Cabernet Sauvignon, 201
cava, 113, 134
Chardonnay, 34, 64, 88, 97, 138, 143, 164
Chianti, 16
cooking with, 37
Gamay, 112, 157

Gewürztraminer, 103, 186
Grüner Veltliner, 50
Malbec, 195
Merlot, 37
Pinot Blanc, 57, 76
Pinot Grigio/Pinot Gris, 32, 37, 73, 137
Pinot Noir, 149, 170, 186
Riesling, 60, 63, 99, 161
rosé, 22
Sancerre, 59
Sangiovese, 16
Santenay Burgundy, 170
Sauvignon Blanc, 16, 29, 59, 100, 175
Semillon, 70
Shiraz, 37, 198
sparkling, 113, 127, 132, 134
Vouvray, 167
White Burgundy, 143
Wondra flour, 135
Wong, Lee Anne, 159, 174

Y
Yogurt
Dill Yogurt, 191–92
Mint Yogurt, 169–70
Tarragon Yogurt, 66

TABLE OF EQUIVALENTS

The exact equivalents in the following tables have been rounded for convenience.

Liquid/Dry Measurements

U.S.	METRIC
¼ teaspoon	1.25 milliliters
½ teaspoon	2.5 milliliters
1 teaspoon	5 milliliters
1 tablespoon (3 teaspoons)	15 milliliters
1 fluid ounce (2 tablespoons)	30 milliliters
¼ cup	60 milliliters
⅓ cup	80 milliliters
½ cup	120 milliliters
1 cup	240 milliliters
1 pint (2 cups)	480 milliliters
1 quart (4 cups, 32 ounces)	960 milliliters
1 gallon (4 quarts)	3.84 liters
1 ounce (by weight)	28 grams
1 pound	448 grams
2.2 pounds	1 kilogram

Lengths

U.S.	METRIC
⅛ inch	3 millimeters
¼ inch	6 millimeters
½ inch	12 millimeters
1 inch	2.5 centimeters

Oven Temperature

FAHRENHEIT	CELSIUS	GAS
250	120	½
275	140	1
300	150	2
325	160	3
350	180	4
375	190	5
400	200	6
425	220	7
450	230	8
475	240	9
500	260	

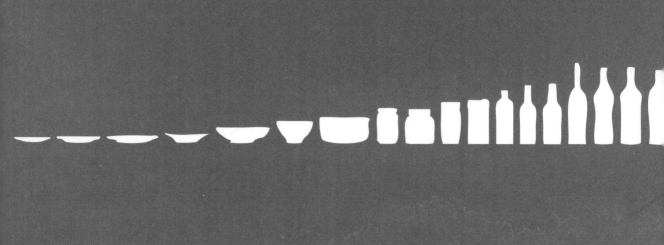